AF606753

JAMES HILLMAN UNIFORM EDITION

4

Uniform Edition of the Writings of James Hillman
Volume 4: *From Types to Images*

Published by Spring Publications, Inc.
www.springpublications.com

First edition

Cover illustration:
James Lee Byars, *Untitled*, ca.1960. Black ink on Japanese paper.
Estate of James Lee Byars, courtesy Michael Werner Gallery,
New York, London, and Berlin

ISBN: 978-0-88214-582-2

Library of Congress Control Number: 2019940548

♾The paper used in this publication meets the minimum requirements of the American National Standard for Information Sciences – Permanence of Paper for Printed Library Materials, ANSI Z39.48–1992.

JAMES HILLMAN

FROM TYPES TO IMAGES

Edited and with an Introduction by
Klaus Ottmann

SPRING PUBLICATIONS
THOMPSON, CONN.

The Uniform Edition of the Writings of James Hillman
is published in conjunction with

Dallas Institute Publications, Joanne H. Stroud, Director

The Dallas Institute of Humanities and Culture
Dallas, Texas

as an integral part of its publications program concerned with
the imaginative, mythic, and symbolic sources of culture.

Contents

ABBREVIATIONS

CW = *Collected Works of C.G. Jung,* trans. R.F.C. Hull, 20 vols. (Princeton, N.J.: Princeton University Press, 1953–79), cited by paragraph number.

UE = *Uniform Edition of the Writings of James Hillman,* 11 vols. (Putnam and Thompson, Conn.: Spring Publications, 2004–).

SE = *The Standard Edition of the Complete Psychological Works of Sigmund Freud,* ed. J. Strachey (London: Hogarth Press, 1986).

INTRODUCTION

by Klaus Ottmann

> Seeing comes before words. The child looks and recognizes before it can speak.
>
> But there is also another sense in which seeing comes before words. It is seeing which established our place in the surrounding world; we explain that world with words, but words can never undo the fact that we are surrounded by it. The relation between what we see and what we know is never settled.
>
> —JOHN BERGER *Ways of Seeing* (1972)

Moving Jungian psychology from types to images, to an image-based archetypal psychology, is James Hillman's concern in this volume.

Archetypal psychology began as a "Postscript," added by Hillman to the 1970 issue of *Spring Journal,*[1] the first to feature the word "archetypal" in its subtitle. For Hillman's archetypal psychology, images are the fundamental productions of the psyche. Images are what makes soul. The "Postscript" was followed by a three-part series of essays that form the core of the second part of this volume, "An Inquiry into Image," "Further Notes on Images," and "Image-Sense," published in the *Spring Journal* between 1977 and 1978.

From Types to Images begins with a discussion of the relation between types and images. It examines Jung's 1921 *Psychological Types* (*CW*6) that has become a central doctrine in psychology as well as the source for a myriad of personality tests, to a great part on account of two eager readers of Jung, Kathrine Cook Briggs and her daughter, Isabel Briggs Myers. "One need not be a psychologist in order to collect and identify types,

1 "Why 'Archetypal Psychology'?," in *UE* 1: *Archetypal Psychology*, 123–28.

any more than one needs to be a botanist to collect and identify plants," Cook Briggs wrote in 1926.[2]

Hillman does away with personality types and the deficient understanding of types inherent in Jung's static typology that by focusing on polarities (e.g., extrovert, vs. introvert) "make us lose the *images* of feeling, or intuition, or extraversion as states in themselves."[3] Instead, Hillman looks to the notion of *Selbstdarstellung* (self-representation) as an image of our emotional nature put forth by his fellow Eranos colleague, the Swiss biologist Adolf Portmann who also advanced a dynamic *Typenlehre,*[4] and to Goethe whose "deep insight into the type concept was that the type is immediately presented *in the image*":

> A type cannot be separated from the image in which it appears. We see types by seeing images; or rather, when we see a type, actually we are seeing an image.[5]

No longer are types opposed to images; they are, according to Hillman, "a special way of imaging." No longer concealing archetypes, they are now seen simply as "empty molds, out of which a pattern of images flows, and the mind, by generating examples, moves from types to images."[6]

Hillman argues for a psychology that focuses on "linguistic images as in poetry. Styles of image-expression as in rhetoric and the transformation of images as in translation and criticism. The genres and taxonomy of images as in symbolism. The phenomenology of images as in dreams, art objects, myths and tales, liturgy, and psychopathology. The rhythms and complexities of image-shiftings as in music. Their valuations as in aesthetics. Their sequences in individual biography (case histories, individuation). Their role in psychological theory—perception, memory, social relations. The epistemology of images. The work with images in psychotherapy, the arts, scientific invention, technology, planning."[7]

---

2 Quoted by Merve Emre in *The Personality Brokers: The Strange History of Myer-Briggs amd the Birth of Personality Testing* (New York: Doubleday, 2018), 46.

3 Below, part 1, chap. 1: "Persons as Types," 30.

4 See A. Portmann, "Selbstdarstellung als Motiv der lebendigen Formbildung," in *Geist und Werk. Aus der Werkstatt unserer Autoren. Zum 75. Geburtstag von Daniel Brody* (Zurich: Rhein Verlag, 1958) and *Don Quijote und Sancho Pansa: Vom gegenwärtigen Stand der Typenlehre* (Basel: Friedrich Reinhardt, 1964).

5 Below, part 1, chap. 1: "Persons as Types," 30.

6 Ibid.

7 From an unpublished 1981 sketch by Hillman for a course to be offered in

These activities of the archetypal imagination are "seen through" by Hillman across the various volumes of the Uniform Edition of his writings. According to Hillman, the language of images belongs less to communication and more to imagination: "Images have their own realm, their own kind of being and cosmology."[8]

Hillman borrows from the philosopher and scholar of Persian philosophy Henry Corbin, who introduced the term *ta'wīl* in regard to images and taught never to reduce "the imaginal to the perceptual, but [to] revert the perceptual to the imaginal."[9] "The practice of *ta'wīl*," as Tom Cheetham writes, "is how we recover the lost speech...The *ta'wīl* is both a mode of perception and a mode of being. It is a way of seeing and a way of living that refuses the literal."[10] And from his friend, the philosopher Edward Casey, Hillman picked up the extraordinary wisdom that an image is not what you see but the way that you see it:[11] "Imaging and imagining... take on as much import as do those images we perceive...To see an image means to shift one's mind."[12] And again, from Jung[13] (via Rafael López-Pedraza), Hillman adopts his "operational motto": "Stick to the Image."[14] a motto echoed in Maurice Blanchot's observation that "image...is not the designation of a thing but the way in which the possession of this thing, or its destruction, is accomplished."[15]

Casey has argued to move from active imagination (wherein "we are ourselves the actors in the psychological play that is produced through

---

Archetypal Studies, which was to include Study of Animation, Study of Images, and Study of the *Anima Mundi* in order to "intensify linguistic and historical awareness" in psychology.

8 J. Hillman, "You Taught Me Language," *UE* 8: *Philosophical Intimations*, 43.

9 J. Hillman and P. Berry, "Archetypal Therapeutics in Ten Brief Theses," an unpublished paper presented at the First Internnational Seminar on Archetypal Psychology at the University of Dallas in 1977, n.p.

10 Tom Cheetham, *Imaginal Love: The Meanings of Imagination in Henry Corbin and James Hillman* (Thompson, Conn.: Spring Publications, 2015), 98.

11 See below, part 2, chap. 3: "Archetypal Image: A High Example," 91n5.

12 Hillman and Berry, "Archetypal Therapeutics in Ten Brief Theses," n.p.

13 Cf. *CW* 16: 320: "To understand the dream's meaning I must stick as close as possible to the dream images."

14 "We take this motto operationally." Hillman and Berry, "Archetypal Therapeutics," n.p.

15 M. Blanchot, *The Work of Fire*, trans. C. Mandell (Stanford: Stanford University Press, 1995), 108.

the forceful elaboration of fantasies that might otherwise remain merely passive"[16]) to archetypal imagination:

> The activity of archetypal imagination moves not only beyond ordinary conscious imagining by constellating contents from the personal and collective unconscious—as occur in active imagining—but also beyond active imagination itself.[17]

In archetypal imagination, "personal conscioussness" encounters "the impersonal, the nonhuman."[18]

Hillman understands archetypal psychology as a "polytheistic psychology":[19]

> It provides for many varieties of consciousness, styles of existence, and ways of soul-making, thereby freeing individuation from stereotypes of an ego on the road to a self. By reflecting this plurality and freedom of styles within the structures of myth, the archetypal perspective to experience may be furthered."[20]

Hillman found the origin of this new thinking about types and images in Jung himself. It was Jung who had written that "everything of which we are conscious is an image, and that image *is* psyche" (*CW*13: 75). As Michael Vannoy Adams has remarked, "before Hillman, to stick to the image was merely one idea among many ideas in Jungian psychology—and hardly a conspicuous idea. After Hillman, it assumed the status of a dictum."[21]

What is archetypal psychology? It is neither a new psychological "-ism" nor is it a vocabulary or doctrine but, by analogy with Roland Barthes's famous essay on structuralism,[22] it is essentially an *activity*. We might speak

---

16 E. S. Casey, "Toward an Archetypal Imagination," *Spring: An Annual of Archetypal Psychology and Jungian Thought* (1974): 17–18.

17 Ibid., 19.

18 Ibid.

19 "Through imagination man has access to the gods." J. Hillman, *The Myth of Analysis: Three Essays in Archetypal Psychology* (Evanston, Northwestern University Press, 1972), 180.

20 J. Hillman, "Why Archetypal, Psychology," *UE* 1: *Archetypal Psychology*, 128.

21 From a presentation by Michael Vannoy Adams delivered at the Montreal Jung Society, Montreal, March 15, 2013 (http://www.jungnewyork.com/very-idea-james-hillman.shtml).

22 R. Barthes, "The Structuralist Activity," trans. R. Howard, *Partisan Review* (Winter 1967). Reprinted in *The Structuralists from Marx to Lévi-Strauss*, ed. R. and F. DeGeorge (Garden City, New York: Doubleday, 1972).

of archetypal activity as Barthes spoke of structuralist activity. According to Barthes, the objective of all structuralist activity, whether reflexive or poetic, is "to reconstruct an 'object' in such a way as to manifest thereby the rules of functioning (the 'functions') of this object... It makes something appear which remained invisible, or if one prefers, unintelligible in the natural object."[23] Similarly, Hillman instigated an active re-visioning, re-imagining, of psychology as a self-generative activity of the soul:

> In archetypal psychology, the word "image" therefore does not refer to an afterimage, the result of sensations and perceptions; nor does "image" mean a mental construct that represents in symbolic form certain ideas and feelings it expresses. In fact, the image has no referent beyond itself, neither proprioceptive, external, nor semantic... An image is given by the imagining perspective and can only be perceived by an act of imagining.[24]

Archetypal psychology "'sees through itself' as strictly a psychology of archetypes, a mere analysis of structures of being (gods in their myths), and, by emphasizing the valuative function of the adjective archetypal, restores to images their primordial place as that which gives psychic value to the world. Any image termed archetypal is immediately valued as universal, trans-historical, basically profound, generative, highly intentional, and necessary."[25]

Barthes, in his brief essay on structuralism, describes the structuralist activity of decomposing, then recomposing the real as "little enough": "this 'little enough' is decisive: for between the two objects, or the two tenses, of structuralist activity, there occurs something new,... and this addition has an anthropological value, in that it is man himself, his history, his situation, his freedom and the very resistance which nature offers to his mind."[26]

At the end of the dialogical second part of this volume, Hillman summarizes his operational goal for his Jungian-trained interlocutor:

> No overarching idea or feeling can guarantee my activities; they must be valid in themselves with each step they take, each move

---

23 Barthes, in *The Structuralists,* 149.

24 J. Hillman, "A Brief Account," *UE* 1: *Archetypal Psychology,* 17.

25 Ibid., 23.

26 Barthes, in *The Structuralists,* 150.

> they make, providing background as they proceed. The soul indeed takes but one day at the time; its entire strategy is tactical.[27]

And he continues:

> The many chapters to which you have so patiently submitted each gave an intention, but not as an overarching theory. An operational inquiry does not separate theory from practice, isolating theory as a set of principles and goals that are then applied in practice. Instead, theory lives in the operation itself and informs its doing. For instance, by sticking to the image, we give it primary place without having to declare a general principle about the priority of images. When we use gadgets to move the images, we demonstrate the depth, substantiality, and analogizing power of images without having to argue a theoretical position about imagination. When we compare the image with the *temenos* of sacred space, we feel the religious implications of the work without having to speak in the language of high-minded spiritual goals, and we have shown how that practice with images is akin to ritual.[28]

New York
March 2019

27 Below, part 2, chap. 18: "Protestor's Last Stand," 220.
28 Ibid.

PART ONE

Egalitarian Typologies vs. the Perception of the Unique

1

PERSONS AS TYPES

Esse is *percipi.*
—GEORGE BERKELEY, *Of the Principles of Human Knowledge*

Three persistent irritations have urged me to this topic. Perhaps you will understand the topic better if I can portray the irritations. The first has to do with elitism. Nature, said Jung, is aristocratic and esoteric (*CW*11:537; *CW*7:198). It is profligate; only few events come to birth, far fewer to full flowering. Jungians are concerned with these rare events, the opus of individuation, working on one's individuality so as to be wholeheartedly all that one is. This requires differentiation (by which word Jung defines individuation—*CW*6:755, 757, 761), elaborating differences within oneself and between oneself and others. This stress upon the *differentness* of individual personality and the private modes of its development means that an avowed Jungian suffers the charge of elitism. So our first problem is how to work with individual uniqueness without at the same time becoming elitist. This problem must be met by every Platonist man of the spirit who at the same time would be a democratic citizen and polytheistic liberal in soul. One way of attempting the dilemma is to examine the other side of elitist fantasy, i.e., egalitarianism.

The second thorn has to do with Jung's *Psychological Types.* This work—begun over sixty years ago—is the part of his opus most well-known to the public, and it is being revived today by many Jungians in hopes of putting their school on a more clinical, scientific, or academic basis. I, for one, feel profoundly discomfited by Jung's typology—and even more by a science of personality based on a scientific method of types. Once the label has been found, the inferiority or superiority identified, then what? How does one imagine further? Moreover, is it not the old drill-sergeant ego who is called on to develop the raw and lazy inferiorities by marching round the mandala through all four functions?

My irritation seems supported by other Jungian analysts. In an international survey published in 1972 on the use of typology among Jungians in active practice, result number one states: "Only half the number of analysts replying found the typology helpful in analytical practice."[1] But surely we cannot so lightly dismiss Jung's major work of his middle period. What relevance has Jung's typology? Why types at all?

Before we proceed into the third worry, there is, curiously enough, a direct connection between egalitarianism and typology right within Jung's book. I am referring to the last few pages, the Epilogue, which opens with "Liberté, Égalité, Fraternité," the cry of the French Revolution whose "egalitarian reforms" Jung praises. But Jung clearly distinguishes social and political equality from psychological egalitarianism, saying "No social legislation will ever be able to overcome the psychological differences between men," and he finds that it serves "a useful purpose therefore to speak of the heterogeneity of men" (CW6:845). His *Types* was conceived to elaborate differences or variety. Yet the Epilogue, like a foreboding afterthought, points to what has since happened; the book has become an instrument of psychological egalitarianism by means of typical categories into which persons can be fit. Instead of helping us to relativize all psychological positions, it establishes them more fixedly. The book has converted into its opposite: it has become an instrument of the egalitarianism it is expressly designed to ward off, and a more insidious kind—psychological egalitarianism. But we shall come back to Jung in more detail later.

Now, the problem of perceiving the unique. This problem is at the heart of therapy. If there is one thing each patient needs, it is to be perceived in his or her uniqueness, and if there is one thing an analyst struggles with unrelentingly, it is to espy a particular and different self in each patient. The desire to see and the need to be seen cannot be overestimated; when such seeing and being seen takes place, it is like a blessing.[2] Despite what is revealed of a patient's psychodynamics, the

---

1 A. Plaut, "Analytical Psychologists and Psychological Types," *The Journal of Analytical Psychology* 17/2 (1972): 143.

2 "Blessing" might also be put as "healing," in that what is required is an insight into essential nature—a seeing. When Paracelsus refuses the first Hippocratic aphorism

typical and archetypal patterns of interior life and the soul's history, until I can envisage this person's uniqueness, I cannot imagine him profoundly enough and therefore cannot recognize who he is. I see individuation, but not individuality. If my work is with an empirical embodied self in its individuality, then how to perceive a self not in symbols and synchronicities, not hermeneutically, but immediately in the person before my eyes, concrete and present.

My misgiving here seems a widespread malaise. The clinician takes few cues from the *kline* (bedside). Instead, he reads blood tests. He is trained to see in groups and typings, a taxonomic eye that coordinates with a prescriptive hand dispensing treatments. A person written about in a case report is far less enunciated than one finds in a novel or biography. Psychiatry texts, today swollen to obesity, are crammed with statistics. But where are the careful descriptions of ill persons, such as we find in Krafft-Ebing and Bleuler. When I attend discussions on candidate selection for analytical training, I am abused by the banal descriptions and unawareness of character in the remarks of my colleagues—and in my own. Something has happened to the sight of the psychologist, and owing to our gradual glaucoma, we turn more and more to committees, objective tests, increased quantities of training. The problem of uniqueness is not merely methodological—the old argument between nomothetic and idiographic, between statistical, experimental psychology versus clinical, between science versus art in psychology.[3] The problem is rather *the* problem of human relations: the experiencing of each other as selves, as

(art is long; life, short), he says this is so only for the poor physician because he is looking (or empirically searching), which is not seeing. The true physician must see the illness as the geometer sees the circle—an imaginative act. L. Braun, "Paracelse, Commentateur des *Aphorismes* d'Hippocrate," in *La Collection hippocratique et son rôle dans l'histoire de la médicine* (Leiden: E.J. Brill, 1975), 345.

3 G.W. Allport's writings are the most sympathetic to this division; in fact, he has been accused of causing it. See R.R. Holt, "Individuality and Generalization in the Psychology of Personality," *Journal of Personality* 30 (1962): 377–404; also P.E. Meehl, *Clinical versus Statistical Prediction: A Theoretical Analysis and a Review of the Evidence* (Minneapolis: University of Minnesota Press, 1954); G.W. Allport, "The General and the Unique in Psychological Science," *Journal of Personality* 30 (1962): 405–22, where Allport proffers the term "morphogenic" to replace idiographic for study of the individual—a term drawing attention to visible shape. The tendency of psychologists (noticed by both Holt and Allport) to misspell idiographic as *ideo*graphic also suggests an unconscious assimilation of uniqueness by conceptual ideation.

individual persons with distinct natures; each person the embodiment of an individual destiny.

How did others do it in other times? So much has depended upon the ability to see the nature of the person before our eyes. For instance, at the French Court in the 1850–60s, the German, Austrian, British, and Russian ambassadors each sent back their reports based on their readings of the enigmatic, ill, and capricious Napoleon III. Cowley, the British Ambassador, read best, and what he said was most in tune with historical events. How did General Haig grasp his French colleagues on the Western Front or decide upon appointments for Commanders of its sections—Haig, who is usually considered a military ramrod, a wholly unpsychological John Bull? Yet his biographers show his concisely summing up character on which terrible decisions rested after the briefest encounter with a previously unknown person. How does a baseball scout perceive the uniqueness in a nineteen-year-old rookie infielder in the bush leagues, size him up not only in terms of skills but see a nature that will fit him into a team and be worth long investment of money and time?

Let me tell you three stories. At Harvard in the 1890s, Professor William James had in his classes a rather wonky, stubby, talkative Jewish girl from California. She was late for classes, didn't seem to understand what was going on, misspelled, knew no Latin—that sort of typical mess, the girl who couldn't get it together, a "typical neurotic," as we might say today. But William James let her turn in a blank exam paper, gave her a high mark for the course, and helped her through to medical studies at Johns Hopkins. He saw something unique in this pupil. She was Gertrude Stein, who found herself as the Gertrude Stein we know only ten years later, far from Harvard, in Paris.

In a Southern small town, a man named Phil Stone, who had some literary education at Yale, took under his wing as coach and mentor a short, wiry, heavily drinking, highly pretentious lad of the town. This young fellow wrote poems, pretended to be British, carried a walking stick, and wore special clothes—all in smalltown Mississippi during World War I. Phil Stone listened to the boy, whom we might call today a "typical *puer*" and perceived his uniqueness. The man went on to become the William Faulkner who was awarded the Nobel Prize in Literature in 1949.

A third tale of the perception of uniqueness: In the year 1831, one of those marvelous old-fashioned scientific expeditions was to set forth;

a schoolmaster named John Henslow suggested that one of his former pupils be appointed naturalist. The lad was then 22; he had been rather dull at school, hopeless in math, although a keen collector of beetles from the countryside; he was hardly different from the others of his type and class: hunting and shooting, a popular member of the Glutton Club aimed for the clergy. He had a "typical family complex," as we might say today, soft in the mother and dominated by a 300-pound father. But Henslow saw something and persuaded the parties involved to include the pupil, Charles Darwin, in his journey.

What did they see, and how did they see it? Is this sort of seeing a special gift, as some have held, or is it possible to anyone—providing nothing stands in the way of such perception, a perception that implies, in these cases, a deep subjective affection, a loving?

Here we can detect an interrelation between two of our problems. For what might have stood in the way of seeing uniqueness could have been seen typically—to have seen Gertrude Stein as a typical neurotic girl, William Faulkner as a typical *puer,* Charles Darwin as a typical family boy with an obsessive hobby but not much "upstairs." Had we seen by means of modern psychology, that is, typicalities, we could have missed the target.

There is also a relation with our other problem, egalitarianism. The sort of perception we just described singled out Stein, Faulkner, and Darwin. The eye that saw them saw them differently and in their differences.

Hearing these tales of Stein, Faulkner, and Darwin—or rather of James, Stone, and Henslow—we could make a psychological maxim of Berkeley's principle: *esse* is *percipi.* To be is to be perceived. Stein, Faulkner, and Darwin became what they were because of having been perceived. Their being was the result, in part, of that.

But first we turn to what might get in the way of such perception—types, and the concept of types. Then we turn to modes other than types for the perception of persons.

The Type Concept:[4] The word *typos* does not quite mean *Schlag* or blow as we have taken for granted. Originally, the way *typos* was used in Greek gave it

4 For the concept and theories of "types," see W. Ruttkowski, *Typologie und Schichtenlehre: Bibliographie des internationalen Schrifttums bis 1970* (Amsterdam: Rodopi, 1974); C.G. Hempel and P. Oppenheim, *Der Typusbegriff im Lichte der neuen Logik* (Leiden: Sijthoff, 1936); A. Koort, "Beiträge zur Logik des Typusbegriffs," *Acta et*

the meaning of an empty or hollow form for casting, a kind of rough-edged mold. From the beginning of its use by Plato and Aristotle, the word had a sketchy, incomplete relief, or outline character, that emphasized a visible shaping quality rather than a sharply struck definition.[5] Even today, in modern logic and epistemology, a type differs from other ordering categories just by virtue of its imprecision.

Owing to this uncertain boundary, types are used most frequently in life sciences and humanities. Types can flow into one another: there is no sharp border between typical historical periods (Medieval and Renaissance), between typical literary styles (heroic and tragic), or between typical groupings of mental disorders, social functions, or even animal species. Fluidity, relativity, elasticity are the most distinctive aspects of the type concept.

Therefore there cannot be any pure types because they are not meant to be pure by definition.[6] A pure type has already become a class where a different sort of logic obtains. My name begins with the letter H, and I

Commentationes Universitatis Tartuensis 38 (1936): 1–138 and 39 (1938): 139–263; A. Seiffert, "Die kategoriale Stellung des Typus," *Beiheft zur Zeitschrift für philosophische Forschung* (Meisenheim-Wien: Hain, 1953); W. A. Lessa, "An Appraisal of Constitutional Typologies," *American Anthropologist* (n. s.) 45 (1943): 7–96; O. H. Schindewolf, *Über den "Typus" in morphologischer und phylogenetischer Biologie* (Wiesbaden: Franz Steiner, 1969).

5 A. von Blumenthal, "Typos und Paradeigma," *Hermes* 63 (1928): 391–414.

6 The very impurity of types in experience therefore necessitates "ideal" types (Dilthey, Jaspers, Spranger, Max Weber), which are not intended to be evidentially verified, but are required as purely imagined backgrounds for understanding human experience. Ideal types are like Platonic ideas (but denied their metaphysical implications—A. Rustow, "Der Idealtypus, oder die Gestalt als Norm," *Studium Generale* 6.1 (1953): 54). But ideal types are unlike Platonic ideas because the way in which they are formed gives them a freakish, caricature-like quality. They are constructed by intensifying, exaggerating, and purifying singular traits at the expense of others and subsuming those others within the salient ideal type as a Gestalt. They exist in no single instance, and are thus unnatural—which is precisely their value for seeing through the natural. The act that forms an ideal type is a *Wesenschau,* an insight into essence, and not a statistical averaging (norms) or a logical reasoning (classes). Neither empirical nor logical methods apply. Rustow (p. 59) calls the principle by which they are formed "morphological." Ideal types require an imagination of Gestalten or forms. Jung's types belong here inasmuch as they are an imagined morphology of consciousness—a phenomenology of the shapes of experience. For examples of ideal types in philosophy, see C. D. Broad, *Five Types of Ethical Theory* (London: Kegan Paul, Trench, Trubner and Co., Ltd., 1930) or S.C. Pepper, *World Hypotheses: A Study in Evidence* (Berkeley: University of California Press, 1942).

was called to military service in 1944. That puts me into two classes with hard edges. There is nothing typical about persons whose names begin with the letter H or who were called up in 1944. We can, however, be classified with H and 44. Classes require an "either-or," types a "more-or-less" kind of thinking. I am either an H or I am not; I cannot be more of an H than an L or a T, or a lesser H or a little H, etc. But with types I am rather more an extravert than an introvert, a point Jung made at the very beginning of his *Psychological Types* (*CW*6: 4–6). Extraversion does not per se exclude introversion.

But it is not easy to keep this distinction between classes and types. Often types are used as classes, and we begin to classify ourselves by means of types, thereby severing our fluid natures into well-defined and mutually exclusive parts. To use a type concept as a class concept has crippling results.

Also for the body politics: when we use types as classes, they become literal stereotypes and work in a Procrustean manner. A typical German or a typical American brings a typical image to mind, and this image has nothing to do with the legal definition of nationality. But should the typical image become the class definition for the national, then all German and American nationals must conform to a stereotypical image, resulting in political exclusion, and even genocide.

We tend to speak of types wherever we try to combine wide general principles together with single particular instances. Then types help to organize a vast number of similar events into rough groupings. (But the events must show similarity—and we shall come back to that). Vast numbers of events are hard to work with. For example, in the 1930s, Gordon Allport and Henry Odbert at the Harvard Psychological Laboratory[7] compiled a list of 17,953 trait names in English applicable to human personality, about as many different words as "alert," "aloof," "alone," "alcoholic," "altruistic," "alluring," "altered," "alive," "all-round," "almighty," etc., to 18,000. This list reveals the immense vocabulary at our disposal in only one tongue for describing human nature. If we are nominalists, these names of traits have no substantial existence or necessary connection to "personality," which is another such insubstantial word. But if we are even moderately realists, then these names point beyond their verbal nature

7 G.W. Allport and H.S. Odbert, "Trait-Names: A Psycho-Lexical Study," *Psychological Monographs* 47/1 (1936).

and might indicate something about the subtleties of human being. As Allport and Odbert say: "Each single term specifies in some way a form of human behavior."[8] And these terms may point to a correspondence between linguistic richness and psychological richness, and perhaps "a correspondence between linguistic convention and psychological truth [may be] very close."[9]

If rich language and rich insight do bear on each other, then here already is one of the reasons for our falling off in psychological acuity, compared with just fifty years ago. We no longer allow ourselves to use naive language of the old days; much of the words regularly used for character perception are old-hat or taboo: ethnic-racial words (Jew, Turk, Okie, Prussian), Biblical words for character (Jeremiah, Ruth, John); class words (blue blood, servant class, street urchin, pickaninny, bastard). The new "-ologies" insist that such terms are prejudices and stereotypes, which do not help seeing but block it. The "-ologies" have substituted another objectified language instead. So now we say "fascist," "neurotic," "overcompensated," "overweight," "underdeveloped," "underachiever," "elitist," "unrelated," "chauvinist," and our perception by means of obscene epithets has moved from a landscape of low race, birth, and region to a landscape of the low body.

But what can we do, unless we are Shakespeare or Joyce, with 18,000 trait names for understanding personality? The problem confronted by psychology-as-science is similar to that which confronts the sciences of nature that have before them one million species of animals or a quarter of a million kinds of plants.

So psychologists, on the model of natural scientists, attempt to order the vast array into smaller groupings. Cattell, ten years after the Harvard study, reduced the 18,000 trait names to 171 adjectives in twelve groups.[10] Another psychologist, Orth, once named 1,500 sorts of feelings. But Thomas Aquinas, René Descartes, and many moderns who think the same way have reduced the panoply of feelings to eleven, or eight, or six, five, or just two basic types of emotion of which all others are composed. Clearly the simplification of words aids the reduction to types. You will notice here that we have entered into a numerical kind of thinking. We

8 Ibid. vi.

9 Ibid., 2.

10 Cf. F. Gendre and C. Ogay, "L'évaluation de la personnalité à l'aide de l'Adjective Check List (ACL) de H. Gough," *Revue suisse de psychologie* 32/4 (1973): 332–47.

have assumed the scientistic eye that sees by means of numbers. Specific qualities, each with its trait names, are viewed as a mass of chaotic quantity calling for ordering by reduction into a few types, as if the less the variety, the more we know.

In short, type concepts fill a particular place in the ordering of events. They serve as intermediaries between a variegated world of huge quantities of bare particulars and the abstract world of general principles and classes—and types partake of both worlds.[11] They are *anschaulich* and descriptive as well as abstract and conceptual. By connecting individual and universal, or variety and oneness, they solve the problem of this *Tagung*,[12] and we could sit down here. But there is more.

One question besetting type theory is this: Are types mental constructs that we impose on the world or are types given with the world? Are they artificial or natural? Have they a logical-epistemological status or an ontological one? When I call you an extraverted feeling type, is this a way of organizing perceptions of you, or am I saying something essential about your nature that is given with it?

Some biologists insist that types are natural groups and that one cannot help but speak of types in the life sciences because they are empirically evident—right before the eyeball, as are the shapes of animals. Types do not have to be constructed; they simply can be observed. For 370 million years and in a variety of more than 800,000 sorts, there is a creature divided into head with antennae, three pairs of mandibles, a thorax with three pairs of legs, often wings, and an abdomen. This type or *Bauplan* is an insect and a *morphe* of creepy-crawly life right there, not a Platonic idea, an ideal artifice, or a nominalistic construction. It is a visible fact of a tangible world.[13]

But in psychology, types are not empirically visible. I may *see* coarse-blonde hair, set jaw, and skillful hands, but I can only *infer* courage or determination. Physical anthropology—measurements of human

11 Both Goethe and Dilthey, if in different ways, made the connection between universal and particular to be the essential characteristic of the type concept and thus the essence of their type theories. Cf. Koort, "Beiträge," 193–95.

12 "Egalitarian Typologies versus the Perception of the Unique" was first presented at the Eranos Tagung (Conference) in Ascona, Switzerland, in 1976.

13 Schindewolf, *Über den "Typus,"* 15; cf. "On the Nature of Natural Necessity," in M. Grene, *The Understanding of Nature: Essays in the Philosophy of Biology* (Dordrecht and Boston: Reidel, 1974), 236: "The very subject-matter of biology... demands a reference to standards, types or norms."

bodies—gives only the grossest sort of information about the psyche of those bodies.[14]

Because psychological types are not directly observable, it has been a major exercise of personality research to make them more visible.[15] Experiments demonstrate or test singled-out factors of personality: cognitive abilities such as reading speed, syllogistic reasoning, word fluency, or motor abilities such as aiming, reaction time, manual dexterity. This is what most experimental psychologists of personality are busy with. Then these low-level multiple factors can be computed and integrated into second- and third-level groupings called intelligence, reasoning, and creativity, and then, finally, high-level types of personality may be empirically verified as clusters of these trait factors. Then a type has some demonstrability. "True to type" means predictable reactions. Then a term like *introvert* becomes operational and a piece of positive knowledge.[16]

---

14 Constitutional typologies (Pavlov, Kretschmer, and others reviewed by Lessa), including the one of left/right brain hemispheres, cannot escape the more fundamental problem of the psyche/soma pairing. As Lessa points out, constitutional typologies are least problematic in areas of biological pathologies, and most questionable when they formulate sociological (criminality—Lombroso, race, class) or psychological differences. B. M. Teplov, "Problems in the Study of General Types of Higher Nervous Activity in Man and Animals," in *Pavlov's Typology,* ed. J. A. Gray (New York: Macmillan, 1964), points to the difficulties of directly relating types of nervous systems with types of behaviors—a fundamental critique of Pavlov's theory. See further A. Portmann, *Don Quijote und Sancho Pansa: Vom gegenwärtigen Stand der Typenlehre* (Basel: Friedrich Reinhardt, 1964). Another sort of psyche/soma correlation is implied by Lavater's physiognomic view (see below) who conceives the connection between physique and character to be *imagistic* rather than literal.

15 "No elements of personality are observable with perfect directness; all are inferred from behavioral indexes," N. Sanford, "Personality: Its Place in Psychology," in *Psychology: A Study of a Science,* ed. S. Koch, 6 vols. (New York: McGraw-Hill, 1963), 5:514. The task of making personality observable is treated thoroughly in *Multivariate Analysis and Psychological Theory,* ed. J.R. Royce (London and New York: Academic Press, 1973).

16 The deepest problem in this method of establishing "high-level" types through "low-level" demonstration of traits lies not where we might suppose: the disjunction between the levels. (Empirical research continues to complain of an inverse proportion between high-level integrative ideas such as types backed with few "facts" and low-level empirical regularities demonstrated by immense data—suggesting an epistemological disjunction between ideal types and empirical traits.) Rather, the problem rests on a fundamental fallacy: the assumption that the low-level concepts are "closer to facts" and directly observable while high-level concepts such as "introvert" are

The chief urge behind the attempts to devise tests for Jung's eight types (Grey-Wheelwright, Myers-Briggs) has been to establish them as observable "facts" acceptable to "science." In the great corpus of Jung's work, his types offer the best place for the succubus of the science fantasy to latch, or leech, on.

Empirical psychology approaches uniqueness in the same manner. Uniqueness is a CPID, a "consistent pattern of individual difference." One must first chart consistencies before one can begin to see what is different. It begins with sames to find differents; groups to find singles; egalities to find oddities. The unique becomes the atypical, abnormal, deviate—an approach taken up here two years ago.[17] This approach separates human uniqueness from human sameness, missing that they are interchangeable perspectives and not literal actualities. At one moment I can view any aspect of myself as common; a moment later, as unique. My very oddness that splits me from humankind can become, in a shift of vision, the common bond that joins me with others. The soul in Platonic usage is always both an all-soul, an *anima mundi,* and an individualization.

The vampiric metaphor I just used is apt for what goes on in typing. In the move to establish a type from a number of personal traits, the traits themselves are sucked out and drained into the larger factors. Actual concrete qualities of personality lose their blood to attitudes and functions. This happens every day when we look at ourselves typologically.

Let us say that I have good thinking and poor feeling. Yet there are specific traits of thinking that I cannot perform—keeping my checkbook accurately, understanding the principles of information theory, *Mengenlehre,* or symbolic logic, or how the television can be repaired. I may still stumble over the correct grammar of "that" and "which" in clauses, daylight-saving-time, or Celsius-Fahrenheit conversions. These may each be

theoretical and indirectly inferred. This assumption has been soundly rebuked by B.D. Mackenzie and S.L. Mackenzie, "A Revised Systematic Approach to the History of Psychology," *Journal of the History of Behavioral Sciences* 10 (1974). No matter at what "level" we operate, we are working with concepts. As Sir Cyril Burt put it: "The theory of the concept is prior to the operation for measuring the concept" ("Definition and Scientific Method in Psychology," *British Journal of Mathematical and Statistical Psychology* 11.1 [1958]: 57). The problem of conceptualization of person and personality in relation to measurement is examined carefully in the papers by Fiske and by Sells in *Multivariate Analysis.*

17 J. Hillman, "On the Necessity of Abnormal Psychology," *Eranos Yearbook* 43 (1974).

miserable inferiorities in my thinking, even though I can perform many other analytical, logical, and systematic activities with precision, speed, and ease. Similarly, there are specific qualities in my supposedly poor feeling function that not only do not conflict with thinking but enhance it, such as feeling the value of a first-rate idea and subtly and aesthetically differentiating it from a second-rate one, or experiencing the ethical consequences of trains of thought or organizational planning. As well, despite this poor feeling function I may nonetheless be a loyal friend, a magnanimous host, a charitable critic of my students, admit and inwardly contain my despairs, and not be afraid to call a spade a spade in behalf of my values. In other words, particular moral and characterological, and even technical proficiencies, are altogether drained off into typological notions. A type consists in traits. Because usually a type is defined as the axial system that holds traits together or simply as their principle of correlation, it has no substance of its own. Its substance is in the traits. To let go the multiplicity and exquisite variety of the 18,000 traits is to lose the stuff and gut of persons and turn them into types.

The emptiness of types, the hollowness implied by the very word, their "invisibility," causes another problem. As Koort[18] has observed, whenever we talk of types, we soon begin talking of examples and cases. Types call for living instances. Jung's book needs its Chapter X to make visible images with anecdotes and persons so that we can imagine all that has gone before. This peculiar process of thought—the need for examples—casts a shadow over all uses of typological thinking, especially in psychology and psychiatry. Is there not the danger of filling in the empty notion with concrete persons, creating cases even in the pathological sense to fill in our typical forms of pathology?

Pavlov's typology requires four types of reactions of higher nervous systems. But empirically only two dogs could be found to fit the phlegmatic type—and since his time, none.[19] One empirical study of Jung's types finds only five of the eight. The study does not question the system, the eight; it questions only its own method that did not find the full array of examples.[20] In other words, once we have begun to think in types, we have to see examples, find them, or invent them. We use

18 Koort, "Beiträge," 255–56.

19 Teplov, "Problems in the Study of General Types," 114–15.

20 L. Gorlow, N.R. Simonson & H. Krauss, "An Empirical Investigation of the Jungian Typology," *British Journal of Social and Clinical Psychology* 5 (1966): 108–17.

the empirical to fill the ideal. When we cast persons into these kinds of being, severe ontological consequences follow.

Another consequent is that types tend to be set up as typologies, as systems. Karl Jasper's typology aims, as does Jung's, to grasp the basic positions of the psyche and the forces that move it.[21] But to do this, he must have system (three main forms, three subforms, and then three further subforms of each of these). He defends this method on the grounds that only systematic schema can provide comprehensive theory.[22] When types want to be comprehensive–and unless they do, they offer no necessity and have little explanatory or ordering power–then, as McKinney[23] shows by analyzing typologies, they tend to become bipolar, set in oppositions. Even a typology of type theories bipolarizes them as empirical versus ideal, epistemological versus ontological, structural versus correlational,[24] bipolar versus triadic.

We may speak of them fluidly, as moving along a register between less and more, but their construction and their language remains dyadic. Tests that would type us always ask dyadic questions. Do you prefer to enter buildings with large doorways or small? Do you prefer red flowers or blue, women with large buttocks or large breasts? Test literature over and again uses the word "versus,"[25] creating a world for an ego to choose between events that hitherto had not seemed opposed or to demand preferences. We understand introversion only as less or moving away from, or versus extraversion, thinking only as less, or moving away from, or versus feeling. Soon, the contrasting poles of *one and the same thing on the same dimension* have become polar oppositions, then contradictions: to think is not to feel; to sense is not to intuit. (Contradiction is, of course, not necessary to type construction, but we are not all "thinking types" who can handle logic, especially not when assessing ourselves and others.) So the polarisation of type construction polarizes us; we feel *either* introverted *or* extraverted. The inferior then becomes the other pole, a cut-off

21 "Einleitung," in K. Jaspers, *Psychologie der Weltanschauungen* (Berlin: Springer, 1919).

22 Ibid., 17.

23 J.C. McKinney, "The Polar Variables of Type Construction," *Social Forces* 35/4 (1957): 300–306; Hempel and Oppenheim, *Der Typusbegriff*, 78.

24 Cf. Hempel and Oppenheim, *Der Typusbegriff*, 4.

25 E.g., P. E. Vernon, "Multivariate Approaches to the Study of Cognitive Styles," in *Multivariate Analysis*, 128–34, a thorough review of contemporary typology scales presented throughout in terms of "versus."

impossibility, or a heroic task to be developed through the "sacrifice of the superior function."[26]

These polarities also make us lose the *images* of feeling, or intuition, or extraversion as states in themselves. We see them only dynamically in tension with an opposite. But in actual life, a "feeler"—who can be depicted in literature or in biography, as a hysteric or depressive syndrome with a host of idiosyncratic traits, or as a child of Luna, Venus, or Saturn—can well be presented without any polarity or opposition. Planetary types, the thirty character epitomes of Theophrastus, and the syndromes of psychopathology as reaction types do not have to be set up in polar systems. Imaginative, depicted types as backgrounds differ from systematic typologies. I would even hazard that systematic typologies are fundamentally anti-imaginal and that the fantasy of types disturbs our appreciation of the image and our ability to imagine.

Here I have myself set up a polarity between imagining and typing, and soon we could be arguing that the more we perceive in typologies, the less we do so in images, and eventually they could become contradictories: to imagine is not to type; to type is not to imagine.

We may circumvent this danger when we remember that typological polarities are themselves an image—an image of a sliding scale along a straight line. Statements about ourselves in terms of bipolar types present fantasies of "where we are placing ourselves" lineally. I locate myself on an axis that offers only two possibilities, more or less, with gradations of advancement or retreat from the goal values of this axis.

Now, "advancement" and "retreat" belong to heroic imagery, so it is not surprising that personality assessments of types usually rely on ego-introspection ("self-reports" through preference questions) and that Jung's four types are conceived as functions of ego-consciousness.[27]

---

26 *Introduction to Jungian Psychology: Notes of the Seminar on Analytical Psychology Given in 1925,* ed. S. Shamdasani and W. McGuire (Princeton, N.J.: Princeton University Press, 2012), 53 (Lecture 6).

27 The association of the functions with ego-consciousness comes out clearly in the "heroic" description Jung gives of a "differentiated" function: it can be recognized by its "strength, stability, consistency, reliability, and adaptedness," whereas an inferior function is quite "unheroic": "lack of self-sufficiency and consequent dependence on people and circumstances ... disposing us to moods and crotchetiness ... suggestible and labile" (*CW*6: 956).

This brings us to the relation of type and image, a subject with a long history that shows types presenting themselves as images. For example, poetic types are persons from literary legends used as *universali fantastici* by Vico. Planetary types are figures of gods displayed in the images of myths. Biblical types are persons of the Old Testament seen as *Vorbilder* of the New. Morphological types are figures in nature seen, in different ways by Johann Wolfgang von Goethe, Georges Cuvier, and William Whewell, as manifestations of *Urbilder.*[28] Goethe's deep insight into the type concept was that the type is immediately presented *in the image.* A type cannot be separated from the image in which it appears. We see types by seeing images; or rather, when we see a type, we are actually seeing an image. No longer is it a matter of the difference between types and images as objects of perception. Now it becomes a matter of viewing one and the same event by typing it or by imagining it, either by means of the perspective of types or that of images. This conjunction of type and image implies also that images are not romantically free of typicalities and predictabilities.

We have come to a new place. Now types are not opposed to images, but are a special way of imaging. Rather than conceiving images typically and organizing our styles of perception into types, we are beginning to see types and their systems imaginally. Now by imagining a type in our minds, instantly the type moves into images that display it. Instead of our having to multiply instances to prove the type, the type multiplies images out of itself. Now a typical introvert is not conceptually defined or described as a cluster of traits. It is my younger brother sunk in thought on the beach under seagulls; myself blushing last night when introduced to the chairman's sleek, lithe daughter. Types have now become empty molds, out of which a pattern of images flows, and the mind, by generating examples, moves from type to image.

When this move of the mind is put into Biblical typology, then Old Testament figures are literal prefigurations of New Testament historical fulfillments.[29] When this move from type to image is put into animal types (Whewell), then a type is manifested in the varieties of itself in living images, and we can reconstruct the prehistoric *Urtier,* the genotype, from these phenomenal images. The power of a type to image itself is taken by Biblical, literary, or biological typology as a literal movement in the world

28 Cf. Koort, "Beiträge," 43–90 and 119–28.

29 Cf. J.A. Galdon, *Typology and Seventeeth-Century Literature* (The Hague: Mouton, 1975), esp. chap. 2–4.

of history, as an emanation from archetypes into images. Then we try to recompose or "verify" a type—or an archetype—by collecting instances. We do not need to think in this manner.

All we need do is recognize that when we are seeing types, we have begun to imagine in a figurational mode. We have begun to personify. We have begun to envision presences as the determining powers and that life is a fulfillment of their predictions. Things run true-to-type in that each thing fulfills its image, imagines itself typically into itself, each image held within the relief of its specific form. It is the typicality inherent to the image that we acknowledge in science by speaking of prediction and in psychology by speaking of the archetypal. It is this typicality in an image that sets its limit and suggests its placing (*topos*).

So the evidence for a type is in the vision that sees its images. The word *evidence* refers to an act of *vision*. Seeing types is a Platonic act that cannot be established by an Aristotelian method. Two eyes, even with microscope, cannot equal that third eye. To restore images to types means seeing types as a mode of imaging that cannot be satisfied by empirically gathered evidence. (It is anyway the type in our eye—the ability to see similarities and to compare—that allows us to see resemblances in what we gather for evidence and in the questionnaires that yield this evidence.) The scientistic search for evidence betrays itself for what it is: loss of morphic vision, an eye unopened to the image.

Jung's Typology: Let us turn now to Jung's types, focusing on only a few considerations.

First of all, his types are formed into a polar construction such as we discussed. The polar construction makes the types not mere random eclectic categories but a *typology*. It is this system that gives them their high-level explanatory power. They are axiomatically connected with one another in a tightly-knit, tension-filled "cross" (*CW*6: 983). This cross is also all-inclusive. Jung claims completeness for his typology (*CW*6: 843; *CW*11: 246), much as Aristotle does for his four causes, Schopenhauer for his four principles of reason, Popper for his four root metaphors, Pavlov for his four types of nervous systems, and Russell for his four types of philosophical statements.[30] The claim to completeness seems characteristic

30 Cf. Teplov, "Problems in the Study of General Types," 113. The types of philosophical statements in Russell and Wittgenstein are discussed by K.R. Popper, *Conjectures and Refutations: The Growth of Scientific Knowledge* (London: Routledge, 1969), 69–70.

of fourfold systems. That is, it belongs to the rhetoric of the archetypal perspective of fourness to present itself as a systematic whole, a mandala with an internal logic by means of which the system defends itself as all-encompassing.[31]

Because Jung's types are laid out axiomatically as a polar construction, the types rest on their "-ology," on principles even more fundamental than the types themselves: the principles of opposition,[32] even mutual exclusion, operating between the pairs of "subject and object," "inner and outer," "conscious and unconscious," "rational and irrational," "superior and inferior," "mind and heart," "actual and possible." Anyone using types in their systematic form is immediately implicated in the premises—and problems—on which the system depends. Jung's typology, presented modestly as a description of empirical functions and attitudes, nonetheless implicates an entire *Weltbild* of oppositions and energies held together by its mandala form. If not overtly an ontology or metaphysics, at least we cannot escape its *Weltanschauung*. It is set forth as the basic structure of our consciousness.

The connection between typology and mandala is also biographical. Both appeared immediately after Jung's "creative breakdown" (Ellenberger), euphemistically termed his "fallow period" by the editors of the *Collected Works* (*CW*6, p. v), what Jung himself calls his "confrontation with the unconscious" (c. 1913–1919). Typology and mandala both serve the same purpose of ordering irreconcilable conflicts. Jung had written on types before his years of self-analysis, but the final formulation as an eight- or sixteen-pointed conceptual mandala came only after this period (published in 1921). Functionally, the interlocking system of the typology and its power of explaining one's differences within oneself and the world, as well as one's differences with the world and one's enemies (Freud and

(In both Pavlov and Russell/Wittgenstein, the "fourth" type gives difficulties or seems of another kind than the other three.) I have discussed the metaphor of the fourfold root as it appears in Aristotle's four causes, Schopenhauer, etc. in J. Hillman, *Emotion: A Comprehensive Phenomenology of Theories and their Meanings for Therapy* (Evanston, Ill.: Northwestern University Press, 1961), 246–48.

31 The system is envisioned spatially, wholly in terms of the subject-object relation. Others have tried to give the typology a temporal dimension, e.g., H. Mann, M. Siegler, and H. Osmond, "The Many Worlds of Time," *Journal of Analytical Psychology* 13 (1968), 33–56.

32 The relation between the kinds of oppositions in Jung is discussed in J. Hillman, "The Dream and the Underworld," *Eranos Yearbook* 42 (1973): 303n101.

Adler as ostensible efficient cause of the book), serve, as does any good system, as an apotropaic or paranoic buttress of egoconsciousness (to which Jung attributes the types) against what he called Dionysian dissolution.

We still turn to typology when we need system. When our ego comprehension is disoriented and anxious, we turn to astrology, typology, archetypology, and the like. Types still bring with them their origins in defense against confusions by means of systems. Appeals to founding Jung's psychology scientifically upon types (Meier) and to relying more on them for understanding clinical psychodynamics (Fordham) bear the same witness to apotropaic system-building for the unpredictabilities of the "confrontation with the unconscious" and its images.

Our moves in psychology recapitulate Jung's moves. Ideas have roots in the necessities of our abnormal psychologies—in Jung's no less than ours. That is why it is so important to understand the internal necessity of his ideas in connection with his psyche, for one and the same psychic process continues in our own work when we use his ideas. They bring with them their roots. When we turn to typology, we need to see when Jung turned, and that he so rarely turned there again as he deepened his work from types to archetypes. Moreover, unlike Meier and Fordham, Jung had no need to establish his types with scientific or clinical literalism, which would turn modes of seeing into things seen.[33]

Despite their mandala structure, Jung does not give his types archetypal significance as such. They are not presented as *Idealbilder, Urtypen,* or *Urformen.* Only the fourfold system is archetypal, not the types.

A closer look at the way Jung speaks of the types, however, suggests that they, too, are archetypal. For what determines type? Here the *a priori* element enters: Jung speaks of a "numinal accent" falling on one type or another (*CW6*: 982). This selective factor determining type is unaccounted for. It is simply given. A numinal accent selects our bias toward

33 Jung's intention with his types was neither scientific nor clinical but Kantian (*CW6*, pp. xiv–xv). Kant is often referred to in this book, e.g., *CW6*: 512, even as an allegory for the superior function opposed to Dionysus for the inferior (*CW6*: 908–10). The Kantian fantasy of the typology thus correlates with the "Dionysian" experiences preceding it (1913–19). On the fourfold mandala as defense against the dissolution of Dionysus-Wotan-Nietzsche, see J. Hillman, "Dionysus in Jung's Writings," *UE6: Mythic Figures* (Thompson, Conn.: Spring Publications, 2016), 15–29. On Jung and Kant, see J.W. Heisig, *Imago Dei: A Study of C.G. Jung's Psychology of Religion* (Lewisburg, Penn.: Bucknell University Press, 1979).

what becomes our superior function that drives the others into the background (*CW6*: 984). We begin to see that the four types are more than mere manners of functioning. There is something more at work in them, something numinal—and "numinal" means "divine." And surely when in the grips of our typical set, as we cannot help but be when we imagine ourselves typologically, the structuring power of the type is like that of an archetype or mythologem. Especially the experience of the inferior function, also referred to as numinous, brings with it a radical shift of perspective, as if there has been an ontological shift, an initiation into a new cosmos or archetypal *Seinsweise.*

An archetypal background for the four functions has already been intimated by Jung himself. He speaks of a philosophical typology in Gnosticism or Hellenistic syncretism (*CW6*: 14; 964) by means of which human beings could be called *hylikoi, psychikoi,* or *pneumatikoi.* Jung does not document this typology, but Shmuel Sambursky considers that these terms were applied less to actual persons than to the imaginal persons of Neoplatonism, especially by Plotinus. These imaginal regions and their beings might thus be the archetypal imagination at work in the functions, giving to them each its numinal accent and each its ontological significance as structuring ground of consciousness.

Then *hylikoi,* or *physis,* with its attendant ideas of matter, body, actual physical reality would be the archetypal principle in what Jung called sensation; *psychikoi,* or soul, with its attendant Jungian description of love, value, experience, relatedness, woman, salt, color would be the archetype within and behind what Jung called feeling; *pneumatikoi,* or spirit, with its attendant descriptions in terms of light, vision, swiftness, invisibilities, timelessness, would be what Jung called intuition; and finally, not expressly distinguished in this Hellenistic triad, *nous, logos,* or *intellectus,* with its capacity for order and cognitive intelligence, would be the archetypal principle that Jung called the thinking function. (Jung himself identifies thinking with *pneumatikoi* [*CW6*: 14].)

This archetypal background gives a deeper sense to what Jung says about the four functions. For instance, if sensation so often brings with it an uncomfortable inferiority; and intuition, superiority; then the reason is not functional but archetypal—the one being hylitic and bearing all the aspersions put upon *physis* in our tradition; the other, pneumatic, windy with the idealizations of the spirit.[34] Or it is hardly a feeling function, as an ego-disposable mode of adaptation through evaluations that can support such redemptive features Jung claims for "feeling" (cf. *CW*14:28–34; *CW*6:488–91; *CW*13:222, and also *CW*8:668–69 where his discussion of evidence for soul turns on "feelings"), unless we realize that "feeling" has become a secular psychologism for soul.[35]

Furthermore, we now can grasp better the connection that Jung makes between the four functions and the wholeness of the "total personality" (*CW*14:261), or Adam (*CW*14:55–57). For now we would be dealing with the root archetypal structures or *cosmoi* of Western human being, our four "natures" as Jung calls them (*CW*4:261, 265; cf. *CW*11:184–85), which, as he says in *Mysterium Coniunctionis,* are an archetypal prefiguration of "what we today call the schema of functions." The four types are thus not mere empirical functions. They are the physical, spiritual, noetic, and psychic *cosmoi* in which man moves and imagines.[36]

The ancients placed these *cosmoi* one on top of the other and fantasied the ideal man moving through them from below to above. Jung, too, imagines the individuating person moving through the functions, not ascensionally in his model, yet still redemptively from one sidedness to fourfoldedness. Although these archetypal powers of the ancients present themselves conceptually, they are nonetheless archetypal persons of the imaginal to begin with.

---

34 Practitioners' descriptions of the *puer* psychology of young men often call them "intuitive" and airy, needing "sensation" and earth. The older language of elemental natures has been unwittingly associated with that of functional types. Actually, the practitioner is discerning young pneumatikoi whose archetypal basis in spirit cannot be reduced to an overdeveloped empirical ego-function of intuition.

35 William Willeford ("The Primacy of Feeling," *Journal of Analytical Psychology* 21/2 (July 1976): 115–33), argues for a special place for the feeling function beyond Jung's polar equalities. Because Willeford takes feeling to be the function of the "subjective sphere" (an idea which brings us again to Jung's early identification of feeling with introversion), he is suggesting that its relation with soul is different and more important than that of the other functions.

36 That Jung did not elaborate the archetypal aspect of the four functions has given rise to many attempts to deal with this hiatus by means of correlations with various sorts of cosmic constants: humours, elements, geometric forms, zodiacal signs, principles such as Love, Truth, Beauty, and Light, alchemical substances (salt, sulfur, mercury, and lead, or a composite tetrasome of four metals), alchemical colors, or even the eight world religions (A. Toynbee, *An Historian's Approach to Religion* [New York: Oxford University Press, 1956], 138).

By this I do not mean to replace intuition with spirit, and feeling with psyche, etc., or to equate them or reduce them. Rather, I am maintaining that the functions have been carrying archetypal projections that gives them, and typology, a numinal accent. *Types conceal archetypes.* The contemporary cult of feeling, for instance, is a disguised psychologistic substitution for cult of *soul.* The frequent attack on *intellect* (metaphysics and theology) through Jung's writings and letters has resulted in poor critical thinking in the Jungian school because the archetypal principle within thinking has been devalued. Unless we recognize the imaginal persons in our personal modes of functioning, these modes lose their numinal accent. Only an archetypal appreciation of the functions can take them out of the hands of the ego. Unless the great root principles of Western man's orientation are seen for what they are, as the modes in which the imaginal operates (functions) in all realms of being, they, and we, are condemned to psychological jargon without numinal accent. Thus we must cling to the types for orientation since they do conceal the archetypal natures of our Western compass.

Jung did not intend his typology to be used for typing persons. Precisely the way in which his types are used and experimented within the Grey-Wheelwright and Briggs-Myers tests—the clinical scientism—is what Jung expressly did not intend. He writes:

> It is not the purpose of a psychological typology to classify human beings into categories—this in itself would be pretty pointless. (*CW*6: 986)

> Far too many readers have succumbed to the error of thinking that Chapter X ("General Description of the Types") represents the essential content and purpose of the book, in the sense that it provides a system of classification and a practical guide to a good judgement of human character... This regrettable misunderstanding completely ignores the fact that this kind of classification is nothing but a childish parlour game... My typology... [is not meant] to stick labels on people at first sight. It is not a physiognomy... For this reason I have placed the general typology... at the end of the book... I would therefore recommend the reader... to immerse himself first of all in chapters II and V. He will gain more from them than from any typological terminology superficially picked up, since this serves no other purpose than a totally useless desire to stick on labels. (*CW*6, pp. xiv–xv)

What then was the "fundamental tendency" of the book if it was not to type persons? Jung sets it out most clearly:

> Its purpose is rather to provide a critical psychology... First and foremost, it is a critical tool for the research worker." (*CW*6: 986).
>
> The typological system I have proposed is an attempt... to provide an explanatory basis and theoretical framework for the boundless diversity... in the formation of psychological concepts. (*CW*6: 987)

Note: not diversity of *human beings* but diversity of psychological concepts. As a critical psychology, a psychology that offers a critical tool for examining ideas, it belongs to epistemology, and it was a necessary consequent of Jung's placing psyche first. As Aniela Jaffé has said at Eranos in 1971, referring to that period between 1913 and 1919 when Jung had been convinced through his own experience of the primacy of psychic reality: "The soul cannot be the object of judgement and knowledge, but judgement and knowledge are the object of the soul."[37] The types were to provide the fundamental psychological antinomies that enter into every judgement in psychology. The typology was intended as a means of seeing through statements about the soul.[38] It was an attempt at a differentiated understanding of the variety of human psychologies (*CW*6: 851–53).

The consequence of using a multiple tool is psychological relativism. This Jung knew; and it is even a corollary purpose of this *Types* to see through and relativize any psychological position. He says in the Epilogue to that work:

> In the case of psychological theories the necessity of a plurality of explanations is given from the start... an intellectual understanding of the psychic process must end in paradox and relativity. (*CW*6: 855–56; cf. 846–49).

Though intended as a Kantian critical tool for research and imagined as a "trigonometric net" or "crystallographic axial system" (*CW*6: 986) of structural principles behind personal viewpoints, the personal creeps in the back door of this the least imagistic of all his major later works, as if the

37 A. Jaffé, "Die schöpferischen Phasen im Leben von C.G. Jung," *Eranos Yearbook* 40 (1971).

38 For a use of Jung's typology as he intended it (the examination of psychological ideas rather than persons), see B. Klopfer and J.M. Spiegelman, "Some Dimensions of Psychotherapy," in *Speculum Psychologiae: Eine Freundesgabe. Festschrift zum 60.Geburtstag von C.A. Meier*, ed. C.T. Frey-Wehrlin (Zurich: Rascher, 1965).

shadow of the book is its Chapter X. There the eight types are depicted anecdotally, imagistically.

And here we all get caught by his book, not for the superb analysis of the medieval universals problem or his examinations of Schiller and Spitteler, Jordan, and James but for how few even read this part of the work! No, we all fall for these descriptions (of the introverted intuitive type, the extraverted sensation type, etc.) and take them literally as empirical persons. Such is the movement of the psyche when reading the book: it moves from the abstract to the *anschauliche*. Types become images. In the hollow rough-edged space the psyche would have an engraved gemstone, a little depiction of a personified image. The evidence that the psyche desires is not satisfied empirically, for it seeks an image: an anecdote, a Theophrastian character, a psychiatric case, a "typical example" from life or literature, a saint, an icon of visible traits that acounts for the numinal accent of my type. Without these personified images to give precise substance to a type, a type more easily rigidifies into a defined class.

Until the hollow of the type be specified with its image, it is our own face we see in typologies. Don't we tend to turn to them most when we are self-occupied, neurasthenic, narcissistically depressed? When we need ego-support? Typologies fascinate and convince because they are methods of mirroring what we most look for—self-perception, recognition of our individual image. And the more we gain this insight into our uniqueness and present ourselves as an individual image, the less fascinating and convincing typology; we say, "no longer fit in." Our individual image has become shaped more distinctly than the empty rough-edged form that reflects us each in its equalizing measure.

And every well-written typology, such as those depictions in Chapter X, in the older psychiatry texts, or in astrological *Charakterkunde* will capture us and equalize us into its image—especially the pathologized image. As we journey through the planetary houses, typical syndrome to syndrome, we become the description, embody the diseases one by one, fit into each chapter. Such is the power of the well-shaped image and such is the suffering of the soul until it be perceived in its own image. Thus within every typological system there lurks the abstract emptiness in which we lose our uniqueness until we have the sense of our own morphological individuality.

2

PERSONS AS FACES

> The world lives in order to develop the lines on its face.
> —T. E. HULME, "Cinders"

Jung wrote: "Since individuality... is absolutely unique, unpredictable, and uninterpretable,... the therapist must abandon all his preconceptions and techniques" (*CW*16: 6). We have been attempting this, abandoning even one of the techniques, typing, derived from Jung. But our problem remains: how to perceive the human phenomenon before us in its uninterpretable uniqueness?

Here we might turn from the empirical and scientistic to the more philosophical psychologies. We should expect help from phenomenology whose very business is to confront the phenomenon directly, from existentialism whose concern is mainly with the existential person, or from the psychoanalytic tradition whose focus of effort is the individual case in the privacy of practice.

But in the first case (phenomenology), "there is no person as such for Husserl, only an empirical and a transcendental ego, united tenously by the body and behavior"[39] as global abstractions, while Merleau-Ponty gives us hermeneutics, interpretative *meanings* of body and gesture across the board, in all of us, as universals. In the second case (existentialism), Sartre "dissolves personal encounter into a petrifying scotophilic *look*—a look that overlooks the crucial minutiae" that are unique and govern one's existence; while Heidegger's concern is neither with the person nor with the particular except as modes of *Dasein,* and this despite all his appeal to the concrete. In the third case (psychoanalysis), Freud and his patient never looked each other in the face during the procedure of their ritual,

---

39 I am indebted to E. S. Casey for the substance and quotations of this paragraph.

and Lacan admits that "a psychoanalysis normally proceeds to its termination without revealing to us very much of what our patient derives in his own right from his particular sensitivity to colors or calamities, from the quickness of his grasp of things or the urgency of his weaknesses of the flesh, from his power to retain or to invent—in short, from the vivacity of his tastes."[40] Again the nomothetic dominates. In philosophical psychologies,[41] as much as in scientistic psychologies, the individual is crowded to the wall by the general. So we must try another approach altogether. Is it possible that the person before us already gives us his individuality? Could it be that his invisible essence is stamped right in his visible presence? Each human being bearing the traits of his uniqueness stamped upon him—this ancient idea is the common ground of all systems of characterology. And characterology, the study of visible signs for discovering the invisible in human nature, is a trunk root of psychology.

The relation between physique and character—as Kretschmer was to call his work—as well as deriving predictabilities from this relation, occurs already among Babylonians. Physiognomic omina revealed fate. Physique was related to character by means of a "when/then" formula—the language of prophetic magic not so very different from the language of predictional science: "When his hair and his face is long, then his days are long, he will be poor."[42] There is no distinction between character and fate. A character statement derived from physique is also a prophecy. When a woman shows features good for bearing children, then she will bear many children. Or according to a man's build: "The man is sinful, he will be killed by a weapon."[43] Taking our cue from Jung, when we read a person or his soul's contents (dreams) in order to predict fate (marriage, travel, psychosis), we are moving away from uniqueness that is

40 The quoted passage by Lacan is from J. Lacan, *The Language of the Self,* trans. A. Wilden (Baltimore: Johns Hopkins Press, 1968), 29.

41 "Typical psychological phenomena are what phenomenological psychologists have traditionally studied (von Kaam, Fischer, Lauffer, Cloonan, Stevick, Colizzi)." E. Keen, "Studying Unique Events," *Journal of Phenomenological Psychology* 8 (1977): 27–43. Keen's solution—a dialectic between typical and unique—falls prey to its own philosophical assumption: typical and unique, general and particular are valid categories and problematically opposed.

42 F.R. Kraus, "Die physiognomischen Omina der Babylonier," *Mitteilungen der Vorderasiatisch-Aegyptischen Gesellschaft* 40/2 (1935).

43 Ibid., 12.

both uninterpretable and unpredictable. To see the essence of a character does not mean that we can predict what will happen to that character. That psychologist who "can look into the seeds of time, and say which grain will grow and which will not" is the witch, says Shakespeare (*Macbeth*, 1.3). Greek treatises on physiognomies—and here the main influence on us is the *Physiognomonica,* the pseudo-Aristotelian treatise on physiognomy—distinguished between character and prophecy, between psychology proper and magical or scientific predictabilities. The basic principle of reading character through physical visibility is stated straight off: "Dispositions follow bodily characteristics"[44] and immediately there follows an assumption presented as evidence: "For no animal has ever existed such that it has the form of one animal and the disposition of another, but the body and soul of the same creature are always such that a given disposition must necessarily follow a given form."[45]

Aristotle next summarizes three different ways of reading persons. We can see them in terms of animal analogies,[46] of geography and race, and of facial display of emotions. We see a person as birdlike or horsefaced, and as Greek or Egyptian, and as displaying the universal signs of anger or erotic excitement. These same three ways of understanding the looks of our fellows have continued to inform our tradition of physiognomics from Aristotle or before until our own day of research on stereotypes in perception and sociology of race relations. Besides these main methods, this little treatise codified observations that still come quick to the tongue: "For those living in the north are brave and stiff-haired, and those in the south are cowardly and have soft hair."[47] Later this sort of north-south division became one between blondes and brunettes. Physical

44 "Physiognomics," in Aristotle, *Minor Works: On Colours. On Things Heard. Physiognomics. On Plants. On Marvellous Things Heard. Mechanical Problems. On Indivisible Lines. The Situations and Names of Winds. On Melissus, Xenophanes, Gorgias,* trans. W. S. Hett (Cambridge, Mass.: Harvard University Press, 1936), 85 (805*a*).

45 Ibid.

46 Perception of persons by means of animal analogies is deep in our language offraits. This language was of course powerfully shaped in English by Shakespeare who has over 4,000 allusions to animals in his plays. Falstaff, Caliban, Richard III, and Ajax have the highest scores for character descriptions in animal terms. See A.E. Yoder's *Animal Analogy in Shakespeare's Character Portrayal* (New York: King's Crown Press, 1947) for statistics and excellent bibliography on the tradition of animal analogies.

47 Aristotle, "Physiognomics," 95 (806*b*). Cf. J. Hillman, *Re-Visioning Psychology* (New York: Harper & Row, 1976), 259n112–13, for a psychological view of the north-south polarity.

anthropology around 1900, and Havelock Ellis as well, produced studies to show that blondes are more "positive, dynamic, driving, aggressive, domineering, impatient, active, quick, hopeful, speculative, changeable, and variety-loving."[48] Jaensch's T-type was to be found, he said, mainly among blondes. Darker persons were of another type showing "romantischen Bluteinschlag [romantic blood impact]."[49]

Though the discrimination of persons according to ethnic, racial, and geographical notions is one of the oldest and most basic habits in the tradition of psychological assessment of persons, it is now fully suppressed. We do not dare discriminate along these lines. Even the term "discrimination" has taken on a pejorative "elitist" sense. We no longer allow ourselves to discriminate differences by means of north and south, smooth and hairy, dark and light, oily and dry. Because we no longer dispose of a richly emotional language for insighting the historical and geographical shadow in the psyche, this entire metaphorical possibility becomes unconscious, returning as literal racial discrimination in the world. But *stereotypes are images,* modes of imagination that present physiognomies of the shadow, allowing me to see my own in contrast. By means of these ethnic epithets I am able to discriminate a region of differences between myself and others and locate each psyche within a distinct landscape, giving it history and soil. Of course, all communal thinking, all egalitarian '-ologies' taboo as prejudices these modes of perceptive discrimination, forcing ethnic images and metaphors into literalisms that project shadow rather than letting see and feel shadow.

These stereotypical modes—animal, geographical, emotional—were part of the physiognomies by means of which the ancient world understood and described persons.[50] In ancient medicine or philosophy, drama or literature, rhetoric or biography (as the *imagines* of the Emperors by Suetonius), character could be differentiated by telltale signs explained by axioms collected in physiognomic hand: books.[51]

48 K. Blackford, *The Job, the Man, the Boss* (Garden City, N.Y.: Doubleday, Page and Co., 1914), quoted and criticized in W. A. Lessa, *Landmarks in the Study of Human Types* (New York: Brooklyn College Press, 1942), 141.

49 E. R. Jaensch, *Grundformen menschlichen Seins* (Berlin: Elsner, 1929), 325.

50 Cf. the superb monograph by E. C. Evans, "Physiognomies in the Ancient World," *Transactions of the American Philosophical Society,* n.s. 59/5 (1969).

51 Evans, "Physiognomies," 6–17, on the treatises and handbooks.

For instance, Emperor Julian was declared demonic by Gregory of Nazianzus[52] in terms that everyone could understand: one had only to look at the man: his unsteady neck, jerking shoulders, unstable feet, unrestrained laughter, effeminacy. None of these traits were proper to the ideal image of Christian physique, and therefore Julian could not be but demonic. Anatomy is destiny. Julian, of course, had his own physiognomer who found his same traits laudatory, and Julian wrote on this very subject himself, insisting to his portraitist: "Paint me exactly as you saw me."[53] His nature was revealed in his face. But our task is not judging Emperor Julian but candidate Carter or our candidates for training as analysts. Let us look at some other approaches, less antique, for seeing persons not as types but as faces.

Darwin. What we have just learned from the ancients is that there is indeed a mode of perceiving persons directly: the person is his self-presentation. And we have learned that it will not be altogether possible to follow Jung's fantasy of existential objectivity and abandon all preconceptions, since when we see persons we see faces, and certain preconceptions–animal, racial, emotional–seem given with the face itself. The weak chin, bull neck, low brow, and fleshy lip are themselves images; the very phrases echo metaphorically. There have been various attempts in psychology, and we shall now be reviewing several to work out *the relation between person and image.* For instance, does a knitted brow always indicate worry and a downturned lip sadness? This sort of question occupied Darwin.

Darwin's study on *The Expression of the Emotions in Man and Animals*[54] was published one year after his *Descent of Man,* and was conceived as part of that earlier book. The work on expression brought further evidence for his thesis of mental continuity or the evolution of the human from other animal species. Even the human face and its variegated expressions so characteristic of what we consider uniquely human and unique in each human, if not divine, has its phylogenetic roots.

Darwin scrutinized the faces of the mentally ill, works of art, higher animals, adults from various cultures, infants, and children. (He had

---

52 Gregory of Nazianzus, *Orations* 4 and 5. Cf. Evans, "Physiognomies," 74–80.

53 *The Works of the Emperor Julian,* vol. 3, trans. W.C. Wright (Cambridge, Mass.: Harvard University Press, 1993), 303.

54 C. Darwin, *The Expression of the Emotions in Man and Animals* (London: John Murray, 1872).

begun keeping a journal of his observations on his own children in 1840, thirty-two years before publishing his findings.) Since then, similar work on similar groups has confirmed Darwin. Facial expression of anger, joy, surprise, sorrow, fear appear early in life. Learning is not required for this appearance. Research with the congenitally blind also supports Darwin's thesis that what we show in emotional physiognomies rests mainly on innate factors that do not require seeing other faces. Cross-cultural studies, which have included such isolated and preliterate peoples as the Fore and Dani of New Guinea, conclude: "The same facial expressions are associated with the same emotions, regardless of culture or language."[55] Darwin further suggested that physiognomy of any face was itself largely the result of emotional attitudes. Repeated emotional experiences lead to the development of permanent facial form (wrinkles, coloring, muscle tensions).

One does not have to accept Darwin's evolutional explanation even while we may accept both the innate expressive *analogies* between human and animal physiognomy and the innate *commonality* in all human faces as one more place where what Jung calls the "collective unconscious" manifests itself. The image that we present in our self-representation or *Selbstdarstellung*—to use Adolf Portmann's term—is the visibility of our emotional nature. Our surface presents our depth.

Szondi. Our next approach runs through Zurich. Type and image come together in the *Schicksalsanalyse* (fate analysis) of Léopold Szondi.[56] Briefly, Szondi is a Hungarian psychiatrist who lived in Zurich, where the Szondi-Institut is still based. He developed a diagnostic test and a therapeutic direction based upon discovering one's type through selecting among forty-eight radically pathologized images. One is shown photographs of the faces of paroxysmal epileptics, catatonic schizophrenics, criminal sadists, severe depressives—eight types in all—that have been culled from the brilliantly precise, descriptive psychiatry texts[57] of the early part of this cen-

55 See *Darwin and Facial Expression: A Century of Research in Review*, ed. P. Ekman (Cambridge, Mass.: Malor Books, 2006), 218.

56 L. Szondi, *Schicksalsanalyse: Wahl in Liebe, Freundschaft, Beruf, Krankheit und Tod* (Basel: Schwabe, 1944).

57 Thirty of the forty-eight photographs were gleaned from W. Weygandt, *Atlas und Grundriss der Psychiatrie* (Munich: Lehmann, 1902). Further examples of Weygandt's descriptive psychiatry (with extraordinary photographs) are found in *Lehrbuch der Nerven-und Geisteskrankheiten* (Hall: Marhold, 1935) and *Idiotie und Imbezilität* (Leipzig/Wien:

tury, when this sort of medical freak show was the delight of adolescents, doing more, I suspect, for their education into the profundities of the psyche than the pornographic substitutes of today.

It is Szondi's theory that the genetic pattern shows in the face: the faces in the test are the most extreme and purest visibilities of basic genetic types. Therefore, should I choose manic faces as more sympathetic, and catatonic faces as most repulsive, my selection derives—so he says—from my recessive genes working through my unconscious sympathies and antipathies. It is assumed that the person whose face I have chosen suffers from the specific type of psychiatric disorder that is potentially present in me owing to my recessive genes. These recessive genes rule the unconscious, forcing us to choose our partners, our professions, our sicknesses, and our deaths. By choosing a specific pathological physiognomy, we discover which specific type of personified monster is unconsciously affecting our destiny.

Before Szondi, as early as 1878, Francis Galton,[58] Darwin's half-cousin and also an extraordinary person in the history of psychology, had begun making composite photographs of criminal and disease types, and of family members, by superimposing one exposure on another until he got the image of a face that brought out what he called hereditary traits. By an empirical technique he arrived at a pure type, an idealized family face beyond individual peculiarities. The type face could be used as a norm for seeing deviations in any individual or, because of the intensification of dominant traits, it produced an image of the family's degeneracy, the "skeleton in the cupboard." Szondi's test asks us to choose among eight syndromes as archetypal modes of suffering; for in our mode of pathologizing our life is styled. As Jung said, types and temperaments determine how we live our complexes.[59] The notion of basic types of archetypal suf-

Deutike, 1915). The forty-eight photographs and the rationale of their selection are discussed in English in L. Szondi, U. Moser, and M.W. Webb, *The Szondi Test* (Philadelphia: Lippincott, 1959), 3-21. Parallel series of images have been devised in other cultures, e.g., F. Farah, *Études comparatives d'une série japonaise, parallèle à la série originale du Szondi-test* (Bern: Herbert Lang, 1975).

58 F. Galton, "Composite portraits made by combining those of many different persons into a single figure," *Nature* 18 (1878): 97–100; "Composite Portraits," *Journal of the Anthropological Institute* 8 (1879): 132–44.

59 Jung, too, saw the temperaments or types more fundamental in choice of neurosis than the complexes (*CW*6: 970, 927–30, 960–61) and his specific theory of psychopathology relates syndromes to typology.

fering appears in the elements of Empedocles and Plato (*Timaeus*), which were modes of *pathos*, ways of being buffeted by fate, being moved by necessity. The four temperaments of humoral medicine are terms—choleric, melancholic, etc.—also derived from pathology. There, too, temperament determined the style of one's fate and diseases.

More specifically, Szondi, and Galton too, touch our theme because they stress that type is seen in the phenomenal face. Genotype is present in phenotype. In the words of Jungian language, for instance, *animus* is not only an opinionated complex reaction or a figure in a dream. *Animus* is visible as a tautness in the mouth and voice, a pallid skin, a graceless tension in arms, neck, and shoulders—a driven, haunted expression. Moreover, the face is the place of revelation of the family ghost, the ethnic shadow, the hereditary taint, the deepest secret—recessive and pathological.

Szondi's theory is elaborated with genetics and statistics, but Szondi's faces, on which the whole work rests, can be taken as a modern variety of Theophrastean characters or overlarge figures such as we experience when reading the great nineteenth-century works of fiction or psychiatry. These figures have overpowering reality so that we identify with them, and are at once drawn in to envisioning our lives in their terms. (Psychiatry books still have this effect; hence we can see ourselves and others so much more vividly and convincingly by means of their diagnostic configurations, those "syndromes" that are vivified personified images.) Szondi insists that this identification through pathology is material and literal. I am suggesting that it is the power of the pathologized image itself that evokes what he calls "psychoshock." Here we go back to *The Art of Memory*[60] and its idea that pathologized images are the most effective movers of the soul. But now we see that what moves the soul most is the "intolerable image"—the face of soft homosexuality, the face of brutal paroxysmal rage—which, because it is so deeply shocking, precisely constellates my repressions, and thus the turns of my fate, even to death.

60 F.A. Yates, *The Art of Memory* (London: Routledge, 1966), 10, 109–10, and as I discussed it in "The Language of Psychology and the Speech of the Soul," *Eranos Yearbook* 37 (1968): 333ff. The notion of the "intolerable image" comes from Rafael López-Pedraza as developed in his *Hermes and His Children* (Einsiedeln: Daimon Verlag, 2012).

Gestalt. Gestalt psychology has made us remember again that the whole world, and not only the human face, presents itself physiognomically. We perceive not just discrete particular sensations–green blotches, bird notes. We perceive significant whole patterns–the palm frond together with a bird's melody in whose total physiognomy there are emotional qualities. And, it is not our subjective ability to empathize (Lipps) or our intentional set of mind (Brentano) that occasions these qualities; nor do we project them into the face of the world. They are there, given in the image. "A thing," said Wertheimer, "is as uncanny as it is black. In fact, it is first and foremost uncanny." Katz says: "The physiognomical qualities of the environment are those that are primary, not cognitive. And this is true similarly for inanimate as for animate things."[61] A paper by Wertheimer in 1912 is said to be the official beginning of gestalt psychology. So it begins during that period of fragmentation of forms that characterizes the consciousmess of many fields at the outbreak of World War I.[62] (We shall come back to this period from quite a different angle later.) Gestalt attempted to deal with the dissociation by denying that consciousness was composed of associated particulars, the fragmentation by insistence on wholes, the surrealist by promulgating laws, the schizophrenic by a religious isomorphism,[63] which united mind, body, and world by means of forms. Its psychology of wholes bloomed at a time when things had

---

61 Both quotations are from D. Katz, *Gestaltpsychologie* (Basel/Stuttgart: Schwabe, 1969), 95.

62 For a list of these many breakdown and breakthrough events in art, music, letters, science, and especially psychology that occurred between 1911 and 1914, see J. Hillman, *The Myth of Analysis: Three Essays in Archetypal Psychology* (Evanston, Ill.: Northwestern University Press, 1972), 164–65.

63 Isomorphism (Köhler, Koffka, Metzger) claims an inherent similarity between the *psychological* patterns in perception, physical patterns in the structures of things, and *physiological* patterns in the central nervous system. The great realms of being–anorganic nature, organic life, and conscious mind–meet in the central nervous system. There is one world united by forms: morphic monism. Isomorphism offers the religious doctrine of correspondences (Böhme, Eckhart, Goethe) in scientific dress. Because of the new dress, the multiplicities in the old correspondence idea are forced into a unity (which then proliferate one hundred and fourteen laws of gestalt). Instead of differentiating the faces of this unity, gestalt abstracts forms and forces. Patterns lose their imagistic content, become formal, even mathematical structures. *Topos* becomes topology. Nonetheless, the religious background remains in the gestalt sense of mission. Karl Lashley called Köhler's work a "new religion," which Köhler willingly acknowledged in his *Die Aufgabe der Gestalt-Psychologie* (Berlin: de Gruyter, 1971), 37.

fallen apart. So we can understand its having been acclaimed as a revolution of vision, even though Ernst Mach, as far back as the 1860s, had begun to show that a tree and a melody are perceived as wholes and not as composites of discrete pieces, and that we perceive two blotches of color differently according to their forms, i.e., we have sensations of a formal, spatial kind.[64]

Gestalt psychology contributes to an archetypal psychology of the image as significant form that precedes and is perhaps different from its cognitive meaning. A gestalt view of the human image, or of any image, gets us beyond interpretations and out of the hermeneutic cages that have trapped our immediate perceptions.

Gestalt has observed that an image is *sinnträchtig* (pregnant with meaning). We could reconsider this "physiognomic character" of an image to be what we call its "archetypal" quality. Then the archetype would not be *behind* the image as a hypothetical *noumenon* in a Kantian sense, not a form to be inferred from or pieced together by amplification and resemblances or to be experienced as an imperative through powerful affects. Rather, the archetypal quality would be *in* the image as its significance because, as the gestaltists say, the image is itself "sinnträchtig." Or, as Jung says:

> Image and meaning are identical; and as the first takes shape, so the latter becomes clear. Actually, the pattern needs no interpretation: it portrays its own meaning (*CW*8: 402).

We are now distinguishing between the meaning of an image and its significance: the first is what we give to it; the second, what it gives to us. It bears the gift of significance; it is fecund with implications; or, in gestalt language, an image has pregnancy.[65] It carries with its own body the potential of archetypal resonance. The archetype's inherence in the image gives body to the image, the fecundity of carrying and giving birth to insights. The more we articulate its shape, the less we need to interpret.

To see the archetypal in an image is thus not a hermeneutic move; it is an imagistic move. We amplify an image by means of myth not in order

---

64 Experiments with infants (between four days and six months) convincingly establish that form perception, especially the preference for representations of the human face over other patterns, is innate. R.L. Fantz, "The Origin of Form Perception," *Scientific American* 204 (1961): 66–73

65 See S.K. Langer, *Feeling and Form: A Theory of Art* (New York: Scribner's, 1953), 8–9, for a discussion of her "principle of fecundity."

to find its archetypal meaning but in order to feed it with further images that increase its volume and depth and release its fecundity. Hermeneutic amplifications in search of meaning take us elsewhere across cultures, looking for resemblances that neglect the specifics of the actual image. Our move, which keeps archetypal significance limited within the actually presented image, also keeps meanings always precisely embodied. No longer would there be images without meaning and meaning without images. The neurotic condition that Jung so often referred to as "loss of meaning" would now be understood as "loss of image," and the condition would be met therapeutically less by recourse to philosophy, religion, and wisdom, and more by turning directly to one's actual images in which archetypal significance resides.

Unless we maintain this distinction between inherent significance and interpretative meaning, between insighting an image and hermeneutics, we shall not be able to stay with the image and let it give us what it bears. We shall have the meaning and miss the experience, miss the uniqueness of what is there by our use of methods for uncovering what is not there. We shall forget that wholeness is not only a construction to be built or a goal to achieve, but, as gestalt says, a whole is presented in the very physiognomy of each event.

But gestalt psychology did not harvest what it had sown. Its work on the image became optics, and it never had much to say about individuality. It soon fell into the usual division of modern psychological thinking: on the one hand, seeking ever more general formulations, as if caught by its own doctrine of wholes, it became scientistically experimental developing one hundred and fourteen "laws" of gestalten, with an algebra of forces, field theory, vectors, brain physiology, visual perception; on the other hand, it became gestalt therapy—Fritz Perls, and groups. The "good" gestalt (Kurt Koffka), where good means "regular, symmetric, simple, uniform, closed, showing uniform direction—in short exhibiting the minimum possible amount of stress,"[66] became both a law to be established experimentally and a psychological aim to be achieved therapeutically.

Nonetheless, gestalt restores a Greek and religious way of viewing the world. The Greeks placed their sanctuaries according to the physiognomic character of the landscape: particular spots spoke to and of

66 L. Zusne, *Visual Perception of Form* (New York/London: Academic Press, 1970), 126.

particular gods.[67] The face of every event bears significance. To read the world, we must read its face, the presenting surface of its landscape and our inscape in response to it. *We must stick to the image.* That is where each particular wholeness lies. Unity is a quality given with the face of each event.

Lavater. Our next avenue again goes through Zurich, one of its most odd and most beloved natives: Johann Kaspar Lavater (1741–1801). Although he was a friend or correspondent of the major figures of his age—Goethe, Mendelssohn, Herder, Hamann, Füseli, nobility, and royalty—and though he preached and published a good deal of personal Protestant theology, he is known mainly for his *Essays on Physiognomy,* or as they were called in German, *Physiognomische Fragmente zur Beförderung der Menschenkenntnis und Menschenliebe,* published in four parts between 1775 and 1778.

The first main thesis that Lavater's work tries to establish is much the same as that of Darwin and gestalt psychology: the universality of physiognomies. His approach, however, is from the beginning subjective. Particular faces produce particular sensations in the onlooker, and "exactly similar sensations cannot be generated by forms that are in themselves different."[68] Lavater extended his notion of "face" also in the manner of the gestaltists. All things have their physiognomic character:

> Do we not daily judge of the sky by its physiognomy? No food, not a glass of wine, or beer, not a cup of coffee, or tea, comes to table, which is not judged by its physiognomy, its exterior; and of which we do not thence deduce some conclusion respecting its interior, good, or bad, properties.[69]

Regional character also shows in the face. For example, of an engraving of a citizen of Zurich, he writes: "No Englishman looks thus, no Frenchman, no Italian, and, certainly, no citizen of Basil [Basel], or Bern."[70]

Lavater also recapitulates the long tradition of comparison between animal and human faces and skulls, the major basis of Darwin's theory and also an idea that some have suggested goes back before Aristotle,

---

67 Cf. P. Philippson, *Griechische Gottheiten in ihren Landschaften* (Oslo: Brógger, 1934) and V. Scully, *The Earth, the Temple, and the Gods: Greek Sacred Architecture* (New York: Frederick A. Praeger, 1969).

68 J.C. Lavater, *Essays on Physiognomy,* trans. T. Holcroft (London: W. Tegg, 1880), 31.

69 Ibid., 16.

70 Ibid., 427.

before Babylonia, to animal totemism. Each kind of animal life bears its distinct nature in its form:

> Were the lion and the lamb, for the first time, placed before us, had we never known such animals, never heard their names, still we could not resist the impression of the courage and strength of the one, or of the weakness and sufferance of the other...As the make of each animal is distinct from all others, so, likewise is the character...the peculiar qualities of a species are expressed in the general form of that species.[71]

Internal significance is revealed in self-portrayal; archetypal nature appears in the image itself. And so, it is the task of physiognomy to read the image, precisely, just as it appears.

It is the *structure* of the image that draws Lavater's eye. Unlike Darwin, Charles Bell, Duchenne,[72] and Piderit—all in the nineteenth century who interpreted the face's expression through movement of muscles, a functional, dynamic view—Lavater's eighteenth-century physiognomy searches out character at rest;[73] its concern is with essence, not with behavior. It is an examination of form rather than expressive emotion (*Wesenschau,* not *Dynamik*).

Lavater, too, had his "good" gestalten. His ideal form is a line that is neither too cramped and rigid nor too soft and flexible, that line, *frei und richtig,* which drops like a string with a lead weight attached. Lavater had engraved this anchored lead-weighted image of the "correct" line pendant with gravity as an allegorical motto on a title page of his work.

The emphasis upon line shows that Lavater thought more as a calligrapher than did the gestaltists. His was the eye that perceived the handwriting of the Creator—his signature in all things—rather than his geometry. God is more the artist who works in images than he is the scientist who works through numbers and laws. The distinction between artist and scientist was applied to Lavater himself by his contemporaries.[74]

---

71 Ibid., 212.

72 G.B. Duchenne, *Mécanisme de la physionomie humaine, ou Analyse électro-physiologique de l'expression des passions* (Paris: Baillière, 1862). Before Darwin's major work, Duchenne had painstakingly elaborated a theory that correlated each muscle of the face with a specific passion; these muscles, being the same for all mankind, cause the universally instinctual facial language of emotion.

73 Lavater, *Essays on Physiognomy,* 12.

74 R. Kunz, *Johann Caspar Lavaters Physiognomielehre im Urteil von Haller, Zimmermann und anderen zeitgenössischen Ärzten* (Zurich: Juris Verlag, 1970).

And this Creator makes each individual different: "It is the first, the most profound, most secure, and unshaken foundation stone of physiognomy that, however intimate the analogy and similarity of the innumerable forms of men, no two men can be found who, brought together, and accurately compared, will not appear to be very remarkably different."[75] God as image-maker and man perceiving imaginatively contrast with God as lawmaker and man perceived typologically. To the artist's idiographic eye, differences stand out; while to the rationalist's nomothetic eye it is similarities, classes, types. Neither Gall and his measurements of skulls nor Carus and his idealized types or models were able to equal Lavater's imagistic eye for individual differences.[76]

In order to describe these individual differences, Lavater insists that one be "inexhaustibly copious in language." He is forced by the immense subtlety of physiognomic expression to "be the creator of a new language."[77] We are reminded of the 17,953 trait names mentioned earlier. Lavater says that poverty of language makes us unable to grasp what we see, perhaps even to see at all. We see what our language allows us to see, a statement drawing support from experimental studies that show a link between having the ability to be an accurate judge of personality and having artistic and literary interests.[78] I am suggesting that the substitution of clinical language for literary, of mathematical exactness for imaginative precision, the learning of observation through microscopic medicine rather than through bedside portraits and biography, and the reliance upon socio-psychological testing instead of moral-characterological scrutiny have all contributed to our decline in psychological perception of the individual person and thus to our age of psychopathy.

Lavater was well aware that nowhere perhaps are we more apt to project than when looking into the face of another person.[79] The problem

75 Lavater, *Essays on Physiognomy,* 13.

76 See R. Züst, *Die Grundzüge der Physiognomik Johann Kaspar Lavaters* (Bülach: Steinmann-Scheuchzer, 1948), 98–100, for a comparison of Lavater's with other physiognomics.

77 Lavater, *Essays on Physiognomy,* 65.

78 P.E. Vernon, "Multivariate Approaches to the Study of Cognitive Styles," in *Multivariate Analysis and Psychological Theory,* ed. J.R. Royce (London and New York: Academic Press, 1973), 68–69.

79 The "argument from projection" against physiognomies actually serves it: when we assume receding-chinned, sallow-complexioned, watery-eyed, thin-haired faces to be lacking in aggressive determination and find men such as General James

of projection when trying to read another human being characterizes all modern psychology, which has devised its methods of distancing, objectivizing, and measuring to be sure that we do not form our judgments by subjective feelings. Yet these "objective" measures to counteract projection seem to make psychologists such poor perceivers. A study by Estes in 1938, borne out by Luft in 1950 and by Taft after that, affirms that psychiatrists and clinical psychologists are inferior to artists, laymen, and even physicists as judges of personality.[80]

Lavater's method for correcting projection was not by recourse to the scientistic distancing of objective techniques. His discipline was psychological:

> In proportion only as he knows himself will he be able to know others.[81]
>
> For this reason, the physiognomist must, if he knows himself, which he in justice ought to do before he attempts to know others, once more compare his remarks with his own peculiar mode of thinking, and separate those which are general from those which are individual, and appertain to himself.[82]

Wolfe, the British hero of Quebec, to put the lie to this assumption ("projection"), whence does the stereotypic "projection" arise if not from the archetypal significance of these physiognomic traits by which we have read "weakness" in Wolfe's face? Cf. J. Brophy, *The Human Face Reconsidered* (London: Harrap, 1962), 164–86.

80 Vernon, "Multivariate Approaches," with full references. The study by J. Luft, "Implicit Hypotheses and Clinical Predictions," *The Journal of Abnormal and Social Psychology* 45 (1950): 756–60, attempted to measure how well clinicians understood a patient as compared with nonclinicians after listening to a case conference summary: "An analysis of variance failed to bring out significant differences between the clinical and non-clinical groups...the psychodiagnostician who had administered the Wechsler-Bellevue scale, the Rorschach, the TAT and one or two other tests, and, who was also present at the case conference, obtained a prediction score equivalent to chance." Taft writes: "Courses in psychology do not improve ability to judge others and there is considerable doubt whether professional psychologists show better ability to judge than do graduate students in psychology"; however, there is "clear evidence that good ability...was related to painting and dramatic avocations but not musical...the ability to rate traits accurately and to predict...responses correlates positively with simple, traditional, artistic sensitivity." (R. Taft, "The Ability to Judge People," *Psychological Bulletin* 52 [1955]: 12–13). Moreover, both Luft and Taft report findings that show physical scientists to be significantly superior, as judges of others, to social scientists. Taft, "Some Characteristics of Good Judges of Others," *British Journal of Psychology* 47 (1956): 19–29.

81 Lavater, *Essays on Physiognomy*, 66.

82 Ibid., 67.

> [Without this discipline of knowing his own heart,] thou wilt read vices on that forehead whereon virtue is written and wilt accuse others of those failings and errors which thy own heart accuses thee. Whoever bears any resemblance to thine enemy will be accused of all those failings and vices with which thy enemy is loaded by thy own partiality and self-love.[83]

Here is a Zurich precursor of the Jung who laid it strongly on Freud that the analyst be analyzed himself before attempting to work with others; the Jung who stressed that the projection of shadow is problematic in all human relationships.

We can learn from Lavater something about this shadow projection. He said: "Whoever does not, at the first aspect of any man, feel a certain emotion of affection or dislike, attraction or repulsion, never can become a physiognomist."[84] Sympathy and antipathy are psychological tools; evidently, these gut reactions of the shadow help us perceive. To hold them off in the name of objectivity does not improve perception but falsifies it. So, too, we injure our perceptual ability by supposedly integrating the shadow. By this I mean that my intense feelings of repulsion and dislike about someone—Richard Nixon, say—are not only part of me to integrate. They are part of the percept of Nixon, part of his physiognomy and given with his gestalt. The more I take the world in as my shadow to integrate, the less I can differentiatedly perceive the world's actual physiognomic character. To call a perception "shadow" generalizes the perception; we are no longer seeing but conceiving. If we do not trust our own eyes to see and ears to hear and to stand for what we feel when we see and hear, we then increase paranoid suspicions about what we are sensing. As our observational precision decreases, vague paranoid impressions veil us in. The task is age-old: to discern the Devil in his actual manifestations rather than to theologize about sin. This does not mean that shadow emotions must be taken literally as truths about the object, but neither are they to be taken as projections, pure subjectivities that belong only to me. Gut reactions are not general, but specific to specific "faces." They call for *precision,* which is neither integration nor projection.

If in Darwin and Szondi genetic inheritance determines physiognomy, and in gestalt psychology, topological laws, in Lavater it is imagination

---

83 Ibid., 68.

84 Ibid., 63.

that determines the visible form. Imagination in the mother forms her child in the womb. Hyperactive imagination produces the giant; imagination in its passivity, the dwarf. "Imagination acts upon our own countenance, rendering it in some measure resembling the beloved or hated image, which is living, present, and fleeting before us...The image of imagination often acts more effectually than the real presence."[85] How did Jung put it? "The psyche creates reality every day. The only expression I can use for this activity is *fantasy*" (*CW*6: 78).

Man is created as an image, in an image, and by means of images. Therefore he appears first of all to the imagination so that the perception of personality is first of all an imaginative act (to which sensation, emotion, and ideation contribute but do not determine). Modern psychological methods of examining images and imagination in terms of sensations or feelings start the wrong way around.[86] Since imagination forms us into our images, to perceive a person as essence we must look into his imagination and see what fantasy is creating his reality. But to look into imagination we need to look with imagination, imaginatively, searching for images with images. You are given to my imagination by your image, the image of you in your heart as Michelangelo, as Neoplatonism, as Henry Corbin would say, and this image is composed not only of wrinkles, muscles, and colors accreted through your life, though they make their contribution to its complexity. To see you as you are is an imagination, as Lavater says, of structure, the divine image in which your essence is shaped.

We have now moved from persons as *faces* to persons as *images.* The imaginative act of seeing requires, Lavater says, a variegated language, self-discipline about projection (knowledge of my own heart and its images), experience of the world—and an eye that sees *instantaneity.* Here words reach their limit, for language must be strung into sentences. They proceed in time, forming narratives, stories. But the image is perceived all at once, as a gestalt, all parts simultaneously.[87] In a letter (and here I am

85 Ibid., 374.

86 This kind of approach is critically reviewed by Mary Watkins in *Waking Dreams* (New York: Gordon & Breach, 1976), 77–90.

87 The contrast between image simultaneity and narrative succession, and the different psychological effects of the two modes, is developed by Patricia Berry: "An Approach to the Dream," in P. Berry, *Echo's Subtle Body: Contributions to an Archetypal Psychology* (Thompson, Conn.: Spring Publications, 2017), 55–77.

relying on a splendid early work of Ernst Benz[88] on Lavater and Swedenborg), Lavater says:

> Every language of this world, even the most perfect, has an essential imperfection—that it is only successive: whereas the speech to the eye of images and signs is instantaneous. The language of Heaven in order to be perfect must be both successive and instantaneous. It must present a whole heap of images, thoughts, sensations, all at once like a painting, and yet also present their succession with the greatest speed and truthfulness. It must be painting and speech together.[89]

Lavater here is echoing both a classical (Horace) and an eighteenth-century idea: *Ut pictura poesis*, the formal and contentual unity of painting and poetry.[90] His vision is thoroughly spatial, and language cannot adequately speak of spatial relations because it talks in time. But Lavater is going beyond aesthetics; he is speaking of the language of Heaven, of angels to whom all is revealed in a flash and who read the character of man and judge him thereby through his image. Here Lavater deepens Darwin. If the expression of man is transcultural and universal, then so must be the eye that reads the expression. As gestalt psychology said, physiognomies is primary and universal, and Darwin traced it to the universals of the animal primitivity of mankind, Lavater transforms primitive and primary to mean *a priori*, the "*Ursprache* of humanity," as Benz says. The image of man precedes the interpretation of man.

Moreover, Lavater continues, in the same passage,[91] the resurrected body will be wholly revealed in its image in which every physiognomic item of the person will express superbly what goes on in us without having to speak a word. Lavater has here moved physiognomies into an angelic mode of perception of the unique subtle body. And he suggests a way of understanding psychosomatic symptoms as expressions of an imagining body that—because it is also a moral body and not merely

---

88 Ernst Benz, "Swedenborg und Lavater: Ueber die religiösen Grundlagen der Physiognomik," *Zeitschrift für Kirchengeschichte* 57 (1938): 153–216. Also, more penetratingly, E. Benz, "Die Signatur der Dinge: Aussen und Innen in der mystischen Kosmologie und Schriftauslegung," *Eranos Yearbook* 42 (1973).

89 Benz, "Swedenborg und Lavater," 199.

90 Cf. "Ut Pictura Poesis," in R.G. Saisselin, *The Rule of Reason and the Ruses of the Heart* (Cleveland: Case Western Reserve, 1970), 216–24; "Ut Pictura Poesis," in M. Praz, *Mnemosyne* (Princeton, N.J.: Princeton University Press, 1970), chap. 1.

91 Quoted in Benz, "Swedenborg und Lavater," 201.

physiological–must bring with them these symptoms, feelings of guilt or sin. The "last judgment" as the ultimate revelation of the shape of personality, the image in the heart on the body drawn, is always going on because it is eternal. To the watching angel, the presentation of a self is in everyday life, where we are being visibly created by our imaginings, which means we are not a product of external forces, not what we do or choose, not what we have stocked in inventory, nor does it matter in that ultimate revelation whether our imaginings proceed via intuition or extraversion or feeling. We are being judged in our images, which gives to the image and all our imaginings an extraordinary moral importance.

3

PERSONS AS IMAGES

Imagism: Lavater's prescription ("It must be painting and speech at one and the same instant") brings us to our last approach, Imagism, the school of poetry in the English-speaking world that appeared during the same crucial years in London, just before and during the World War I, as did gestalt psychology in Berlin and Jung's *Symbole der Wandlung* in Zurich. Although Imagism was hardly a movement and lasted briefly, most major poets in the English language since then were in it or affected by it.

In the words of Ezra Pound, an aim of Imagism is "to paint the world as I see it,"[92] to put the concrete event as subjective experience into precise images. Imagism recapitulated several traditions: French symbolism, Japanese Haiku, Classical lyrics.

Here are a few lines from H.D. (Hilda Doolittle), the Grecian purist of Imagism. She was first Pound's fiancée in Philadelphia, then the central woman of a tiny London coterie, then an analysand of Freud's (she wrote beautifully of her analysis with him), and finally a person some of you may have known, for she lived many years in Küsnacht where she died in 1961. "Evadne" (singing of being loved by Apollo):

> His hair was crisp to my mouth
> as the flower of the crocus,
> across my cheek,
> cool as the silver cress
> on Erotes bank;
> between my chin and throat
> his mouth slipped over and over.[93]

---

92 In a letter to William Carlos Williams, 21 October 1908, in *Imagist Poetry,* ed. P. Jones (London: Penguin, 1972), 16.

93 H.D., *Collected Poems 1912-1944,* ed. L.L. Martz (New York: New Directions, 1983), 132.

One of Pound's, "The Encounter":

All the while they were talking the new morality
Her eyes explored me.
And when I arose to go
Her fingers were like the tissue
Of a Japanese paper napkin.[94]

And a passage from early Eliot, "La Figlia che Piange":

Stand on the highest pavement of the stair—
Lean on a garden urn—
Weave, weave the sunlight in your hair—
. . .
So I would have had him leave,
So I would have had her stand and grieve.[95]

In these lines, the image tells a story, is the story, and each love story collapses into the instantaneity of the image. *Ut pictura poesis*; event as tableau to be seen.[96] The surface, concrete and visible, implicates invisible volume and depth, like sculpture. Pound called Imagism "another sort of poetry where painting or sculpture seems as if it were 'just coming over into speech.'"[97] To bring this out, a poem called "Autumn" from William Carlos Williams:

A stand of people
by an open

grave underneath
the heavy leaves

celebrates
the cut and fill

for the new road
where

---

94 E. Pound, *Lustra* (London: Elkin, Mathews, 1916), 47.

95 T.S. Eliot, *Collected Poems 1909-1962* (New York: Harcourt Brace & Company, 1991), 26.

96 Cf. M. Benamou, *Wallace Stevens and the Symbolist Imagination*, chap. 1: "Poetry and Painting" (Princeton, N.J.: Princeton University Press, 1972).

97 E. Pound, "Vorticism," *Fortnightly Review* 96 (1 September 1914): 461; see further, T.E. Hulme's 1908 "Lecture on Modern Poetry": "This new verse resembles sculpture rather than music," in M. Roberts, *T.E. Hulme* (London: Faber and Faber 1938), 269; and my mention above of Michelangelo (poet and sculptor). Emphasis on sculpture is emphasis on image, structure, and space rather than on line, story, and time.

an old man
on his knees

reaps a basket-
ful of

matted grasses for
his goats.[98]

Here, people, open grave, new road, old man on his knees, grasses and goats form a whole wanting nothing, a gestalt that is a unique perception or *a perception that creates uniqueness.* It comes into being with the perception, in the uniqueness of the image. To be is to be perceived: *esse* is *percipi.* And now we begin to understand that the act of imagistic perception does not merely see or reproduce a uniqueness that is there. Rather, this act creates uniqueness by its imagistic mode of perception. Uniqueness is created by *poesis,* shaping images in words. But first the imagistic eye that sees in shapes. For images are not simply what we see; they are the way we see. Thus the perception of uniqueness begins in the eye that sees imagistically,[99] whereas the eye that sees by means of scientifically constructed types will always conceive uniqueness as a problem.

Lavater, his friends said, was an artist despite his system. One had to have "his eye and his heart"[100]—and that was his true method. Scientific method depends on repeatability; if an opus in science, an experiment, say, cannot be duplicated, it loses validity. A depth psychology concerned with soul in its individuality cannot proceed as a science. Hence Jung's remark that individuality means the end of technique, the end of prediction and interpretation, which also means the end of "scientism." In place of the scientific fantasy of method for psychology, I am suggesting the imagistic; instead of measurement, precision. I am suggesting that we see the complex in the patient's image and not only adduce the complex from his material. But psychologists do not have to become artists and poets, literally. We need but see as if we were. And speak so.

---

98 "Autumn," in *The Collected Poems of William Carlos Williams,* vol. 1: 1909–1939, ed. A.W. Litz and C. MacGowan (New York: New Directions, 1986), 449.

99 "An artist makes you realise with intensity… something which you actually did not perceive before." T.E. Hulme, *Speculations: Essays on Humanism and the Philosophy of Art,* ed. H. Read (London: Kegan, Paul, Trench, Trubner, and Co., 1936), 168–69.

100 See Shakespeare's Sonnet 46: "Mine eye my heart thy picture'd sight would bar."

"Use no superfluous words, no adjective, which does not reveal something . . . ," says Ezra Pound, "Go in fear of abstractions."[101] And Frank Stewart Flint says, "Use absolutely no word that does not contribute to the presentation."[102] To find the words for your image I need Lavater's rich, variegated language, the Allport-Odbert list of 17,923 trait names. Our usual psychological language fails the precision of the image. What is revealed with such terms as "introvert" or "mother complex"? Morever, these terms of typicality–unless imaged–bring further perceptions to a halt. Our language also fails the emotion. Hulme points out that emotions come in "stock types"–anger, sorrow, enthusiasm–words that convey only "that part of the emotion which is common to all of us."[103] Measurements of these emotions do not make the concepts or experiences more particular. Whereas art in images, defined by Hulme as "a passionate desire for accuracy,"[104] presents each emotion precisely. Here, image speech takes precedence over emotion speech. When we react to a dream image in terms of its emotions, or describe ourselves as "suicidal," "depressed," or "excited," we are again typifying, and moving away from the etching acid of the image.

Let us remember here that a complex presents itself first of all as a cluster of precise images revealed in instants of time in the word association test. In one of Jung's early experimental works from 1905, he demonstrates a pregnancy complex. But this has been adduced from the words "stork," "bone-bed," "flower," "red," "blood," "pierce," "heart" (*CW*2: 605). These words phrased by an Imagist or a Haiku writer would restore to the complex its imagistic precision.

Jung's "complex," Pound's definition of "image," and Lavater's "whole heap of images, thoughts, sensations, all at once"[105] are all remarkably similar. Pound calls Image "that which presents an intellectual and emotional complex in an instant of time"; "the Image is more than an Idea. It is a vortex or cluster of fused ideas and is endowed with energy"; "a Vortex, from which and through which, and into which, ideas are constantly

101 E. Pound, "A Few Don'ts by an Imagiste," in *Poetry: A Magazine of Verse* (March 1913): 201.

102 F.S. Flint, "Imagisme," in ibid., 199.

103 Hulme, *Speculations*, 162.

104 Ibid.

105 J.C. Lavater, *Aussichten in die Ewigkeit: In Briefen an Herrn Joh. George Zimmermann*, vol. 2 (Zurich: Orell, Geßner, Fueßlin und Comp., 1773), 106.

rushing."[106] Thus the movement, the dynamics, are *within* the complex and not only *between* complexes, as tensions of opposites told about in narrational sequences—stories that require arbitrary syntactical connectives that are unnecessary for reading an image where all is given at once.

The preference for image, structure, or sculpture does not imply a static psychology. Rather, I am in search of a ground for psychodynamics other than narrational sequences; the battle of opposites, stages in a process, the pilgrim, the hero, or the developing child—which all keep us confined to an ego psychology. Moreover, the dynamics of story become types—the typical motifs of fairy tales, the typical stages of emotion in Freud and Erikson, the typicalities of individuation in religious disciplines. Actually, it is narrational processes that are static: their typicalities can be interpreted and predicted. We know where they are headed. To conceive images as static is to forget that they are numens that move. Charles Olson, a later poet in this tradition, said: "ONE PERCEPTION MUST IMMEDIATELY AND DIRECTLY LEAD TO A FURTHER PERCEPTION..., always one perception must must must MOVE INSTANTER, ON ANOTHER."[107] Remember Lavater and his insistence on instantaneity for reading the facial image. This is a kind of movement that is not narrational, and the Imagists had no place for narrative: "Indeed the great poems to come after the Imagist period—Eliot's *The Waste Land* and *Four Quartets*; Pound's *Cantos*; Williams's *Paterson*—contain no defining narrative."[108] The kind of movement Olson urges is an inward deepening of the image, an insighting of the superimposed levels of significance within it.[109]

106 These definitions of image by Pound come from his various writings and can all be found in *Imagist Poetry*, 32–41. Further on complex and image, see J.B. Harmer, *Victory in Limbo: Imagism, 1908-17* (London: Secker & Warburg, 1975), 164–68.

107 "Projective Verse," in *Selected Writings of Charles Olson*, ed. R. Creeley (New York, New Direction, 1966), 17.

108 *Imagist Poetry*, 40.

109 H.D. later turned narration into image itself by writing a novel in which the stories, as she says, were "compounded like faces seen one on top of the other" or "superimposed on one another like a stack of photographic negatives" (quoted by Jones in *Imagist Poetry*, 42). Cf. Berry, "An Approach to the Dream," 60: "An image is simultaneous. No part precedes or causes another part, although all parts are involved with each other... We might imagine the dream as a series of superimpositions, each event adding texture and thickening to the rest."

This is the very mode that Jung suggested for grasping dreams—not as a sequence in time but as revolving around a nodal complex. If dreams, then why not the dreamers? We, too, are not only a sequence in time, a process of individuation. We are also each an image of individuality. We each turn in a vortex, and each movement in that vortex, that complex, opens another perceptive insight, reveals another face of our image.

Conclusions: Let us draw out several threads that have been running through our work this morning. First, we may reflect that typologies, for all their service in organizing a variegated world of multiple particulars, arise only in a mind that perceives the world in this way. "Chaos" and "order" lie in the eye that perceives as such. "Chaotic multiplicity," "bare particulars," "10,000 things" are not givens. They are abstract generalized images hermeneutically applied to the images that are given. The given itself is shaped; everything comes with a face. It is neither a given of nature nor an axiom of logic that the world *is* a chaotic mass of bare particulars, which then require typing. The world does, however, become such when we remove its face, when we remove its significant subjectivity. So, too, is each of us, each animal and plant, a mass of bare particulars when each is denied its physiognomic character, when stripped of its self-presentation, de-animated, de-personalized. Then we must typify to order our atomistic data, put the world back together again, and breathe some life into it by means of a constructed set of personified images which, we have suggested, types cannot live without. Despite Jung's statement that his typology is not a physiognomy, it is. Even his types could not leave their ground in descriptive exemplary images.

To follow this further: if a de-animated world requires typing, then when we type each other in psychology, are we not de-animating, *de-souling*? Are we not at the moment we perceive in terms of feeling and thinking, Gemini or Virgo, mesomorph or ectomorph, extravert or introvert, turning the world into a mass of bare particulars, a distribution of traits, a "more-or-less" without precision? "To be is to be perceived." When to-be-perceived as a type is to-be-perceived not as a face, then we are collected into rough-edged bins and roughly handled in terms of resemblance.

But notice here how resemblance is not conceived vertically, as an *epistrophé* in likeness to the image in which I am created and am continually being created. Instead, resemblance—also in Wittgenstein's use of the idea—is conceived horizontally as a likeness to others across the sample.

Conceptual types without images. Egalitarian. No longer am I the image I embody. I have become identified with what is not unique, my resemblance with others. My image has been fed to the type. My sense of image lost, my identity seeps out; and so I seem to have no specific shape that can be grasped individually.

Therefore I become a problem. I must be interpreted and predicted about, requiring hermeneutic and scientific methods, and also psychological ego-strengthening to regain an identity that had been given with my image. Regardless of Christian faith in persons and philosophies of humanism and personalism, it is the loss of person as *image* that opens the door to collective techniques of handling persons. Persons in bins can resemble each other only in their commonality. So we would climb out into individualism by heroic acts of rugged will. Ego is the phantom risen, the idol erected, when the image cannot be seen.

Imagism has blessed the problem of this *Tagung*—Variety and Oneness—by cursing both its houses. We can see through both as fantasies of number. That polar construction between multiplicity versus the unit, unity, and oneness is again a typology that can seduce us from perceiving uniqueness. Both these fantasies of number, and the problem between them, arise when we do not stick to the immediately presented image whose anomaly is its integrity, its uniqueness. Uniqueness is anomalous; in our oddness is our integrity, our individuality.

Also, the egalitarian-*versus*-elitism opposition arises from conceiving ourselves numerically, as units. Then to single out any one unit as unique creates an elite particular over and against the equality of the others. The mistake here lies in assuming that units, or bare particulars, are primary, whereas they are secondary numerical constructions. They result from a class concept—the unit—which has already egalitarianized uniqueness by reducing distinctions. Uniqueness is not a special kind of unit (CPID), different from all others, since each unit, before it is classified as such, is from the beginning different and unique.

Unity, too, need not be conceived numerically. Rather, we have been speaking of unity throughout as a quality of perception, the way in which each image is marked by the particular lines of its physiognomic character. Did not the Greek word *charassein* (from which "character" derives) originally describe the act of one who engraves, scratches marks, or inflicts wounds. Where units may be added into larger unities, the specific markings that characterize each uniqueness have no common denominators. Oneness as a number dissolves into an image or into the quality of integrity given with each different image. With the dissolution of unity into a quality of the image, oneness can no longer be set up as a goal of integration. This goal is seductive only to its counterpart: ourselves conceived as uncharacterized, unimaged, unperceived units.

The character of uniqueness together with its painfully anomalous marks gives each person his or her integrity, his or her sense of being odd and unlike all others, and therefore irreplaceable. This further gives that dignity in the face of death, which Miguel de Unamuno calls *The Tragic Sense of Life.*[110] The loss of any unit can be reproduced according to type or replaced by a spare part; the loss of uniqueness is irreversible.

Our second concluding thread draws out the animal analogy, opening the man-animal relation in a new way.

Modern psychology tries to reach the animal by getting inside its psyche. We try to imagine about animal perception, their images, language, and dreams. We have been anthropomorphic, attempting their consciousness in terms of ours.

Let us instead, by following physiognomies, attempt to perceive the animal in man—not merely in Darwin's and Lavater's sense of visible analogies. For what is being said in these theories is that there is an animal in man—an old religious idea, and we may look again at man theriomorphically, by which I do not mean merely genetically or in an evolutional sense. I mean, rather, that the gods themselves show their shapes the world over as animals, so that the animal is also an *imago Dei,* a face of our eternal nature. By perceiving the animal in man we may perceive rudiments of divinity, essential archetypal modes of consciousness—leonine, hawklike, mousy, piggish—essential natures in the psyche that suppose paleolithic indelibility and are our guardians.

The perspective I am suggesting here considers that the first psychological difference between humans and animals resides in how we regard each other. Humans regard animals differently than animals regard animals (and humans), so a first step in restoring Eden would be to regain the animal eye.

---

110 M. de Unamuno, *The Tragic Sense of Life in Men and Peoples,* trans. J.E. Crawford Flitch (London: Macmillan, 1921).

Here we are taking up Jung's idea—presented first at Eranos[111]—that image and instinct are inseparable components of a single spectrum. As there are images in instincts, so we might say there are instincts in images. Images are bodies. Animal images in art, religion, and dreams are not merely depictions *of* animals; they are also showing us images *as* animals, living beings that prowl and growl and must be nourished; the imagination, a great animal, a dragon under whose heaven we breathe its fire.

Darwin considered the animal *expression* in physiognomy to be primary. Gestalt responded by considering the animal *perception* of physiognomy to be primary.[112] If the world presents itself in expressive shapes like animals, then there must be an eye that can see shapes, as animals. To read lines on the face of the world we need an animal eye. This eye not only sees man as animal but by means of the animal—seeing with an animal eye. To this eye, image and type appear together. There is no abstraction of one from the other, no "-ology." As T.E. Hulme, the Imagist, put it: "We must judge the world from the status of animals, leaving out 'Truth,' etc."[113] Wallace Stevens[114] states in his poems that the animal is the first idea, the myth before the myth, whose perception is of physiognomic gestalt, as a "lion roars at the enraging desert."[115] This bird before the sun of our ordinary round and mind, this "dove in the belly" perceives, and creates with its response, the innate intelligibility of the world. This animal comes in our dreams, this animal—or is the dove an angel?—perceives, *sub specie aeternitatis,* the brute eye that reads character in the flesh, and, like Lavater, instantly feels like and dislike. The animal

111 C.G. Jung, "Der Geist der Psychologie," *Eranos Yearbook* 14 (1946). Revised and augmented as "Theoretische Überlegungen zum Wesen des Psychischen," in C.G. Jung, *Von den Wurzeln des Bewusstseins* (Zurich: Rascher, 1954), and translated as "The Nature of the Psyche" in *CW* 8.

112 David Katz, after reporting on experiments with animal patterns of recognition, says: "The understanding of alien soul-life must be something entirely primitive... an expression is the very first thing outside of itself to be grasped by a primitive being" (*Gestaltpsychologie,* 94).

113 T.E. Hulme, *Speculations,* 229.

114 For some of these "animals" in Stevens, see his "Notes toward a Supreme Fiction," "The Hermitage at the Center," "Song of Fixed Accord," and "The Dove in the Belly," in *The Collected Poems of Wallace Stevens* (New York: Alfred H. Knopf, 1954).

115 "Notes from a Supreme Fiction," in *The Collected Poems,* 384.

eye perceives and reacts to the animal image in the other, the form we display in our *Selbstdarstellung.*

Jung (by insisting on the archetypalness of images), Adolf Portmann (by drawing us to the shape and self-display of life), and the Imagist poets have made it possible to perceive the brute world under our noses as distinct and unique images.[116] They show us the way of returning the natural world to its imaginal significance—the most difficult task for a mind that cuts itself off from the animal, divides the universe into mind (Hulme's "Truth, etc.") and nature, and then attempts to rejoin them by "natural science." Then the mind, pulling away from the divine sensate animal, our soul's protective angel, falls into the nature it would leave, but now mentally putting the soul down into the scientistic, naturalistic fallacies.

Another thread is political. No governmental system depends more on the perception of the individual person by the individual person than does democracy. For what sense has our vote if we cannot read the faces and voices and bodies of the candidates. Many millions cast their votes many times for Richard Nixon despite the exposure for decades of his visual image. Does it help to analyze his personality, to find him an introverted thinking type, or anal, or paranoic-psychopathic if we cannot see what is directly revealed? And, evidently, we cannot see, and so people get, as Joseph de Maistre has said, the governments they deserve. We lose our ability to discriminate among qualities of men when we let slip the qualitative language for differentiating personalities, for then how to "tell" one man from another, except grossly, roughly as demagogic popstars. Know your man by his decibel count. If even we, psychologists trained to focus on individuality, cannot or dare not discriminate, then how can or dare we oppose the "ogical" views of man? If even psychology sees man as exemplifying typical functions, then there are no essential differences among human kind. We are functions, or functionaries, of groupings, an inventory of consumer tastes, actuarial probabilities, marketable skills, and opinion.

---

116 William Carlos Williams complains how difficult it is "lifting to the imagination those things which lie under the direct scrutiny of the senses, close to the nose... The senses witnessing what is immediately before them in detail see a finality which they cling to in despair, not knowing which way to turn. Thus the so-called natural or scientific array becomes fixed, the walking devil of modern life." "Prologue," in W.C. Williams, *Kora in Hell: Improvisations* (Boston: The Four Seas Company, 1920), 17.

Once a new Caesar had to exhibit himself, as Emperor Julian did to his troops, often and again, that he be seen, his person judged by his stance, his tone, his *Selbstdarstellung.* Once a candidate for admission to the Pythagorean academy was judged—not by a battery of psychological and intelligence tests—but Pythagoras, says Iamblichus,

> surveyed their unseasonable laughter, their silence, and their speaking... what their desires were, with whom they associated, how they conversed with them... He likewise surveyed their form, their mode of walking, and the whole motion of their body. Physiognomically also considering the natural indications of the frame, he made these out as manifest signs of the invisible manners of the soul.[117]

The physiognomic eye could break the types into which we have been cast by concepts and statistics. Then I am no longer a typical intellectual, a typical Swiss, leptosome, Jungian, Jew, urbanite American, middle-class, or any of the other comforting places to shelter from the confrontation with me as a vivid calligraphic idiosyncrasy, an image close to your nose, with hands and handwriting, with gestures and intonations, eyes and mouth and creases, syntax and vocabulary, pelvis, gait, and skin-coloring, with a long ancestral history and biography of actions that present myself. Then the imagination bewildered by this complexity searches for and seizes upon revelatory images to create a distinct individual.

However, by breaking the conceptual types, imagination re-uses them to feed the image. Typical perceptions of "intellectual," "Swiss," "American," "middle-class," "Jungian," etc.—each a stereotype that sociologists abhor as prejudices and psychologists condemn as shadow projections—return to narrow, limit, and add to the image the fixity of sculpture. Stereotypes solidify, as *stereos* means firm, solid. They fill in the type of a person with images of his ethnic, historical, psychiatric, and animal shadows. Stereotypes help us discriminate ancient depths of difference in visible surfaces, and Jung's old term "racial unconscious" can be revived not in a literal genetic sense but in this sense of shadow images that deepen our inner soil.

The seduction of typology goes further, you see, than the equalization of our external world. It is indeed no mere parlor game. It also flattens our inner perceptions of self—our dreams, complexes, behaviors. Our

117 *Iamblichus' Life of Pytagoras,* trans. T. Taylor (London: J.M. Watkins, 1818), 37–38. Cf. R.A. Pack, "Physiognomical Entrance-Examinations," *Classical Journal* 31 (1935): 42–43.

dreams become anxiety dreams or rebirth dreams, our complexes mother or father, our behaviors *puer* or *animus.* Types all. The archetypal persons become typological configurations, and the gods dissolve again into the allegorical systems of the rationalizing mind, that iconoclast, that slayer of the dragon, that god-killer.

Not only is each person an image, and this image is his invisible divinity presented, but each particular *aspect* of a person is a *face,* each face an *image,* this dream and this symptom, this behavior and this desire, is also a distinct image, a tale condensed into a depiction, a visibility that needs no interpreted meaning, gives no certain feeling, a vortex that expands and solidifies a cluster of multiplicities rushing through it.

The image is itself—this room, you, others, me, the thigh on the hard chair, the attention fading in and out, appetite rising, the light through the leaves, palm rustlings and heat, stereotypically Eranos through forty years; yet, uninterpretable and unpredictable, a presentation, like an animal in its own display that is type and image at once and cannot go beyond itself, only deepen within itself; a presentation that sets limits to mind, keeps mind held within the image. As images are psychic reality and the source of every mental act, every meaning and feeling, so they are the dissolution of all mental acts, their end in image. Wallace Stevens said this in his late poem "Of Mere Being":

> The palm at the end of the mind,
> Beyond the last thought, rises
> In the bronze decor,
>
> A gold-feathered bird
> Sings in the palm, without human meaning,
> Without human feeling, a foreign song.
>
> You know then that it is not reason
> That makes us happy or unhappy.
> The bird sings. Its feathers shine.
>
> The palm stands on the edge of space.
> The wind moves slowly in the branches.
> The bird's fire-fangled feathers dangle down.[118]

118 W. Stevens, *The Palm at the End of the Mind* (New York: Alfred A. Knopf, 1971), 398.

PART TWO
An Inquiry into Image

1. Symbol and Image
2. The Context of Image-Making
3. Archetypal Image: A High Example
4. Archetypal Image: An Ordinary Example
5. Emotion and Image
6. Reduction and Analogy
7. Archetypal Reduction
8. Radical Relativism and the Click
9. Image-Words: Concepts vs. Images
10. Images as Percepts: An Analogy with Painting
11. Images and Pictures
12. ~~Image as Temenos~~, IMAGE AS Idol: Analogies with Religion
13. ~~Image-Making~~ POIESIS: WORDPLAY
14. Gadgets or Imagistic Mechanics
15. Aesthetikism
16. Image-Body or Acting-Out
17. Image-Sense
18. Protestor's Last Stand

1

IMAGE AND SYMBOL

There is no better way to start our inquiry than by laying out a piece of material on which we can perform our experiments and demonstrate our methods. For this shall be an operational exercise, showing what can be done with images, how they work, and why they are important.

To begin in this straightforward manner also requires risking a rough definition—not so that it will confine the inquiry but so that we have both a stated point of departure and also of retreat, for definitions allow us to come back to a first clearing whenever we get entangled in the forest of endless distinctions and clever arguments.

By image, then, I propose this definition, simple and clear (before it accretes further attributes from the ensuing investigations): an image is nothing more than a complex depiction in any medium that is precisely qualified by a specific context, mood, and scene. We shall put this definition to use at once when tackling our first obstacle—the distinction between symbol and image. For it shall be our first contention that symbols are not images, but that a symbol can become an image when particularized by a specific context, mood, and scene. Let's see how this distinction between symbol and image works in regard to a piece of psychic material, such as this dream:

> In some kind of a cave, a dark cavern. The whole place slopes backwards and downwards from where I'm standing. There was a big dead white swan with arrows sticking out of its breast at all angles. I think there were five of them. I felt I could not breathe in there and turned desperately around toward daylight—brilliant—hurrying out without looking back. But in my hurry I seem to lose control of my leg, the right one, I guess at the knee, and my leg wobbled in all directions as I hurried.

In this dream, the arrow, cave, swan, five, knee, etc., are the symbols. I can look them up in a dictionary of symbols or in an index to Jung. This research is the first step of "amplification." By finding more about these words than my own personal associations (I hurt my knee when I was about three years old; arrows mean to me St. Sebastian; I was always told swans are beautiful but dangerous), I am gaining a wider cultural context, something about how these symbols appear to the imagination in general through the history of art, religion, and folklore.

So I shall find that caves are places of refuge, where mysteries occur, where gods are born or children kept, where secrets, treasures, and cries are hidden, and that they are often imagined as entrances to an underworld. And I may discover that swans are birds of high inspirational gods: Eros, Aphrodite Urania, and Apollo. They have to do with love and with death in mythologies, with longing and long-distance flights; also these white waterbirds belong among the *anima* phenomenology of tall-necked princesses and water nymphs and maidens, and especially with curious combinations of ugliness with beauty, of water with air, of proud savagery with extreme softness. And so on about arrows, fives, knees, breasts, brightness, etc.

The field of this sort of knowledge is symbology: the study of symbols. The conscious use of swan and arrow, cave and knee, in a poem, painting or ballet is symbolism. (Conscious use here means employing them for emotional and aesthetic effects, especially those that enlarge an event toward universality. Another kind of conscious use is employing symbols to convey a definite meaning that is transparently disguised in the symbols, i.e., allegory.) One who uses symbols and schools that urge using them in this manner are called symbolist. Symbolists can create haunting impressions by the use of traditional cultural figures, or by juxtaposing them in interesting ways, or by suggestively altering their usual form. Symbols, per se, are neither good nor bad, and *symbolic* works can range from majesty to kitsch. *Symbolization* as a spontaneous psychological act generally refers to a curious bunching of significance into compressed form, whether the form be a sensuous image, a concrete object, or an abstract formula. Symbolization takes place nightly in our dreams and daily in our speech. It is such a basic activity that it is as incomprehensible as consciousness itself and, in this basic general sense, not subject to our inquiry. So when I speak about *symbolizing,* I mean more specifically seeing images symbolically or turning images into symbols. (A very great deal has been written about what I have just put in this paragraph, but our paragraph will serve for a preliminary orientation.)

A symbol holds at least one main idea in an image—the cave holds the idea, e.g., of mystery, and presents it in sensuous form. (However, a symbol also holds an image in and by and to its main idea—a troubling consequent we shall return to later.) Both image and idea have in common something general in human experience that is durable through time. That is, a symbol condenses a set of conventions that tend toward universality. Wherever and whenever cave, swan, arrow appear, they tend to bunch a closely similar cluster of ideas. This very conventionality is a clue to the recognition of symbols. It is also what accounts for the majesty of their kitsch. For symbols bring the depth and power of history and culture, the generally human experiences of the universe, which are both ineffable truths and banalities. A swan is a good example of this. It can be immensely forceful or utterly trite, depending on—well, what? Depending, first of all, on *how* the swan, the image, appears.

Consequently, two ways now open up. We can approach images via symbols, or symbols via images. If we focus on the whenever and wherever of an image, its generality and conventionality, we are looking at it symbolically. If, on the other hand, we examine the how of a symbol, its particularity and peculiarness, then we are looking at it imagistically.

Therapy usually approaches images through symbols, and there are distinct advantages to this method. Since the disadvantages shall frequently engage us in the following pages, let's first review the advantages.

First, when confronted with a dream and in search of its meaning, we fill in the gaps of our personal associations with our knowledge of symbols, just as Freud said. We learn this symbolic approach during analytical training. The approach is also a necessary consequent of Jung's emphasis upon the manifest dream: if a lion appears, it is a lion and not a tiger or a bear. Since the dream has been specific, we must be equally so if we wish to approximate its meaning with our interpretation. We must know how lions differ from tigers and bears so that we are to the point and less waffling about the dream lion as "animality," "instinct," "power," or "father image"—statements that could as well be said about tigers and bears—and eagles, even oak trees, rocks, and locomotives. So the symbolic approach helps locate an image within the tradition of the imagination.

A second advantage of the symbolic approach is that it relieves the dream of its narrowly personal oppression. We do therapy just by amplifying. For by looking up a symbol, we reconnect, remember ourselves with the wider imagination. The symbolic approach opens a wide door into the riches of culture.

A third advantage follows from the second. Symbols have scope and echo. Any event seen symbolically takes on size; it gets universalized, gains transcendence beyond its immediate given appearance. One feels in touch with big meaning. Symbols give grandeur—and the delusion of grandeur. But now we are entering the disadvantages, so let's move on.

When we look attentively at the two ways, symbolic and imagistic, we find they are not real alternatives. For there are no symbols as such, only images. Every psychic process is an image, said Jung. Symbols appear, only can only appear, in images and as images. They are abstractions from images. (Else we couldn't look them up.) The only symbolic swans we can find as such are in a dictionary or index. Every other swan—Swan matches, Swan Lake, wild swans on the river Coole, or raping Leda, or pulling Aphrodite's chariot—is located in a specific context, mood, and scene. Each symbol is articulated, vivified or deadened, by the image that presents it. *A symbol cannot appear at all unless in an image.*

But maybe a symbol is a certain sort of image—a big universal one? A great white bird lying dead is surely a symbol. Think of the albatross. But this won't work either because we have lost the image of a swan in a cave, a particular cave with its particular feeling, and a swan dead with or from arrows in its breast, and particularly five arrows and presented together with my emotions and my action.

In other words, images that are generalized and conventionalized (dead white bird) have had their characteristic peculiarity erased. They no longer can rightly be called images. Any image that is taken as a symbol, by being stepped up to universal size, loses the precision of an image. The symbolic approach prevents the imagistic, mainly because the symbolic approach offers generality at the cost of precision.

Finally, a dream is an image because of this specific context, mood, and scene. It is not a symbol. This is evident from the fact that you cannot amplify a dream as such, only its symbols. They can be taken out of a dream, researched, painted, interpreted—but all this is not the dream, not the image. To put this another way: a dream is an entire image, no matter how fragmentary, how equivocal, which intrarelates its own images that in turn may contain symbols. A symbol may be an element of an image, but there can be images without any symbol at all.

Enter the PROTESTOR: *Hold it! All this may be right if you want to set up a new theory, but it has little to do with how Jung defines symbolic:*

> *Every view which interprets the symbolic expression as an analogue of an abbreviated designation for a* known *thing is* semiotic. *A view which interprets the symbolic expression as the best possible formulation of a relatively* unknown *thing, which for that reason cannot be more clearly or characteristically expressed, is* symbolic (CW *6: 815*).

Your distinction between symbol and image is nothing else but Jung's between sign and symbol. You are turning symbols back into signs, whereas one of Jung's major steps was to distinguish the two and give psychotherapy a fresh theory of symbol. Jung's theory of symbols insists they are wholes, not elements. His theory points to their fundamental ineffability, their mystery, and paradoxical ambiguity. That's why they "live" and can transform our psychic life forward. But you know all this as well as I, so why do you talk about symbols in terms of dictionaries and amplification. To think you can get the meaning of a symbol by looking it up is to miss Jung's theory altogether.

Let's look at what therapists generally *do*—including Jungian ones— rather than at what they say. You'll see there's a gap, a real distinction between Jung's *theory* of symbols and the *practice* of looking them up. This lets me lay out my method in these notes. I want to be operational. I want to inquire by sticking to the actual phenomena. I want to talk about what we do and not what we think we do. This is to distinguish between Jungian method and methodology. Methods are the ways we go about things and methodologies are the "-ologies" we invoke to justify our methods. The first is actual tactics; the second, the headquarters' strategy, the theoretical definitions and plans, and the propaganda.

I can put this difference between what we actually do and what we think we do also like this: To the question "What is a horse?" I can legitimately answer by defining or describing a horse. I can also legitimately answer by pointing at a horse or horses. If a child asks, I can answer best by *pointing at.* Moreover, and of first importance, pointing at can also be done by telling a dream with a horse, quoting a line of verse, fantasying a horse. Pointing at means horse-in-presentation, horse-in-image. Rather than answering by stating what a horse is, we answer by telling or showing what a horse is *like*: a horse is like the animal we saw pulling the milk wagon in that film last night; it's like our dog, but much bigger and with a shiny coat, and you can sit on top of it and ride fast; do you remember the policeman in front of the parade?—well, he was riding a horse.

By this method of pointing at, I am trying to return to the phenomenon: symbol in operation rather than symbol in definition. This difference can get out of hand: if the definition or description of horse no longer seems to cover what I see when I point at a horse, then our understanding of horses gained from theory (definition) is becoming delusional. It no longer conforms with actual horses. I think this has been happening with "symbol" in analytical psychology.

What goes on in the trenches of psychotherapy seems very different from the plan. When therapists speak or write of a dream with an egg or a coffin, the egg or coffin does not remain within the image, within its precisely qualifying context, nor does the egg or coffin remain "the best possible formulation of a relatively unknown thing" (Jung's definition of symbol). More likely, the egg tends to be an "abbreviated designation" (sign) for fertility or growth or femininity; and the coffin, the negative mother or death. The symbols become stand-ins for concepts. Where theory declares them unknown, in practice we simply know what they mean at a glance. Our practice with symbols no longer accords with our theory of them.

This state of affairs has come about through the progressive development of symbology. We no longer practice Jung's theory of symbols for they are no longer unknowns as they once were. We have suffered a historical change. Freud, Jung, and the second generation have reclaimed vast amounts of this "forgotten" language. Consciousness today is wide awake to symbols of all sorts. The task now is to get back to the unknown that only a few years ago lay in the symbol by exploring the image. (After all, our main concern is neither with symbol nor image but with the unknown that is the source of all depth psychology.)

Dream as image brings us back to the unknown. We stick to it in the image. There is nowhere else to go. And it can tell us about itself. So we set aside our collective consciousness that knows what dreams are, what dreams do, what they mean. The practice with dreams as images suspends our theory that relies on a symbolic approach. We do not want to prejudice the phenomenal experience of their unknownness and our unconsciousness by knowing in advance that they are messages, dramas, compensations, prospective indications, transitional objects, transcendent functions. We want to go at the image without the defense of symbols.

PROTESTOR: *That's naive. Even if you throw out or bracket the usual assumptions, you will just replace them with others. You have to have an approach of some sort–tools. What do you do with dreams?*

My first assumption is that a dream is an image and that an image is complete just as it presents itself. (It can be elaborated and deepened by working on it, but to begin with, it is all there: wholeness right in the image.) Next, we assume that everything there is necessary, which further suggests that everything necessary is there. Hence the rule: "Stick to the image," in its precise presentation: the cavernous place slopes down and back; I hurry without looking back; the arrows stick out at all angles from the breast; the swan is big (not small) and dead (not sick, or lively, or swimming) and white (not without color, or black).

Something marvelously therapeutic happens when you affirm the image just as it is. You are relieved of guilt for its supposed faults: you don't have to coach it into shape or edit out its errors. Because the swan, the arrows, the knee are as they are, things are as they are–an affirmation that in turn affirms the psyche. You are standing in your soul as it is. So you see, affirmation of the image also means affirmation by the image. You become more familiar and therefore more comfortable with necessity.

Even if the images were less detailed ("any number of arrows," "some arrows," or "I think there were some arrows"), whatever is said is necessary to the precision of the image. Don't take precision as some sort of fine-grained Ektachrome replication of detail–the more and sharper, the better. Precision means whatever is actually presented. Simply: the actual qualities of the image. Vagueness, dullness, indifference–and imprecision too–are also qualities. ("I felt 'blah'"; "The dream was vague"; "I could only catch a fragment"–this, too, is image precision.) The more precision, the more actual insight.

PROTESTOR: *Still, you do want to fill out the vagueness with more details. Would you ask the dreamer what clothes he had on in the cave or whether there was blood around the arrow wounds?*

Who said there were wounds? The image says "arrows sticking out of its breast," not "into its breast." No mention of wounds.

PROTESTOR: *That's just my point: to get more precise about what's happening, we have to fill out the gaps in the dream by asking questions, by imagining further. Then the image becomes more complete and defined.*

Precision doesn't only mean defined in the sense of unambiguously complete. Working with images doesn't intend to relieve them of their power to suggest. Ambiguity may be essential to what they are actually saying and doing. "Full" does not equal "better," nor do the questions that a dream suggests have to be taken literally and answered. That a dream fosters questions by its absences is exactly part of its precision. Precisely this or that area or connection or figure is left open and vague. Maybe nature abhors a vacuum, but dreams don't. What's not there is there—as an absence. The image composes itself in the best manner possible, and it is your job and mine, we who receive images, not to score them for what is missing and ask them for more but to see precisely their actual precision.

PROTESTOR: *Their "actual precision" is presented literally by the image.*

Now we are in trouble, because you are both right and wrong. Yes, in order to be precise, we must literally stick to the image, to what is actually said and shown. So we are definitely literal in the sense of being mimetic like a simple photocopy. Yet we are never literal in the sense of univocal, unquestionable, opaque, for that is what I call literalism. At the first approach to any event, we can't help but be literal. We must see and feel and smell what is actually there; the image as it displays itself. But when we claim that it is all there is, that what is there states one thing with one voice, without question or doubt, that it is evident and self-satisfied, without underlying implications and suggestive overtones, without the potential misreadings and misapprehensions, then we have moved from the literal to literalism. That literal first level is the fixity that allows displacement. It's the furniture before the rug is pulled out from under, before the text is seen through.

PROTESTOR: *I begin to see now why you always equate literalism with monotheism. Monotheism for you is more than one-sidedness. For you it's a repressive notion, a way of scrutinizing an image so that it has only one voice, one sense.*

Let's keep going on with our main theme, the distinction between images and symbols. In contrast with an image, a symbol stands out from its mood and scene, as the five arrows in the swan, taken as a symbol, become "the arrow" or "arrow." As such, a symbol has no syntactical location or tonal shading, no feel to it, no necessary relation with its surrounding. There is nothing intrinsic to the arrow, that it be in a swan, in the breast of a swan, or that there be five of them. It is this salience of symbols that allows us to amplify them. This salience also encourages analyzing, taking the dream apart, looking up each symbol, one by one, and finding meaning through a process of decoding their *inter*relationships. The symbolic approach tends to break up an image; it is iconoclastic.

The imagistic approach considers each aspect of the dream as image (swan in the cave, arrows in the breast, hurrying toward daylight) and that these images are all *intra*related. No image can be dealt with apart from the others, and the enlightening of any one image sheds light on the others. Images are intrinsic to each other: in the dead-swan-cave, my hurrying is toward brilliance, which is a not-looking-back hurrying; it is an away from sloping downwards hurrying, and not looking back is for me to hurry. All the images of the dream adhere, cohere, inhere—this *inhesion* is fundamental to an image. Patricia Berry[1] has already so well argued all this about the dream as an image so that I do not need to do it again. She calls this the "simultaneity" of the image.[2] All parts are co-relative and co-temporaneous. (In philosophical language, the parts are linked by "internal relation.") A similar point about simultaneity and intrarelatedness is made by Rudolf Ritsema in his *I Ching* translation.[3] He speaks of it as an "imaginal language."[4]

1 "An Approach to the Dream," in P. Berry, *Echo's Subtle Body: Contributions to an Archetypal Psychology* (Thompson, Conn.: Spring Publications, 2017), 55–77.

2 Ibid., 60.

3 *The Original I Ching Oracle or The Book of Changes: The Eranos I Ching Project,* trans. R. Ritsema and S.A. Sabbadini (London: Watkins, 2005).

4 Ibid., 18.

2

THE CONTEXT OF SOUL-MAKING

PROTESTOR: *You defined image as a specific context, scene, and mood. Then, making precise contexts, scenes, moods ought to constitute image-making. Is this all? Is there something further in image-making that has not yet been articulated?*

We'll work with an example: "I am standing on the veranda, watching the sun go down and feeling sad." More precisely: "The veranda is plain pine wood, just built onto the house. It gives on to fields with hills, behind which the sun goes down heavy, slow, and red. There is damp heat in the air, and my sadness is felt in the limbs as a numbing, and in my face as a drawn sagging of my cheeks and around my mouth. Not bitter, not sweet, not desolate–just down and sad."

So I have precisely qualified the scene and the mood. Do we now have an image? It seems not to have any pregnancy beyond this careful description, a description that could be exhaustively extended in the manner of Marcel Proust, Henry James, or Thomas Mann, or exhaustingly in the manner of phenomenology, or shown in pages and pages of detail drawings or photographs. At best, we would have accurate reporting, but without significant echo. No sense of importance. The veranda scene and its mood wouldn't take hold of us because it would have no appropriate fit with anything further. This fitting in, or weaving in, must then be context.

What else characterizes context? To find the answer, let's start down several wrong paths.

1. Context is nothing other than the whole scene and mood, the physical sensations and visibilities, the emotional feelings and positions of myself within it–a *full description.* If this were the answer, then context would be redundant; scene and mood would be enough to establish an image.

2. Context is *allegorical.* The sunset as "story" of life sinking, decline of blood into night, confirmed by the mood of sadness. But this won't do

because we have already shown at the outset that the symbolic view—and allegory is one of the symbolic moves—prevents the imagistic view.

3. Context is *memorial.* Other sunsets evoked by this one, other sadnesses evoked by this sadness, film and literary echoes, personal remembrances, recent events in the day ("a hard day behind me" analogized with "a hard life behind me.") This notion won't suffice either because it limits context to personal memory. If context is personal, then the image is only *my* image, not *an* image, and dependent upon reconstruction through my memory of scene and mood. Then context is merely the world of the historical ego and created by the historical ego out of its memory. To define the context by memory is like considering a dream or a poem to be composed of my day's residues and reducible to them. This notion of context appears in overly personal art work and dream interpretation that, to have any significance, requires knowing the author's associations and intention. The images do not carry over to the viewer. They have no life of their own and so must borrow from the artist's and dreamer's life.

4. Context is *selection.* It is nothing additional to scene and mood, but the selection of significant detail in scene and mood. That the veranda is newly built and of pine wood is irrelevant, but that the veranda was finished that day and that this is the first sunset after completion of it—that detail is significant. Significant detail eliminates the need for the extenuation of details—drawn mouth and sagging cheeks, damp air and hills.

Now we are getting warmer. For if we ask how to select a significant detail, we find, as in the veranda example, that the one we select allows us to *suppose* something. I now suppose that the person feels sad because the veranda is finished (not because of damp air or pine wood), and I may suppose further that experiencing the sadness of ending so strongly in the body may be an intimation of death, and yet further suppose that those efforts to build a place to stand and observe this accomplishment has actually led to noticing the sinking sun, decline, and coming darkness.

All these suppositions have been implied by the image—but only because a significant detail has been enunciated. Now we sense some obscure internal connection between the sunset, the sadness, and the just-finished veranda. This inherent relation, this implication, is not an explicit allegory that symbolizes the sunset into life itself, nor is the obscure relation the personal memory of my carpentry, and my personal associative twists to sunsets, verandas, sadnesses—i.e., that I love long summer sunsets; that we had a veranda at my grandfather's house in

Tennessee; that when I feel sad I like to have a drink and write a poem. These latter are subjectivities I paste onto the significant detail, like ornamentation and personal conceits in literary works. No, the significant detail (the completion of the veranda that day) is given with the image. It is a fact like the setting sun and the sadness in my limbs.

Without the significant detail we have only standing on the veranda, the setting sun and the sadness in my body—simply one of many scenes and many moods of the day. Nothing strange. It passes without noticing unless arrested by a detail that hooks into the psyche, touches my pathology (death), and deepens the scene and mood into an image.

PROTESTOR: *You are identifying context with significant detail. Either they are the same, and therefore one or the other is redundant. Or they are not the same, and you have to spell out the differences.*

The difference is easy. The significant detail works like a leading thread into the invisible weave, or context, of the image. The detail itself is not the context, but because of the detail we suppose some obscure psychological implications beyond a mood and scene, a deeper weave that ties mood and scene together, and presto, an image! The detail makes the supposing of implications possible.

PROTESTOR: *You have hung your argument on your supposition about death. Finishing the veranda may be a fact of the image, but supposing it to be the significant detail is not. The image says nothing about intimations of death. I could suppose something quite different. I suppose, for instance, that you feel sad at sunset when the veranda is finished because you realize you should have been a builder, that you truly love carpentry, not writing and thinking and talking, and that you have been on the wrong track all your life, and now the sun sets. Too late. Same significant detail; different supposition.*

Let's suppose another: Finishing the deck reminds me of my brother, killed in the war, getting the news on an afternoon like this, that he was a cabinetmaker, did beautiful work. I feel the beauty of him, his work, the evening. My sadness is neither that of finishing and death (option #1) or of accomplishment as an indication of what I should have been (option #2) but the melancholy of beauty, love, and remembrance.

Each of these suppositions derives from the same detail: finishing the veranda at sunset. What counts here is not what we suppose but that we suppose. The detail opens up the supposings. They, in turn, refer to implications in the image so that it all weaves together, inheres, fits. That's context.

This all sounds very much like the old idea of unity: that every work of art has a unity that makes it a work of art. But I believe I am saying something more. Unity doesn't echo outside of the work; it keeps the image self-enclosed. Whereas the fit of the context means fitting not only together within itself (unity) but also woven with wider patterns (context).

PROTESTOR: *Context has now come to mean broader implications folded obscurely into the image. Are you saying that unless there is an implication, there is no image? Are you saying that no matter how strong the mood and rich the scene, we still need something more to make an image, and that something more is an implication? If you say no, then you still haven't defined context. If you say yes, then what is the distinction between context and implication?*

First of all, let's put what we've been doing within its own context. Berry's essay lays out three terms for three phases: Image, Implication, Supposition. She carefully restricts image to what is actually there, the intrarelation of its parts, its emotion, sensuality, texture, etc. Implications emerge from the image, and suppositions follow from these internal implications. In the example above, however, we worked in the reverse direction. We started by supposing some implication in the image of sadness at sunset on the veranda. By beginning with supposing, I am saying that image-making requires suppositions. Supposing helps to suggest implications and, because of these implications in a scene or mood, we have an image. An image implies, unless the image implicates us in supposing it is not an image. You see, suppositions involve us psychologically.

Though supposing is crucial, it must, however, stick to the image and be implied by a significant detail. Otherwise, the suppositions are wild and wooly, revealing only a personal bias or ideological allegory—e.g., I suppose the sadness on the veranda has to do with your drunk father who used to have his sundowners on the back porch. That supposition has nothing to do with the significant detail (that the veranda was just finished); and skews the image to fit into an arbitrary context, that of your father complex, alcoholism, etc., given not by the detail but by your ideological supposition.

So, to say it again: supposing doesn't make the context. The context is already in the image and draws us into supposings—and, puts limits to these supposings. By providing a unity, the context limits an image, even if its scene has confused amount of detail and conflicting moods. The context says: only here, in this specific weave, does it all fit together and make sense, only these details, as they are woven, allow the image to open up, carry weight, begin to matter. The context thus limits abstracted meanings, hypothetical explanations, and symbolic interpretations. It both promotes many suppositions and holds them in check.

PROTESTOR: *I need more examples. Show me again how it works.*

Let us say that instead of "just finishing the veranda that afternoon," some other statement were put into the mood of sadness and scene of sunset, such as: a) "just come out to study for tomorrow's bar exam"; b) "just put down the phone after hearing about my daughter's divorce"; c) "just beaten the dog for stealing the lamb shank"; d) "just been mulling over a sense of 'out-of-touchness' with my dreams."

If you were in drama school, you would walk onto the veranda scene in the same sad mood, but in each case there would be a different quality to your entrance. This is because of that additional factor, that significant detail, beyond scene and mood. They are woven through with further implications owing to the dog, the exam, the daughter, etc. Now we have an image; and what finally made the image was its fitting in with something psychologically immediate.

The mood and scene now resonate implications in that one or another of these four themes reflects in the mood and scene in a particular concrete and sensuous way. My having beaten the dog gives to the numbing and sagging of my sadness a different quality from the numbing and sagging that accompanies having just heard of my daughter's divorce. Different suppositions arise about the sadness in each case. Also, different details of the scene and mood move into the foreground as others become less significant, depending on the context. That is, damp heat in the air and the sun setting slow and heavy gives a sensuous concreteness to the moods of (a) study and (d) mulling but may be less relevant to (c) having beaten the dog.

I have got to insist here that psychological immediacy is not personal immediacy. An image leads beyond the person in the image or to whom it happens—myself having beaten the dog, mulling, or studying. Memory and allegory restrict images to personal immediacy, as if psychological = personal (*my* experiences, *my* interpretations). The psychological immediacy of a living image provokes anyone to begin supposing and sensing into its implications and thus to find himself or herself in the image, woven into context. We feel entangled, or caught. It doesn't let us go. That's also how the context sets limits.

Clinical language might call context the "presenting complaint," that is, the limiting psychological entanglement that the patient brings to therapy, or better, what brings him to therapy: beating the dog, daughter's divorce, etc. The presenting complaint refers to immediate psychic realities. "I finished this veranda and dropped into a terrible depression." The clinician begins to expand the context by asking for specific moods and scenes so as to begin supposing, searching out implications. Where in your body is the depression? What happened that day? Who were you thinking about?

PROTESTOR: *Aren't you getting too clinical? Does the context, and thus an image, really require this kind of overt psychological problem?*

No, it does not. If it did, imagine what our painting and literature would be like! Nonetheless, I am comparing it with the presenting complaint in order to stress the tension-laden, perplexing urgency (immediacy) of the context. A comparison with clinical talk gives to context a certain pathologizing flavor, that sense of inescapable importance for soul that pathologizing brings. Besides, I do want to suggest the peculiarity in an image. Images, you know, are very odd arrangements.

They are heightened intensified moments. Psychology of the imaginative arts talks about hyperbole, condensation, foreshortening, tension, symbolization, catachresis—that is, terms that refer to a non-natural or *contra naturam* aspect of imagination. Deformation and distortion are quite essential to the imagination, as our dreams show. So by making this clinical analogy, I am deliberately keeping us in touch with the pathologized side of the image and its entangling relation to our individual peculiarity and how it makes us suffer. I am bringing out the fact that we not only "make" images but "suffer" them as well.

Let me explain context yet another way, this time by an analogy with the Jungians. For them, a dream must be placed in its context in order to be understood. Some of the context for them is the conscious situation of the dreamer. Some of it is the course of other dreams in the last weeks and in the same night. Some of it is the whole anamnesis of the dreamer (life history and case history, the immediate problem, the character, type, pathology, culture, ancestry, the transference relation, and so on). For Jungians, a dream has bearing only within a context and the context provides bearing for the dream image.

The Jungians are saying that an image doesn't just float freely. It fits in somewhere, and the fit makes it feel necessary and valuable. To find where an image fits and how it fits requires a lot of puzzling and playing (suppositions). Curiously enough, this searching for its fit or context is itself archetypal, going back to Plato and picked up again by Jung as the "myth of meaning"—"meaning" not as interpretation or even as archetypal *epistrophé* (placing or returning an image to a specific god) but as fitting. For Plato, what is right and good and true and beautiful is what fits, or what artists call what "works."

When Jungian therapists extend the context widely by amplifying into symbolism and cultural history, they are weaving an image into a network, fitting it into a wider web of psychological implication. They are saying: yes, this image belongs to you (and your personal loss of your brother, or your own death), and it also belongs to all of us, to collective humankind, to the self and God. Its importance transcends your importance; in fact, this large context gives the image its amplified resonance so you can hear its value for you, personally.

Context is therefore another way of speaking about psychological involvement. The sad veranda fits within a net entangling me in implications beyond my personal sadness and my personal carpentry. The personal has now been taken beyond itself into the image. "Beyond" refers to the dimension of soul that psychology since Heraclitus calls "depth." The sense of soul, given by context, indicates an inherent relation between image-making and soul-making.

I think the soul wants to be made. After all, why so much worry over our dreams, our poems, and our paintings, getting them right, making them "work," fussing over how they fit into our lives, other lives, the world. Isn't the psyche itself causing this obsessiveness, urging us to articulate our images for its sake, as if the psyche desires to fit in somewhere, find a context for its continuous production of fantasies, thoughts, feelings, and baroque inventions? The psyche seems to want the mind to suppose and speculate, the hands to craft, and so it gives with each image some significant detail to catch our notice and draw us in. And that's the job of our art, whether artists, scientists, or therapists—to pick up on the significant detail.

But now I better conclude: By context I mean the psychological entanglement within a mood and scene. I could call this entanglement "resonance," "implication," or "depth." Whatever the term, I mean something more than just tying bits of mood and parts of scene or even their full interrelation as a unity. Entangled in an image is its implication whose depth amplifies into the wide world. Hidden, obscure, suggested only, nonetheless these implications suppose that the ultimate context of an image is the *anima mundi,* the soul of the world.

PROTESTOR: *I need to hear this, feel this, since I am so used to fitting images into the context of my life, its problems and wishes. This keeps me locked inside my interpretations and keeps the soul locked inside my life. Too small, too transitory, and probably too selfish.*

Then let's reverse the question. Not how does an image fit with my context and belong to me but how do I fit and may better fit with it?

3

ARCHETYPAL IMAGE: A HIGH EXAMPLE

Jung says archetypes *per se* are unknowable, irrepresentable, unspeakable. Let's take this not as a metaphysical but as an operational statement. Let's work with it, see how the irrepresentable/unspeakable works in images.

Already we have progressed from archetype as noun to archetypal as adjective. This is no mean progression! For we have just slipped through one of philosophy's oldest brambles and all its tangled, thorny questions about participation between universals and particulars, noumenals and phenomenals, possibles and actuals.

Instead of beginning with two distinct events—archetype and image—and asking how they relate, we begin with one event: archetypal image. We do not have to remove "archetypal" from "image," for evidently when we do, archetypal eludes our abilities and becomes unknowable, irrepresentable, unspeakable. We would be blocked at the outset by the unknowability of what we were inquiring into. Clearly, it becomes a more fecund way of proceeding to inquire into just what modifications, if any, occur to an image when it is declared "archetypal." This way, we are more likely to come upon what archetypal actually points to than were we to begin with the theoretical question, what are archetypes. In fact, we do not even have to distinguish archetypal from image; we need ask only what in particular about an image draws the modifier "archetypal." So our focus remains on images.

What, then, is it about an image that we term archetypal? The first answer, symbols or the symbolic, simply displaces the problem. (If symbols made images archetypal, then we have only put our problem somewhere else. Then the question becomes, "What is the difference between archetypal and symbolic?" Unless we can discern a distinction, we have to admit they are identical, so that one or the other of the two terms is redundant.) But I think we can face the symbol answer head on by looking at our dream example.

Is this dream archetypal because of its symbols (cave, arrow, swan, dark-bright)? If so, then any dream (image) that contains a symbol is archetypal. It is enough to have a tree, an animal, or even another person (child, shadow, *animus, anima*) in a dream for it to be archetypal. Extension to absurdity—yet, let's grant the proposition that it is symbols that make images archetypal. Let us try to operate with the proposition even though we can't draw the line between what is a symbol and what is not. (Are cars symbols? Supermarkets? Supermarket baskets? Brown bags? Check-out lines? Checkout girls? Boys who carry bags to cars? Leashed dogs awaiting?)

PROTESTOR: *Not so fast! Jung once said: "Whether a thing is a symbol or not depends chiefly upon the attitude of the observing consciousness"* (CW6: 818). *So those checkout girls and brown bags can indeed be viewed as symbols. I am sure I could amplify them in mythical and ritual terms so that you, too, could see their symbolic nature.*

Jung's shifting the symbol problem from a kind of object to a kind of attitude in the subject seems to help—but does it? It is like Edward Casey's statement that an image is not what you see but the way that you see.[5] The appeal is to a kind of seeing. But what is this kind of seeing? If seeing with a symbolic attitude means seeing things as symbols, we are merely in a new begged question that is being answered with a new tautology.

So far all we can say is that because of Freud and Jung we can now sense symbols where once we couldn't. They developed our symbolic consciousness. Freud helped us to see (or hear) "brown bag" as a sexual (female) symbol, and owing to Jung, we can recognize "checkout girls" as *anima* figures, and passing through their narrow examining lanes into the wide world, as a *rite de sortie.* Once we are in a symbolic attitude, we can indeed see anything as a symbol. But we have entered this symbolic attitude and see symbols because we have learned what symbols are by amplification, by symbology (Freudian, Jungian, Tarot, Christian, etc.). So the symbolic attitude, too, is based on what we do or have done enabling us to see something as a symbol.

But to the dreams: Let's look at one in which there are eight big symbols. And we state they are symbols by pointing at what people do in order to call them such.

---

5 On the *act* of seeing, see E.S. Casey, *Imagining: A Phenomenological Study* (Bloomington: Indiana University Press, 2001), 170: "There is always more to be seen, as well as more ways in which to see what has already been seen."

They store them and find them in collective depositories: dictionaries, indexes—of myths, fairytales, and folklore, of motifs in the arts, religions, and depth psychology. First, the dream stripped down to its symbols. First operation:

> By a *river,* a *baby* plays with a *lark* and a *pearl. Flowers* are growing around. A *hag* carries a *box* of *shit.*

Now, tell me why this doesn't work?

PROTESTOR: *There is no emotional happening; no one to whom it happens. It is as if it doesn't matter. It is an image without deeper significance, and therefore it cannot be called archetypal.*

I believe this image cannot be fairly called archetypal because it fails the "criterion of decorum."[6] The image is improperly expressed. Eight loaded symbols are washed out in a trivial statement. The indifferent declarative style does not suit them. Symbols alone don't do the job; there must be something else for an image to be called archetypal. This something else seems first of all a matter of style—or, style makes things matter. (Classical rhetoric would agree. *Elocutio* or style must accord with the topic.) We need not only symbols; we need a genre to embody them. Otherwise it's like washing out the image power of a Christ, green and bleeding on the cross, in a sentimental nineteenth-century Italian-school painting. The vehicle must carry the symbol. So, second operation:

> Once upon a time by a *river* there was a *baby* who played all day and every day with a *lark* and a *pearl. Flowers* grew all around the baby and one day a *hag* came by carrying a *box* of *shit.*

Now we have put the symbols into the genre of fairy tale, satisfying, I believe, the criterion of decorum. (To have put them into epic or tragedy would have been "undecorous.") But still the image doesn't seem to deserve the epithet "archetypal." It is as if the tale has only got started. What little there is of narrative is a fragment. There is no conflict, no plot, no moral tension that takes hold of us when we read.

Jung says that archetypes are carriers of meaning. This image bears no significant message. If one can say "so what" to an image, it is hardly archetypal. So, a third operation:

---

6 See R. Tuve, *Elizabethan and Metaphysical Imagery: Renaissance Poetic and Twentieth-Century Critics* (Chicago: University of Chicago Press, 1947).

> I was watching a *baby* by a *river* playing with a *lark* and a *pearl*. *Flowers* were growing around the baby when (or "but suddenly," or "until," or "however") a *hag* came by carrying a *box* of *shit*.

Two things have changed. First, there is a dreamer, an observer with whom one can identify; and second, there is a rupture, a peculiar "hiatus" in the image (Chapter 14) caused by the introduction of a disjunction. The image now has an internal tension, the inklings of a plot, even a smoulder of anticipation.

PROTESTOR: *I still cannot feel it to be archetypal. It's simply not* big *enough. Even though it has the tone of a tale (decorum) and is packed with well-known universal images (symbols), it remains remote and artificial. I know this could be said about most archetypal images—mandalas, cosmic clocks, heavenly visions, fairy-tale castles—yet there is nothing here that offers mystery, emotion, or meaningfulness. Let me rewrite the eight symbols into what I would call a truly archetypal image. The fourth operation:*

> A hag, *who looked like my mother's mother, had a screaming* baby *in a* box, *which she was either removing from or putting into a* river. *Suddenly, a* lark *dove down scattering* flowers *and* shit *all over them, and now in the box was a* pearl. *I felt frightened at first and then relieved.*

You see what I have done. Now there is emotion in the image itself ("screaming," "suddenly," "dove down"). Then there is the dreamer's personal engagement ("I felt frightened," "my mother's mother"). There is an ambiguity: "either removing from or putting into." So we don't know what the hag is up to, a mystery of positive and negative. Then there are the definite mythological motifs of the old woman (mother's mother, double mother, Great Mother) endangering a child by exposure, the helpful animal, rescue from above and by opposites (flowers and shit). And finally the whole thing is now a narrative. A story of transformation has happened. Can't we call this image archetypal?

We best test a hypotheses by attempting to falsify it. Therefore, let us rework the image by *removing* everything we have used to build it toward "the archetypal"—disjunctive hiatus, narrative, smoldering anticipation, the opposites and ambiguity, emotional involvement, and the mythological motifs, including the transformational plot. Not more of these but less. The fifth operation:

> By a pale-blue and shallow *river* a sitting boy *baby* plays about idly with a singing *lark* in his right hand and a reflecting *pearl* in his left around the baby narcissus and dandelion *flowers* are growing a *hag* carries a *box* of *shit*.

This last version is a return to the first. The motifs of transformation, opposites, abandoned child, overt ambivalence, helpful animal, and dreamer-observer have all been excised. So has the emotion and the narration. Even more, the punctuation is gone disorganizing rhythm, syntax, and emphasis. Everything that we had been building up to get at "the archetypal" is gone.

The principal difference between the fifth version and the first is that some our symbols have now been *precisely specified.* Even if no expressed emotion, there is *mood* and *scene.* The symbols—without introducing any new connections between them or any affects—now provide a context for each other. (You may recall that I said at the beginning that these italicized items were important for making symbols into images.)

Reading and re-reading the image, hearing and re-hearing, we learn that sitting by a shallow river is sitting as a baby, and sitting as a baby is to have a singing lark in the right hand, and that happens when a box is in a hag's hand. When narcissus and dandelion flowers grow, the river is pale blue and shallow, and a baby plays idly. Idly playing is baby-playing even if with a reflecting pearl. What does a baby boy do with a reflecting pearl? A baby plays idly with it, and that happens when the river is pale blue. When boys play, hags carry; when hags carry shit, boys play larks. And is it all just going by, like a river going by and a hag going by?

More: What exactly is playing idly? Playing baby? Is it playing *about* (rather than straight playing *with*)? When there are pearls and larks, the flowers are "dandylions" and narcissus, and these flowers are growing a hag. Reflecting pearl, pearly reflection, is in his left—not hand. There is no left hand. Maybe, pearly reflection. Maybe, pearly reflection is "left around the baby narcissus" (just as it says without punctuation), and when the pearl is left around (because there is no left hand? because the hag carries?), then the river is shallow. But anyway, we do know this happens when he is sitting and playing idly with a right-hand lark or is having a right hand-lark. Flowers all around him are growing a hag, even while larky singing goes on together with playing about pearls, and a box of shit.

As we go through this chant, this singing the verses of an image as if it were a round or fugue (or written by James Joyce or Gertrude Stein), a deeper significance begins to resonate. The image amplifies itself without the act of amplification; that is, its volume increases through what Berry calls "restatement."[7] In alchemical terms, what we have been doing is an *iteratio* of the *prima materia*: going over and over again the same opaque "unpsychological" stuff, giving more and more possibility for connections to appear and psychic patterns to emerge. Psyche emerges, but not in straight messages given by interpretative meanings. Rather, psyche emerges as we merge with or get lost in the labyrinth of the image. Restatement and *iteratio* are also a mode of admitting one's lostness in front of the image, which in turn heightens the value of the image.

If this had been your dream in therapy, one analogy after another would have struck home in regard to your fantasies and behaviors, your ambitions, your styles of reflection and sexuality, attitudes toward yourself, life, old women, boys, growth, and shit. The dream would have gathered value, that all-encompassing sense of importance we tend to call archetypal. "Archetypal" now is the result of an operation, given not with the image but with what happens with the image—a function of *making* rather than a function of *being*. The image grows in worth, becomes more profound and involving, that is, it becomes more archetypal as its patterning is elaborated. We are following Jung here quite strictly:

> Image and meaning are identical; and as the first takes shape, the latter becomes clear. Actually the pattern needs no interpretation: it portrays its own meaning (*CW*8: 402).

It portrays. It makes a picture of its own meaning—not one supposed by interpretation. As shape emerges, meaning emerges. Image-making = meaning. And all this without our usual interpretative moves.

PROTESTOR: *But I must intervene, for I think you did interpret. You did slant the chant in one direction only—toward condemnation of playing idly. You are against sitting like a baby and reflecting and having a lark. I could have re-sung the whole thing, bringing out the importance of singing, the left, the reflection, which lets the river of life carry away one's shit just as the old woman does. In other words, the image could be read to feel the supportive role of mother nature and the value of playful idleness.*

No doubt an image catches us in a complex; of course, we slant the chant in the direction of the complex. There is no objective, no scientific, no pure work with images. We are always ourselves in the image and unconscious because of it.

7 Berry, "An Approach to the Dream," 71.

However, your reading or chanting of the image, Protestor, singles out one or two motifs and arranges them to accord with a meaning ("supportive role of mother nature and the value of playful idleness"). You have left out the words: pale blue, shallow, narcissus; you have not faced the actual words, such as "dandelion," "plays about," "the baby narcissus" (boy disappears). I grant my slant, but it is not the same kind as yours. For you have not stuck to the image, whereas mine derives from it and returns always to it. Moreover, I would now add your protest to the chant, as an additional rabbinical commentary below the line, a further enrichment rather than an alternative interpretation. I insist: what we did was not reductive interpretation. It was simply a phenomenal approach to the image, letting it "show itself."

Maybe we should notice some of the more usual moves of interpretation so as better to realize what we did not do with the image:

1) We have not amplified the symbols (hag, river, pearl, etc.) by referring to their folklores, mythologies, and the like.

2) We tried not to single out or weight any part with more importance. We did not imagine the dream out from a central figure like "the shallow river," or in the other case, "the dead swan." This may be a valuable move in skewing the configuration into a new image for the sake of some therapeutic aim, but such a move is essentially reductive rather than imagistic. It puts the images in service of an overall view of them.

3) We did not read the images symbolically, i.e., river, old woman, and shit as symbols of the Great Mother of Life (Kali). This leads to your interpretation, Protestor, which actually distorts the image. For here the river is pale blue and shallow and not like an old woman and not shit-bearing. (The interpretation would, of course, take this approach further by insisting that the pale blue and shallow aspects are an *anima* fascination having as their other pole the hag and shit, just as Kali presents these contrasting "side.")

4) We did not use a developmental model, assigning psychodynamic functions to the images: the swan as "dead feeling-function"; the hurrying with our bad right leg as "inferior extraversion"; the hag as a still "untransformed mother complex."

5) We neither put emotion in, searched for it, nor abstracted it out (as a fear dream, a pleasure dream). We tried to let the feel of the image stay in the image, the mood in the scene.

6) We did not press the image into a narration of dramatic sequences: Sitting and playing while life flows by leads to narcissus flowers and ends up in the shit of the mother complex. Or, in the other case, coming out into daylight is the result, the end of the story, the dramatic resolution. Remember: an image has no lysis. An image goes on and on without "resolving." An image can have no lysis because it is not a drama—unless we look at it as such.

7) Without drama we do not need an agonist. The dreamer thus plays no central role as hero, but is interwoven in specific ways into the pattern of the image.

8) We did not moralize the image by finding some parts positive and others negative or by judging it regressive or progressive.

9) We did not programmize it by deriving a course of action from it (dream as message): "You should not let the feminine carry the shit for you." Or this dream warns you about "your weak right side," the "death-dealing power of Artemis or Apollo" (five arrows), or to "go back into the cave again and talk to the swan to revivify it."

10) We did not sexualize it, which could have happened in terms of playing with birds and pearls in the hand.

11) We did not pathologize it, which could have happened in terms of seeing woman as hag whose box has shit in it or, in the other case, by concentrating on the symptomatic knee and anxiousness.

12) We did not personalize it by identifying the figures with the dreamer or any person in his entourage. Thus we never addressed the dreamer directly, and yet the image always addressed him indirectly, and his entourage by its analogies. We might have personalized by showing the "ego attitude" and then by addressing the dreamer as if he were that figure in the cave or by the river. Often this addressing the dreamer becomes a dressing down of the dreamer for what he should have done in the dream: at the turning point you made the wrong move, and so sprained your knee; if you hadn't turned wrong, you wouldn't have sprained your knee, and it would have come out all right; you shouldn't run from the dark or go too deep into the unconscious for you get overwhelmed; or you have killed your animal and can't face discovering this fact.

13) So we did not try to correct the dream by saying how it might better have been.

14) We did not mythologize, which could have happened with narcissus, reflection, and water, nor did we assign the image to an archetypal locus in the mother complex or the *puer* nor to any god.

Nonetheless, and this is quite remarkable, many of these very implications of the image—and again I rely on Berry—emerged as we went through our chanting and weaving. The interpretations appeared indirectly. All we did was "stick to the image," i.e., stay faithfully close to the actual text. As Berry has pointed out, text and context refer to weaving:

> The word *text* is related to weave. So to be faithful to a text is to feel and follow its weave... the dream is sensate, has texture, is woven with patterns offering a finished and full context... Image in itself has texture.[8]

What I have done in the example was put into operation her approach to the dream.

8 Ibid., 60.

4

ARCHETYPAL IMAGE: AN ORDINARY EXAMPLE

PROTESTOR: *The entire venture so far has depended on poetical images. My goodness—swans! And now larks and baby boys! Let us see something archetypal made of this dream, a bread-and-butter dream without high-blown symbols, maybe no symbols at all:*

> *My sister is driving my* Chevy *and has a* beer *beside her. She pulls up at the* curb *to call about getting the* kitchen sink *repaired. I can see through the* window *of the phone booth that she hasn't got a* dime.

As we already have shown in the supermarket/brown-bag example, we can see symbols anywhere once we go to work on the nouns through amplification. So here, too, we can "find" symbols: the Chevrolet as psychodynamic chariot, the sister as soul, the beer as fermented ritual drink usually made or distributed by women, the dime as a piece of silver . . .

But in this nitty-gritty example (in the genre of social realism) we are put to forego poetic echoes and symbolisms. We are challenged to be archetypal without being symbolic, without relying upon half-hidden values stored in "big" words (flowers, pearl, shit, etc.). So let's start playing and put our ears to work.

When my sister drives my Chevy, a repair job needs doing. When my sister drives, she calls. She calls about the sink; that stops her driving. How does this kitchen-sinkery sister tie in with driving my Chevy? And what has it to do with beer that is beside her when she drives. When she has a beer, she hasn't got a dime. Is she beside herself with beer? I see through to my sister in a booth. I see through only when my sister is pulled up, boothed, curbed. Only when she calls. When there is a calling sister, there is no driving sister. Alternatingly, there seems to be a driving sister and a phoning sister, and what happens in-between is pulling up. Pulled up short or pulled up high? What does this image say about my driving? Who drives my car? I seem only able to see into it when it is boothed, for then there is a window to her and she is inside the glass containment. Boothing is a way of being in touch (phoning), even without a dime. It is also a way of distancing (*tele*), being glassed in. Though she has a beer when driving, she hasn't even a dime when curbed and calling. She is curbed for one reason: to call about sink repair. Her kind of sink, her place of sink, is in the kitchen. A kitchen kind of sinking. Sinking is her mode of kitchen, for in the kitchen is where she sinks, and to repair the sink is the purpose and cause of both her pulling up and no longer driving.

By this, I think, we have learned that an image does not have to contain any symbols or motifs that usually are considered archetypal. An image does not have to be shocking, freakish, or sick. An image does not have to have its emotion literalized ("I felt frightened"). There do not have to be big affects or explicit emotional words to make one feel the mood in an image or its emotional weight. Emotion as mood, as textural feel, is given with every image. None of the overt implications of an image have to be literally evident because through precisely portraying the patterns, as Jung said, the implications emerge.

We do not have to know whether to take the sister on the subjective level as part of the dreamer or on the objective level as referring to an actual woman. We do not have to know whether this actual sister drinks or not, whether the dreamer is a man or a woman, has a sister or seven of them, whether there is a money problem now constellated in the therapy, or any of the other "information" that supposedly clarifies the dream. As we play through the dream work, one analogy after another resonates with many aspects of the dreamer's life: my inner soul, my outer sister, my drive problem, my curb problem, my drinking problem, my money problem, my problems of communication, my sinking depression, how I call for repair, how I get insights, how I get stopped, and so on. These analogies can all be spun out of the dream's implications, and the analogies receive precision by the intrarelation of the whole image. It is like looking at interlocking mechanisms at work: when this happens, then that happens. Cogs. I am given images for my problems and how they actually function in relation with each other. Even further problems, formerly unconscious, begin to emerge as I go through the weave of the image. Also, further implications of these problems and suppositions about them emerge.

The implications and suppositions in my chanting were mixed. I would consider all the "when/then" and "only" statements to be implications and all the questions and conclusion ("hence") to be suppositions.

Now, what about archetypal? How does it come in? We have refused it entry through the symbolic, and in later chapters we shall equally refuse the identification of archetypal with emotion and with universality. So, in answer, I think we must refer the "archetypal" to these multiple implications of the image. What makes an image archetypal is that so much wealth can be got from it. An archetypal image is a rich image, even though its surface shows only a can of beer in a Chevy at the curb.

This subliminal richness is another way of speaking of its invisible depth, like Pluto is another way of speaking about Hades. Our exercise with the image gave us a new appreciation of the unfathomable nature of any image, even the meanest, once it dies to its everyday simple appearance. It becomes bottomlessly more layered, complicatedly more textured. And as we do our image-making, even further implications appear, more suppositions and analogies dawn on us. An image is like an inexhaustible source of insights. Mythologically, we are now talking about Hades who in the Neoplatonic Renaissance was the god of the greatest depth, mystery, and insight.

The depth only appeared, however, as we went deeper into it, quite got lost in it; and as we did go deeper into it, it got deeper. On the one hand, its inhesion became more evident–it became more and more internal, coherent. It began to feel necessary. Every part was necessary to every other part, an economic stringency, everything belonging. On the other hand, it became more and more mysterious and unfathomable. That is, the image became at the same time more coherent and more hidden. Heraclitus might have called this "the hidden harmony," which also refers to the underworld.[9]

There is an invisible connection within any image that is its soul. If, as Jung says, "image *is* psyche" (*CW*13:75), then why not go on to say, "images are souls," and our job with them is to meet them on that soul level. I have spoken of this elsewhere as befriending,[10] and elsewhere

9 Heraclitus, fr. 47: "The hidden harmony is better than the visible" (trans. G.T.W. Patrick). Cf. J. Hillman, "The Dream and the Underworld," *Eranos Yearbook* 42 (1973).

10 J. Hillman, *Insearch: Psychology and Religion* (Putnam, Conn.: Spring Publications, 2014), 47–50, 80, 104.

again I have spoken of images as animals.[11] Now I am carrying these feelings further to show operationally how we can meet the soul in the image and understand it. We can actively imagine it through wordplay, which is also a way of talking with the image and letting it talk. We watch its behavior—how the image behaves within itself. And we watch its ecology—how it interconnects by analogies in the fields of my life. This method is indeed different from "diagnostic interpretation." No friend or animal wants to be interpreted, even though it may cry for understanding.

We might equally call that unfathomable depth in the image "love" or, at least, say we cannot get to the soul of the image without love for the image.

Once we get into the soul of the image, many of the other interpretative moves (mentioned in the previous chapter) become unnecessary. They may be regarded as means to give the image soul by literally connecting it to the dreamer's person. But the hidden connections are best, Heraclitus said, and this because the connections are there *a priori* in the person of the dreamer who dreamt them. The connections do not have to be forced into literal (outer) life by personal associations or personalistic interpretations. The method I am sketching can make dreams and images "matter" without having to reduce them to the personal. So all those distinctions between inner and outer, personal and archetypal, subjective and objective are heuristic at best. When we work the image through by means of metaphorical analogies, the hidden connections ramify on all levels into all places. These connections also operationally prevent separations into such theoretical pairs.

Two things to observe in passing. One: our method can be done by anyone, in or out of analysis. It requires no special knowledge—even if knowledge of symbols can help culturally to enrich the image, and knowledge of idioms and vocabulary can help hear further into the image. By letting the image itself speak, we are suggesting that words and their arrangements (syntax) are soul mines. But mining doesn't require modern technical tools. (If it did, no one would ever have understood a dream or an image until modern psychology came along!) What does help mining is an eye attuned to the dark. Two: our method is not to be taken literally, as if all dreams must only be played through according

11 J. Hillman, "The Animal Kingdom in the Human Dream," *Eranos Yearbook* 51 (1982); reprinted in *UE9: Animal Presences* (Putnam, Conn.: Spring Publications, 2008).

to "Hillman's New Verbal Technique." The demonstrations here are not of a new method but of a mode by means of which certain theoretical and practical considerations concerning images can be exposed. There are all sorts of things one can do with dreams and other images (Chapter 14 below). Of main importance is that we recognize what in analysis we have been doing and been taking for granted and now what else we might be doing, what else images can be heard to say when listened to more acutely.

PROTESTOR: *I am still waiting to learn what it is that makes an image "archetypal," besides what you called the "multiple implications of an image."*

We have found our axiomatic criteria—dramatic structure, symbolic universality, strong emotion—not required in our actual operations with an image.

We have found, instead, that an archetypal quality emerges through

a) precise portrayal of the image;

b) sticking to the image while hearing it metaphorically;

c) discovering the necessity within the image;

d) experiencing the unfathomable analogical richness of the image.

Since any image can respond to these criteria, any image can be considered archetypal. The word "archetypal" as a description of images becomes redundant. It has no descriptive function. What then does it point at?

Rather than pointing *at* something, "archetypal" points *to* something, and this is its value. By attaching "archetypal" to an image, we ennoble or empower the image with the widest, richest, and deepest possible significance. "Archetypal," as we use it, is a word of importance (in Whitehead's sense),[12] a word that values.

We found that the word does not single out one image from others: the Chevy-beer-dime image offered as much richness and depth as did the cave-swan-knee image, even though the latter was more symbolic. Even while not adding anything descriptive, the word "archetypal" does value the image by pointing to fecundity (Langer) and generativity

12 "There are two contrasted ideas which seem inevitably to underlie all width of experience, one of them is the notion of importance, the sense of importance, the presupposition of importance. The other is the notion of matter-of-fact... It is the basis of importance; and importance is important because of the inescapable character of matter-of-fact. We concentrate by reason of a sense of importance." A.N. Whitehead, *Modes of Thought* (New York: The Free Press, 1968), 4.

(Erikson). We need the term to encourage our searching, to make us feel the transcending importance of the image. The fecundity and generativity suggested by "archetypal" is of a special kind in a special direction. This has been indicated by my use of words such as unfathomable, patterned, hidden, rich, prior, deep, necessary, permanent. These are the words we have used to give a sense of value. All images gain this value as their volume extends by means of our image-making work.

Should we carry this conclusion over to other places where we use "archetypal," to our psychology itself, then by archetypal psychology we mean a psychology of value. And our appellative move aims to restore psychology to its widest, richest, and deepest volume so that it resonates with soul in its descriptions as unfathomable, multiple, prior, generative, and necessary. As all images can gain this archetypal sense, so all psychology can be archetypal when it is released from its usual surface and seen through to its hidden volumes. "Archetypal" here refers to *a move one makes rather than a thing that is.* Otherwise, archetypal psychology becomes only a psychology of archetypes.

"Only a psychology of archetypes" would mean a psychology that takes "archetypal" as an adjective derived from a noun, "archetype." To this noun we would then be forced to address any question about archetypal. This further leads to a denotative sense of archetypal, as descriptive of fundamental structures, posited abstractions, which have been adduced from myths and religious texts, social institutions (like the family and state), animal behavior (like nest-building), philosophical and scientific ideas (like causality), and art forms (like epics).

In most contexts where we come across the word "archetypal" especially in relation with image ("*that* is an archetypal image"), archetypal could readily be replaced by one or another of the backgrounds on which it relies: mythical, religious, institutional, instinctual, philosophical, or literary.

PROTESTOR: *But there is a difference of feeling between saying "the circle is a scientific or philosophical idea" and saying "the circle is an archetypal idea." Archetypal adds the further implication of basic root structure, generally human, a necessary universal with consequents. The circle is not just any scientific idea; it is basic, necessary, universal. Archetypal gives this kind of value.*

Troubles begin when the value implication is taken literally. Then we believe that these basic roots, these universals *are.* We have moved from a valuative adjective to a thing, to invented substantialities called archetypes that can "back up" our sense of archetypal value. Then we are forced to gather literal evidence from cultures the world over and make empirical claims about what is, by definition, unspeakable and irrepresentable.

We do not need to take archetypal in this literal sense. Instead, the implications of basic, deep, universal, necessary—all those implications carried by the word "archetypal" add richer value to any particular image. Unfortunately, however, the literal sense of archetypal prevails. So when an image is called archetypal, this conventionally denotes that we are in the presence of a basic instinctual pattern or a root philosophical idea or a universal religious theme. If that is what archetypal has come to mean, then where is psychology? Have we not slipped away into metapsychology, or even metaphysics, examining an empyrean of abstractions, gathering evidence to literalize them even further. If that's where we are, let's either stay there and work it out with our colleagues in these fields of religion, philosophy, and social institutions or return to psychology as an ongoing operation with the soul's images where the term "archetypal" connotes rather than denotes, gives importance rather than information, evokes rather than describes, and by recognizing value furthers inquiry into our images.

A descriptive definition of "archetypal" would turn our inquiry down old tracks. We would then be inquiring into images in terms of their archetypes, and we would end up back in symbology: images *of* the Great Mother, *of* the Hero, *of* the different gods. To go in this direction would be to follow on the heels of analytical psychology, which could and should have meant an analyzing psychology, and an analyzing *of* psychology, and instead has come to mean a psychology of analysis by analysts for analysts. Similarly, we would be following what happened to depth psychology, which first meant a deeper psychology, deepening psychology below mere conscious functions, but which then became a psychology of literalized depths or "the unconscious."

To the question "what is an archetypal image?" we answered with an inquiry into the image (and not the archetype) and thus came out somewhere unexpected. It has led us to revision "archetypal" itself, for we found it didn't "say" anything directly about the image. Now two modes of operating with the word "archetypal" begin to appear, descriptive and valuative. And these can be two directions in our work. We can press further and more precisely into a descriptive psychology of the archetypes, and we can work further at revisioning psychology in the valuative sense of archetypal. This revisioning of archetypal implies that the more accurate term for our psychology in its operational definition is revisioning. In what we do we are more revisionist that archetypalist; or, we evoke archetypes (gods and myths) in order to revision psychology. The value of a psychology of the archetypes for revisioning psychology is that "archetype" provides a metaphorical tool of widest, richest, and deepest volume. It conforms with the soul value we wish to give to and find in our work.

The danger of the first descriptive mode is that it can become literal; the danger of the second, that it can become wholly a phenomenological exercise. The first can coagulate so that before we know it we are strangled in a new typology—gods and goddesses as stereotypical models on a tight network for placing everything. The second operational mode can get dissolutional so that all we do is move words around in an existential vacuum, anything as good as everything else in endless widespread analogies. Pragmatic phenomenology and archetypal psychology need each other. Phenomenology needs the sense of mythic structures in the background and their deep values; archetypal psychology needs the deliteralizing, sometimes humorous, sense of metaphor in the foreground. So, too, the two senses of archetypal, descriptive and operational, need each other. Both occur together in images from which both derive in the first place.

5

EMOTION AND IMAGE

Before we can move further, there is a set of prejudices lying in the way: our familiar assumptions about emotion. For example, don't we all believe that emotional images are more important than non-emotional ones? Don't we think that dreams that affect us strongly deserve more attention than those that don't? And don't we tend to believe that the best way with an image is to get into its emotion so that it can make us cry or hunger or remember with pain?

Sometimes we go so far as to hold that images are only emotions in disguise, and that our dreams translate desire, anxiety, and guilt into fantasy images so that we may sleep without disturbance of these affects. Other times we work the translation in the other direction. Then we use images to get out of overpowering excitement: instead of raging or longing, we try to convert the affects into images—write a dialogue or a poem, model clay figures, or mush with finger paints. This active imagination, as the technique is called, however, is less for the sake of the images than to save ourselves from being devastated by emotion. Emotion, rather than image, remains the primary concern.

Because our assumptions hold that emotion takes precedence over image, we believe the therapeutic job with any image is to get to its emotion, either digging for it in the image or by transfusing it into the image from the therapist's own red blood. (Some therapists insist on responding emotionally to dreams and paintings, showing their distaste, their amusement, even their salaciousness and fright, for this is supposed to bring home to the patient that the depicted material is an emotional event.)

PROTESTOR: *I should hope so! Otherwise the dream is just a ship that passed in the night or a ghost ship with nobody aboard.*

Stick to the image! Do you see how your assumption is interfering with an appreciation of the image as it is? If the image comes without overt emotion, then to infect it with an emotion is like adding ideas to it—associating or amplifying. It is a kind of violation, replacing its inherent emotion with yours. You may consider emotions of the very greatest importance, but try to suspend this consideration when regarding images. To inquire carefully into the image we have to set aside assessment of them by means of emotion.

PROTESTOR: *Before we do, at least agree that those images showing emotion or releasing it are the ones to pay most attention to. Please answer this general question: "Are emotional images the more important ones?"*

If I answer you philosophically, we would have to examine our value systems, where we place emotion in our hierarchy of importances. But that is not our way of working here. Operationally I can only say: see what happens when you make the move of giving emotional images preference over others. This leads to subsuming other events—persons, rhetoric, geographies, memories, implication—as lesser than emotion. This further leads to judging dreams, soul itself, in terms of affect. And this in turn tends to take you into a quantitative assessment of value, since affect is usually considered an amount of feeling and can be measured more readily than many other psychological events. This results in such commonplaces as "to be real is to feel, and to be very real is to feel very much"—the more emotion the better the image.

Let's call this overvaluation of emotion the hysterical perspective or the hysterical defense against the seemingly schizoid silence of the image. (Your "ghost ship" that is without "any body," slipping and gliding through dark regions, presents this fear of the cold dark silent underworld and its images without blood.)

We could also work over the emotional perspective by drawing support from Wimsatt's "affective fallacy."[13] He demonstrates that to judge a poem by using the criterion of emotion leads down the blinding alley of enthusiasms, impressionism, sentimentalism, subjectivism, and away from the poem as such. I believe that the affective fallacy is profoundly disrespectful of the image, not taking what is given but asking that it be presented with a show of feeling. It dishonors the image. But now I am arguing, and I want to inquire. Also I don't want to borrow from literary criticism but, rather, find our own convictions.

---

13 See W.K. Wimsatt, Jr., *The Verbal Icon: Studies in the Meaning of Poetry* (Lexington: University of Kentucky Press, 1954).

So, Protestor, we can better answer your question by turning to examples of the emotional assessment of dream images. People report: "I awakened from dreaming of my grandmother baking cookies, feeling completely at peace and self-contained. It was a positive image." They say: "I felt marvelous making love with him in that dream; I never had such a completely free orgasm in my whole life." And they say: "It was a horrible dream—I lay in cold sweat not daring to open my eyes, and when I did, the thing on my chest was my ex-wife smiling at me. Her teeth! A witch!"

Here the images have been appreciated in emotional terms. The images have been graded plus or minus according to their concomitant emotion. Simply: a good orgasm means a good image, and a horrible cold sweat means a bad image.

PROTESTOR: *I would say something more. I would say that the plain image of my grandmother baking is not as important, not as valuable, as the image of her baking that leaves me self-contained and at peace. I am a diehard, and I won't let go of my belief that an image with emotion is better than one without, never mind all the labyrinthine consequences that you just spelled out. What does bother me is your neglect of the emotional aspect of the image.*

So we have two things to clear up: that "bad emotion equals bad image" and that "no emotion equals bad image." I'm keeping them together because I think they can be dealt with in the same demonstration.

Take the example of the woman and her orgasm. If she "had the best orgasm ever" while making love in a dream with Fritz the Cat, an invisible devil, or her younger brother, are we to judge the value of these three figures by the standard of her emotion? Does "best orgasm" mean or equate with best lover = positive figure? If so, then there is no difference in value between a mechanical cartoon figure, a transparent evil spirit, and her closest flesh and blood. There is no difference in importance between the amusing, the sinister, and the brotherly. They have become equalized by the orgasm. Moreover, since it was a positive experience, as she says, then it is a positive image, a good dream. (If this approach were used for judging a poem, we wouldn't get out of Freshman English; yet we use this very method in considering our souls.)

Maybe my point is still not vivid enough, or maybe it's too simple. Let's take your grandmother baking cookies with emotion and without emotion. Because the emotion gives you the sense of peace and containment, you assume that the cookie-baking grandmother is a good and wholesome image. Had you been more wary from fairy-tale reading, you might suspect this cookie grandmother. You might wonder whether the peace and containment wasn't lulling you into being devoured, the effect of being held by her in a cage as Hänsel was kept in the gingerbread house. Even if you were not wary from fairy tales, the precision of the image might help you more specifically appreciate what is going on.

PROTESTOR: *But the emotion of peace and containment are specifications of the image.*

Right! Now you are in another place. Now you are no longer assessing the image by the emotions, no longer taking the emotion out of the image and judging the image by these unreflected standards: a good image because a peaceful feeling. Now you are seeing that when there are peaceful feelings, there is a grandmother baking cookies, and when she bakes cookies, you awaken feeling self-contained.

The image has brought discrimination to your feeling; it is now more complicated: both ambiguous and specific. The emotion has helped articulate and qualify the feelings of the image.

Now back to your persistent question. Is an image with emotion better than one without? It is better, inasmuch as the emotion gives an indication where the imager (dreamer) is likely to be caught in the image since we identify with our emotions. They carry us away; they possess us. The overt emotion does not make the image more valuable, important, useful, or deeper in itself. Its "betterness" consists solely in the value *for therapy*: because of the emotion we can get closer to how and where a person is involved in an image.

The other part of your question still remains: Does bad emotion equal or indicate a bad image? Let's say our image this time is a big black dog showing its teeth, and the emotion is panicked terror. Black dog and panicked terror are part and parcel of the one experience. Because terror usually signals danger, the black dog is assessed to be dangerous: hence bad emotion equals bad image. (I could have coupled terror with standing at the top of a skyscraper, finding a hairy spider in my cereal box, running from a crowd of Nazi boys.) As well I could have used other so-called negative emotions—despair, murderous rage, pettiness—coupled with images that become "bad" because the affect has signaled this. Our emotions are kinds of cognitions. They tell us something about the world as well as ourselves, something about the situation within which they arise.

Here the panicked terror says there is something to be panicked about—a danger.

This kind of reasoning in regard to images is the "naturalistic fallacy" I examined in *Re-Visioning Psychology*.[14] That fallacy means taking emotions literally, just as we would were they to appear in the usual, daily, natural world, where panicked terror tells us something about the image that evokes it and our relation with it. For the natural perspective does call a dog "bad" when it makes us terrified; a lover "good" when he brings marvelous orgasms; and a grandmother "good" when we feel peace in her presence.

In imagination other rules obtain. Our perspective is no longer natural. Dogs, lovers, and grandmothers all have further significance than what first meets the eye. Images are not adequately approached naturally; they require a metaphorical sense. So we realize that making love with brother is not actual incest with actual brother but has to do as well with inner brother, soul brother, brothering, brotherhood, etc. Consequently we do not take the black dog literally; we recognize that the image is presenting me with my blackness, and that this blackness is showing its teeth, and it is a big blackness that is as alive as a dog (is very dogged indeed), and moreover that my terror comes in this shape and size.

Further, because image and emotion are part and parcel of the same event, the terror is not only of the dog and in response to the dog but part of the dog, even partly is the dog, and that this dogged hound is my terror as well as my blackness and my bigness, and where teeth are, and that I am dogged by my own terror, which I ever turn from, by calling the dog "bad," and that this condemnation may even be forming the dog into big and black and terrifying because of my identification with terror. Image and emotion are inextricably enmeshed. My dog comes in this emotion of terror, and my terror comes in the figure of this dog. Since the dog is an image, a fantasy going on in the soul, *so, too, is the terror.*

We are discovering that if we take the image metaphorically, we have to take *the emotion metaphorically.* But our prejudice has been taking only images as metaphors and leaving the emotions literal, and then using the literal, natural signals of emotion to assess the images. We have been taking emotions just as they come, at face value, without doing any psychological seeing through. The literalization of emotion is the reason why

14 J. Hillman, *Re-Visioning Psychology* (New York: HarperPerennial, 1992), 84–86.

you, Protestor, have all along been insisting that emotions are more real and more important than images.

To judge an image by an emotion splits the actual event and uses one part against the other. Moreover, the multiple connotations of the event—the grandmother baking cookies giving me peace, the smiling ex-wife on my chest giving me terror—are reduced to a single denotation: good peace and bad terror. This is to literalize. And this is why it makes us feel so sure and safe when we have found an emotion and use it as the Archimedean fulcrum for evaluating a dream. We forget that emotions, too, must be seen through and kept within their images. They, too, must be imagined.

By "imagining emotion" I do not mean imaging emotion, turning emotion into images through techniques of active imagination. I mean keeping it as emotion, holding on to it even while letting go of the identification with it. This we do by feeling it and by suspecting it, taking it as fantasy, all at the same time. It is a double process of seeing it through and seeing through it simultaneously.

PROTESTOR: *Why do we need to see through our emotions? If there is anything I really got from my analysis, it is to trust my emotion, follow my instincts, have courage of the heart, find what I feel, and go with it. This sounds simple and like acting out, but I don't mean it that way. I mean that emotion is where the deep self lies, and one must listen to emotion. Emotion carries my individuation. You show this yourself in your book.*[15] *That is why all along I have been wanting to use emotion as my touchstone for value.*

I'll reply to this feeling question by turning to a real thinker. The thinker is Thomas Ernest Hulme, the philosophical founder of Imagism, the movement that generated much of the style of poetry in English of this century. This style is like our imagistic psychology and our image-focused psychotherapy. It, too, sticks to images and teaches us how to make them. It, too, scorns symbolisms and generalities, compares images with painting (space, not time), and—for purposes here—examines the relation of image and emotion.

Hulme says: "The average person... does not even *perceive* the individuality of their own emotions."[16] "Language... only conveys that part

---

15 J. Hillman, *Emotion: A Comprehensive Phenomenology of Theories and Their Meanings for Therapy* (Evanston, Ill.: Northwestern University Press, 1960).

16 T.E. Hulme, *Speculations: Essays on Humanism and the Philosophy of Art,* ed. H. Read (London: Kegan, Paul, Trench, Trubner, and Co., 1924), 166.

of the emotion which is common to all of us."[17] "We only see stock types [of emotion]."[18] "If you are able to observe the actual individuality of the emotion you experience, you become dissatisfied with language."[19] "Ordinary language communicates nothing of the individuality and freshness of things... Creation of imagery is needed to force language to convey over this freshness of impression."[20] "In any writing which you recognise as good there is always... an attempt, by the adding of certain kinds of intimate detail, to lift the emotion out of the impersonal and colourless level, and to give to it a little of the individuality which it really possesses."[21]

Let's pretend, Protestor, that you and I are the average person Hulme is talking about. He says: "One may have difficulty at first sight in seeing that one only perceives one's own emotions in stock types." He asks us to see that anger, fear, and sexual arousal, personal as they may feel, are general collective events, universal in their expression, even their facial expression. They are stock types.

It's hard to take that my paralyzing fear in front of the dog's teeth or under the ex-wife's smile is a stock response. Even harder to accept that the "marvelous orgasm" in sleep and the awakening "feeling at peace and self-contained" are common unindividualized events. Hardest of all is to realize that emotion, because it is stock and common, generalizes experiences and, while leading to the "deep self," also makes us all alike.

Therapy that turns to emotion first in the name of the individuality and creativity of the deep self may actually be turning patients into stock types from central casting. Don't we see this in the Woody Allen caricatures of the therapized person whose emotions are stock types and whose language about them is devoid of actual images? We must take great care when translating the emotion of an image into the narrowing concepts of feeling, such as anger, aggression, hostility, rage, resistance, etc. The image defines aggression with such precision, with such imagination! Whirling propellers, a Turk with a scimitar, iron gates, cats' claws, orange-red slashes... infinite differentiation.

17 Ibid., 162.
18 Ibid., 159.
19 Ibid., 162
20 Ibid., 163.
21 Ibid., 165.

If we go back to our lady of the orgasms, what does individualize her experience is "intimate detail" (Hulme), i.e., the image of Fritz the Cat, or the invisible devil, or her younger brother. The image distinguishes her orgasm from each of the others she has had and all the others that have happened on this planet. Her superlatives "marvelous," "the best ever" do not provide that "intimate detail" that would "lift the emotion out of the impersonal and colourless level, and give to it a little of the individuality which it really possesses." Only by precision of the context, mood, and scene, the specifics of imagery, can we get hold of the individuality of the emotion.

If there is any relation, then, between emotion and creative originality of dreams, dances, paintings, poems, it is contrary to what we might have expected: emotion wipes out the little intimate differences that make for originality, reducing originality to a typical event. Instead of what we actually dreamt or painted, and the subtle complexities of its feelings, we are left with "I was depressed," "afraid," or "panicked"—each a word that can be used for hundreds of experiences.

6

REDUCTION AND ANALOGY

The whole business of working with images is to make them matter. Analysts try to make them matter by employing various kinds of reduction. "Going up the driveway and into the house" means entering the vagina and wishing to return to the mother – sexual reduction. "Going up the driveway" means coming to this hour and my office and our relationship = transference reduction. "Going up the driveway" refers to your attitudes toward home, wife, and family = personalistic reduction. "Going up the driveway" presents the root condition of life on earth, traveling, dwelling, and homecoming = existential reduction.

All these reductive interpretations, the very reductive move itself, arise as naive psychological attempts to materialize the dream. As if by concentrating the dream down to a single meaning, it would be reduced to an essential, to be more tangibly felt and have more impact.

PROTESTOR: *You've spent most of your time telling us what we should not do with images. What do you do when "sticking with the image"?*

The first way to make the dream matter is by analogy—and analogies have to return to the original image, unlike associations that form into a chain away from the image and unlike what I call "interpretations" that translate an image into something else: a memory, a symbol, a concept, a meaning.

Analogy follows another notion of matter, that of extension. By spreading the dream out, disclosing connections all over the place, an image takes on weight and can even make me feel that I am walking on its ground, that I am everywhere in the dream rather than it in me.

Analogy is a word used in comparative anatomy for referring to a relation where there is a likeness in *function* but not in *origin.* For instance, there are analogies between the hag with the box of shit and images of crones in legends, witches in fairy tales, the goddess Kali, putrefying corpses in coffins, even memory images of my grandmother, or a smelly old schoolteacher: they look alike, function alike, feel alike. But we do not have to go one step further and claim the hag is an image *of* the Great Mother archetype; for this relation expressed by the genitive "of" would then be one of origin: as if the mother archetype generates hag (and other images) *of* the archetype. Analogies keep us in the functional operation of the image, in the patterns of similarities, without positing a common origin for these similarities. The operative term is "like." This is like that. A dream:

> There is a black dog, with a long tail, that shows its teeth at me. I am terribly afraid.

Analogizing is quite an easy procedure. We simply ask the dreamer, "What is this dog, this scene, this fear, like?" Then we get: It's like when there is a sudden sound, and I jump with fright; like coming to analysis and expecting you to pounce on everything I say; like anger—sometimes I get so angry (or hungry) that I could savage anyone who gets near me; like my ulcer that gets angry and hungry at the same time; like my mother used to look—her teeth; like going home after work in the dark and being afraid my wife will bark at me, jump at me; it's like dying—I'm so afraid—it's so vicious and low and degrading; it's like a film I saw when I was little with black dogs in it and had to leave the movie theater because I was so terrified; like the Jackal god Anubis; like Mephistopheles in Goethe's *Faust*; like when I get sexy—I want to tear into the meat and just eat and screw like a dog in the street, anywhere; it's like the dog was a snake with a long tail. And so on.

Here we see a main difference between analogizing and reducing. Should any one of the above analogies be taken as the meaning of the image, I would lose the others. I would have narrowed the image down to only one place where it matters. Analogies are multiple and don't lose the others; they don't lose the dog either. They keep the image there, alive and well, returning to it each time for a fresh sense of it. Interpretation translates it into a meaning. And most interpretations are reductive in one way or another.

Analogizing is like my fantasy of Zen, where the dream is the teacher. Each time you say what an image means, you get your face slapped. The dream becomes a koan when we approach it by means of analogy. If you can literalize a meaning, "interpret" a dream, you are off the track, lost your koan. (For the dream is the thing, not what it means.) Then you must be slapped to bring you back to the image. A good dream analysis is one in which one gets more and more slaps, more and more analogies, the dream exposing your entire unconsciousness, the basic matters of your psychic life.

PROTESTOR: *I hear you saying: more equals good. The more you can say about the dog, the better it is and the surer you are about not knowing what that dog really means! This leads you all over the map. And I can't see the difference between Freud's method of associating all through memory, or Jung's method of amplifying all through history and culture. They each have the effect of losing the image, which is your very concern to stick to.*

Moreover, analogizing seems impractical. In therapy we need to get down to where it's really at, to essentials. Surely, some of these analogies are more relevant to the patient's problem than others. Is there no hierarchy among the analogies? Are they all equally good? Doesn't analogizing in therapy finally depend on an "A-ha" experience, the "click" in the patient that tells you when to stop, when you've got to it?

Knowing when to stop and where to stop is the whole art of any art. This is an animal-knowing, an animal sense of essential—not instinctive only, not given only, but a refined skill coming from practice with images. But it's not that damned magical click, one of the great delusions of therapy.[22]

22 See below, chap. 8: "Radical Relativism and the Click."

7

ARCHETYPAL REDUCTION

There is an important passage in Patricia Berry's essay where she takes on both the symbolists and the structuralists. First, her target is the symbolist who gives a meaning to "red bird" relatively independent of how and where and with what it appears (its context, mood, and scene).

> Because images with contents are always structurally positioned within a dream, we cannot speak of them apart from this context. A red bird in one dream and a red bird in another never carry exactly the same content, since neither their structural relation (positioning) within the dream nor the other dream images with which they are structurally related are identical.[23]

Then she moves in on the structuralist who tends to neglect the particularity of content, seeing it only as a function of its relations within the image. And the reverse is also true. Because structures are made up of images with contents, we cannot speak of them apart from these contents. Identical dreams with only a single content different—a black bird rather than a red one—would make for different meanings. In other words, it is not the position alone that makes for a symbol's meaning; rather, it is both position and content. The red bird is not the result of structural determinants (laws of force, binary oppositions, grammar, linguistics, or whatever), but is itself one of the determinants shaping the dream. The image is itself an irreducible and complete union of form and content, and for us cannot be considered apart from either: "Image is both the content of a structure and the structure of a content."[24] Berry is telling us two simultaneous things: first, we cannot study images only symbolically but must always regard their intrarelations (which we might call

23 Berry, "An Approach to the Dream," 64.
24 Ibid.

here "their structure"); second, we cannot take images only structurally (contrasts: male/female, foreground/background, first/last, dominant/submissive), but must see what specific contents are being related.

The archetypal approach (in such works as Rafael López-Pedraza's *Hermes and His Children*,[25] Murray Stein's articles on Hephaestus, Narcissus, and Hera,[26] and my own writings on Pan, Saturn, Dionysus, Athene, and other mythic figures[27]), though attempting to keep structure and content interpermeating, all verge closer to the content or symbolist line than to the structural or relational line. Archetypal reduction has tended to mean content analysis, as, for instance, my listing of qualities and attributes of the *senex* (leaden, black, winter, rigid, lame, outcast, etc.). By their qualities ye shall know them. This method leads qualities backwards (*re*duces) to a mythological motif or figure. An image is backed by a myth, and the act of leading events and behaviors back, finding their mythical backing by examining the content of their imagery, has been our method of *epistrophé*, or carrying a human phenomenon to its archetypal source.

PROTESTOR: *This sets up a new typology, an "archetypology," like in the books of Christine Downing and Jean Bolen.*[28] *We could classify dreams and themes into a new dictionary that tells us what belongs where and to whom. Masturbation belongs to Pan; reflection to Narcissus and Echo; cooking to Demeter; the mating instinct to Hera; sensuality to Aphrodite; scientific objectivity to Apollo; hysteria to Dionysus; and so on. I am simplifying here, but isn't this what "archetypal reduction" really amounts to?*

All of us who have done this sort of archetypal reduction have warned again and again against making one-to-one correlations and against using gods as diagnostic categories. We have insisted that archetypes are

25 R.López-Pedraza, *Hermes and His Children* (Einsiedeln: Daimon-Verlag, 2003).

26 M. Stein, "Hephaistos: A Pattern of Introversion," *Spring: An Annual of Archetypal Psychology and Jungian Thought* (1973): 35–51; "Narcissus," *Spring: An Annual of Archetypal Psychology and Jungian Thought* (1976): 32–53; "Hera: Bound and Unbound," *Spring: An Annual of Archetypal Psychology and Jungian Thought* (1977): 105–119.

27 J. Hillman, *Pan and the Nightmare* (Putnam, Conn.: Spring Publications, 2007); "Senex and Puer: An Aspect of the Historical and Psychological Present," in *UE*3: *Senex & Puer* (Putnam, Conn.: Spring Publications, 2013); "Dionysus in Jung's Writings" and "Athene, Ananke, and the Necessity of Abnormal Psychology," in *UE*6: *Mythic Figures* (Thompson, Conn.: Spring Publications, 2016).

28 See C. Downing, *The Goddess: Mythological Images of the Feminine* (New York: Crossroad Publishing Co., 1981) and J.S. Bolen, *Goddesses in Everywoman: Powerful Archetypes in Women's Lives* (New York: Harper & Row, 1984).

better viewed as perspectives toward events rather than things in events or origins of events.

We have also warned that behaviors can belong to or be viewed through many perspectives. David Miller and Ginette Paris[29] have cautioned against taking polytheistic indeterminancy with monotheistic singleness of meaning.

PROTESTOR: *These warnings indicate a lacuna in your method. It is as if you had constructed a faulty path that you try to rectify by setting up signs all along the way: watch out for the holes; you can easily go astray.*

Let's then try to correct the path itself. Suppose we were to rectify our method by going back to what Berry wrote concerning the complete instantaneity of form and content in the image. Then any overvaluation of content and explication of imagery through content only would be corrected by the structure, the positioning of that content.

Take Berry's red bird. As she says, it can't tell us to which myth it belongs, unless we see in what relations it stands with the rest of the image. Is it the only figure, and thus central and dominant, or is it one bird among a flock, one color among many? Is the bird paired in contrast with a black bird, say, as in her example? Is the rest of the image full of "female" content—cows, girls, harvested fruits? Is it an ascending fire bird? Where is it anyhow? Caged? In the bush? Flying freely? Is its redness blood red, cardinal red, ruby red, robin red, autumn red? Each of these words—"blood," "ruby," "autumn"—gives red a different coloring, not only a different hue. Is it big like a cockatoo or tiny like a hummingbird? And what is its size and place compared with other elements of the image? Is its mood quarreling, singing, or feeding its young?

Moreover, how does the red bird function in the image? What does it do with the rest of the imagery? Is it merely there, or does it resolve something by bringing a message, start something by eating a worm, or set off a feeling by appearing at a window or falling dead?

Here I am trying to get at the *imagistic precision* of the red-bird symbol not only by examining its specific quality but also by discovering its structural relations within the image (dominance, tension, action, gender,

29 David L. Miller, *The New Polytheism: Rebirth of the Gods and Goddesses* (New York: Harper & Row, 1974); Ginette Paris, *Pagan Meditations: The Worlds of Aphrodite, Artemis, and Hestia* (Thompson, Conn.: Spring Publications, 2017) and *Pagan Grace: Dionysos, Hermes, and Goddess Memory in Daily Life* (Thompson, Conn.: Spring Publications, 2018).

placement) and its functions there (eating, bleeding, signaling). All this scrutiny belongs to what Berry calls the positioning of the image.

This positioning puts a brake on any rash assumptions as to which archetype the red bird can be assigned (helpful animal, spirit-bringer, totem, ghostly lover, fire-inspirer, etc.).

Another example should make this clearer. Let us take different images of a stone wall in order to see just how positioning affects content.

1. A stone wall surrounding a tall castle. There is a scaling ladder perched precariously against the wall.

2. A stone wall with a fishing pole extending from it, and a fish quivering on the line.

3. A stone wall of tombs, draped in black.

4. A stone wall with towers, banners on the towers, and slits in the wall for spears and arrows.

5. A stone wall at the edge of a city with people of all kinds going back and forth through its gate.

Even if we agree that stone walls traditionally belong to the phenomenology of Saturn (as a god of resistance, imprisonment, and fortification and as lapidary lord of stone), each of these five walls has particular characteristics. They each have different positioning within the whole image. The first wall surrounds; it keeps things in or out. Though it does support a ladder, it does this precariously and not the way the second wall supports a fishing pole. The first wall encloses, while the fifth wall both separates and makes passage possible. And the kind of opening in the fifth wall is different indeed from the slits in the fourth. Then the third wall functions yet differently again for it is in mutual relation to no other image, but is the image itself and, like a tomb, has swallowed all characteristics except the solemn celebration of its own death power.

This scrutiny of the position of the walls now suggests that no single archetype can embrace them all. We can no longer assign this image exclusively to Saturn. In the first image, we have a wall for tall deeds, for precarious escape or rescue. Let us call it a Heroic wall. In the second, we have a wall that serves as a base for fishing up life from below, a meditative *senex* wall—or a *puer-senex* wall in which wall-cum-quivering-fish brings together that moment of life and death, repose and excitement, much as the wall and the pole together present an image both solid and sensitive. Then we have a third wall—the tomb body in black drapes of the mourning Mother, *mater dolorosa, tellus mater*; a fourth wall belonging to the god of war, his erection of walls, his pointed weapons and noble flaunting phallicism; and a fifth, the wall of the border, at the edge, allowing the commerce and exchange of Hermes.

There could be many more stone walls, e.g., the beautiful Shulamite is a towering wall in the Song of Songs. And, there could be more complex stone walls belonging to several gods at once.

The upshot is that we cannot satisfactorily reduce our stone wall into any one mythological place. Archetypal reduction fails because the more careful we are in scrutinizing the content and its structural positioning, the less chance we have of simple attribution of contents to gods.

Nevertheless we did, in fact, perform a subtle kind of archetypal reduction. We attributed the five wall images each to a different mythical figure. Our attempt to find a built-in method of avoiding reduction has still not quite succeeded. We need yet another factor besides the *content* and the *structure* of an image.

This third factor is *rhetoric,* which acts as a truly independent factor not reducible to either the content or the structure of an image. By this I mean that a stone-wall image will not always necessarily speak in a Saturnian style. The painting or dream will not necessarily have to be done in grays, sparse, orderly, stone upon stone, remote. Nor must the stone wall that offers a passage to Hermes necessarily have to speak in a painting or a dream in a hurried ambiguous manner, as if marked with scurrilous graffiti and concealed messages.

One dreamer might describe the first image (castle wall with scaling ladder) like this: "Granite blocks. Archaic. A forbidding atmosphere chilling and desolate. A little old rickety ladder perched on one side. I felt oppressed, and there was something suspenseful in the air."

This very same wall could be described by a second dreamer as: "Stone wall. Part of a castle? Ladder up side of wall."

A third: "There was this marvelous castle surrounded by a stone wall, and suddenly there was this ladder—yet when I turned my head it wasn't there anyway. I think it was leading up to the top (why?... to get someone, to let people out). I hate heights. I might have been on the ladder or in the castle. Like feeling shut off. I didn't know what I was supposed to do or even why I was there, but the wall made a heavy impression..."

And a fourth: "Stone wall all around a castle. I won't stonewall it; not me, Jackson. Go get somebody else to try that ladder. I don't care if I never get out of China."

These four dreamers have expressed the same content in four different styles. The first is careful about aesthetic details, about how the wall feels to him; he never fails to speak the sensitive rhetoric of mood. The second jots down facts in his appointment book as he travels, mainly the nouns from his dreams; no mood, no scene, no significant detail or psychological reflections. He keeps his images under tight control. The third takes everything quite personally, involving himself with guilt or with opinions or with affects in every image. The fourth does a sort of linguistic punning interpretation within the dream itself, through wordplay ellipsis and associative implications. Let me signify these four rhetorical styles in diagnostic terms, such as (1) hyperaesthetic or neurasthenic, (2) paranoid defensive, (3) hysteroid, and (4) schizoid *puer.* One could concoct further dreamers and their varieties of rhetoric. But our aim is already served. We have recognized that besides the wall-as-content and wall-in-relations there is the factor of rhetoric.

Even if we let the wall "belong" to Saturn and the whole imagery (with castle and ladder) too, how do we handle the fact that it is articulated in a hysterical or schizoid style? To what archetype does the image then belong? Saturn surely hasn't much to do with hysteroid or schizoid styles.

If we are *content* archetypalists, we reduce the rhetoric to a defense against the content. That is, we say, the wall as a manifestation of Saturn constellates depression and all the *senex* phenomena that Saturn brings with him. The rhetoric of hysteria, of overpersonalized involvement, is the person's habitual (ego) reaction to the threat of the wall. He is already being walled by the image and his rhetoric betrays what he does when walled—he gets hysterical, personal, guilty, talkative. We are still able to maintain our archetypal reduction in which the content (wall backed by Saturn) is the main determinant for reading the image.

However, if we are *rhetorical* archetypalists, then we would notice foremost a person's style of articulating an image. We would start off with this hysteroid theatrical mode as determining factor and assign the dream, because of its language style, to Dionysus. (Same holds true for painting. Is the image painted with lots of fluidity, no hard edges, dripping, and bleeding over borders?) Then the contents, such as the stone wall, would be considered the psyche's arbitrary move that introduces elements of another archetypal perspective into the dominant style. The metaphor gets mixed. Catechresis. Rhetoric going one way, content another; hysteroid and paranoid; Dionysus and Saturn. But just this condensed, peculiar, awkward tension is what makes both dreams and art break free of formal norms and become interesting.

PROTESTOR: *What's your point here? All we seem left with is a set of conflicting views, each able to claim its support by pointing to an archetype. The image of castle-wall-ladder in terms of its contents becomes Saturnian; in terms of its structural relation, Heroic; in terms of its rhetoric, Dionysian. The various archetypal reductions seem to annul or at least seriously lame one another. Is this the point?*

By trying to pursue consequently the idea of reducing an image to an archetypal background we discovered that *we can never be certain when we arrive at that background.* Any statement that an image belongs to Hera or Hermes (or that a person is a child of Mars or Dionysus) must be taken as a conjecture rather than as a declaration. The coalescence in an image of content, structure, and rhetoric means that we cannot point *at,* in a denotative sense, any single god or mythical figure. We may at most point to (suggest, connote) a god or mythical figure by means of analogy.

Although our reduction of reduction has led to uncertainty, it has not been useless, because now when we claim this or that image "belongs" to Saturn, say, and not to Aphrodite, we will be obliged to explain that our assessment derives either from the content (stone walls and not roses), or the structure (isolated and not interconnected), or the rhetoric (abstract and not sensate).

PROTESTOR: *I still must ask why have we come down this long road, past red birds and so many stone walls if none of this journey makes us more certain about the archetypal placing of an image? Just what does archetypal reduction serve in regard to images? I'm assuming it serves something since the search for backgrounds has been a main thrust of archetypal psychology from its beginnings.*

We have come down this road in order to demonstrate that the entire process of archetypal reduction—no matter how painstakingly carried out and no matter on what we perform it (content, structure, or rhetoric)—has in it a fault so grave that it cannot but self-destruct. We had to show this rather than merely state it, for "pointing at" is our method. We had to come down the road to find this fault: *the assumption that images can belong to something beyond themselves.*

The archetypal reductions such as we have all been doing in our writings on Pan, Demeter, Athene, Hermes, etc., cannot be taken literally as establishing what belongs to what. What must be taken literally, however, is the maxim "stick to the image." This means not to lead the image *into* archetypes and myths but to enter the image *by means* of archetypes and myths. Myths become ways of seeing the image; they are perspectives toward it rather than facts of it or contents in it. Then, by regarding the stone wall, castle, and ladder heroically, we are able to see its ascensional vertical possibilities, the implications of danger, rescue, and escape. And how it implicates the dreamer, painter, or therapist in heroic fantasies. Or, differently, by regarding it through the Dionysian mode (theatrical rhetoric), we can feel its enclosure not as security but as imprisoning.

Indeed, the emotions we feel and thoughts we have about an image tell us not only where the image belongs but, even more, where we are standing. This opens the whole endeavor of archetypal reduction backward into the subject. We are re-subjectifying the observer, returning our comments and interpretations back to ourselves.

PROTESTOR: *Perhaps seeing images as belonging to gods is a case of old-fashioned projection! Perhaps we project them into the image from where we are standing. Your critique is merciless, for you are saying that the revelatory power of an image is like a theophany—we suddenly see "its myth"—and this we literally, naively, mistakenly assume to be in the image, wheras it's all in our minds. If I've got you right, this theophanic reduction, this belief that images have gods in them, is the fault we have been pursuing; in fact, there are no gods there at all.*

There are very strong and long-held arguments that say that gods do reside in images. That's why Hebrews, Muslims, and Puritan Protestants make a radical cut between gods and images. Their laws and iconoclastic campaigns recognize in reverse the theophanic power in images. And this power is still there in the cave walls of Lascaux, in tribal body paint, and polytheistic ritual statues, orthodox icons, masterful paintings—and also in certain ads that persuade us to change our behavior and buy something and in certain movies on which we model our talk, our walk, our fashion. The relation of gods and images remains still, as it did for hundreds of years from early Church councils to Cromwell in England, the subject of furious debate and even horrendous deaths.

But that is not my tack since we are not simply making assertions and staking claims. I would rather respond to your assertion that "there are no gods there at all" by saying that the gods are still there (in the images), but "there" is as much "here" (in the act of observation) as in the image. The gods are to be discovered in the structures of our vision when we encounter an image and the language of our response when we speak about an image. The gods come forth in our gaze and our words.

To think this way is the therapeutic approach to archetypal reduction. We are reducing our consciousness from its inflated objectivity—that it believes it sees the mythical backgrounds and divine figures—to a subjective sensitivity about the limits of its own regard. After all, isn't our interest in images mainly because of our selves as therapists? We are analysts of images inasmuch as we are analysts of our unconsciousness in regard to them.

PROTESTOR: *You are returning everything to phenomenology, treating gods and myths wholly as subjective perspectives, dissolving their power and our ability to make distinctions within the imagination. If these gods and myths are located, as you say, in the beholder's regard, why can't they be located equally and simultaneously in the image? Are they not the formal cause of both, so that a true archetypal perception is like-seeing-like, a consciousness viewing the image, and an image imbuing consciousness with the same perspective, both within the same myth?*

But if this last is too idealist or too Platonic, then let me point out that the fundamental fault you have found in your demonstration rests on one even more basic. You have considered archetypal reduction to be a narrowing toward a single background. When this single background can't be established you believe the whole reductionist intention faulty. What you are assuming is that the archetypalist is a symbolist: that he is attempting to discover what gods the images are symbols of. But this we have dismissed long ago.

That journey past stone walls demonstrated to me at least the deeper value of archetypal reduction. The different experiments brought out the variety of significances of the single image. I saw its fecundity, which lay in the multiple perspectives, the many gods that emerge from the wall.

Archetypal reduction is also useful for therapy. A reduction that places a stone wall in the realm of the mother of death, for instance, narrows the image for the sake of using it to dig more deeply into the psyche of the person to whom this image occurred. For this person we now can suppose that walls are tombs, that stasis, limitation, and solidity evoke death, and that this stone wall brings with it a mother-earth-death cosmos in behavior, symptoms, feelings, and concepts. The image has worked like an emblematic key that opens into much deeper territory, the mythical dimension that is the psyche's basic order, its causa formalis. *Assigning the wall to an archetypal background does not reduce the wall, nor does it leave the image. Rather, it places the wall into a field of implications, and even expectations, so that we can make more imaginatively vital and rich the person's psyche. It is a pragmatic heuristic move, a soul-making move. The motherness of that wall, for example, tells me that the wall does not exist except in perspective and that by reducing to this perspective we can unearth much more than the wall.*

You have accused archetypal reduction of failure because it did not, could not, arrive at a fixed place for an image. This is a monotheistic desire. You have forgotten your "as-if." (That mother's wall is an "as-if," not to be taken as a literal belonging-to, symbol-of.) Remember, archetypal reduction is a polytheistic move that assumes from the start a variety of placings, a variety of backgrounds, and a toleration of them as possible perspectives. No conflict here between three alternatives (Heroic, Saturnian, Dionysian) such as you set up in your monotheistic model that required that one of them be right. You imply an intolerance among placings, a wrong and right alternative, the oppositional duality of a monotheistic consciousness. However, it is the very nature of a polytheistic psychology to reduce into manyness. Our journey demonstrated that beautifully: its failure was precisely its success. The success now lies in the way your demonstration could move consciousness from its insistence on singleness of meaning. Your argument, you see, is not really with archetypal reduction as such but with the way it is used as symbolism, as literalism—monotheistically.

Protestor, you have really learned how to see through and into my latent hard-core monotheism! I rest my case against archetypal reduction to take a breather on the nearest stone wall. Sitting here, a red bird comes by and says: "But what you just heard was radical relativism. Any perspective is as good as any other—mother, hero, Saturn. How arbitrary, even cynical. No truth in anything; so, how then decide what's best?"

We shall have to look into this in the next chapter.

8

RADICAL RELATIVISM AND THE CLICK

An Icelandic proverb says: "Every dream comes true in the way it is interpreted." This states several curious things about dreams and their interpretation: dreams come true; dreams come true because of interpretations; there are many truths since there are many interpretations. So the maxim takes us into the heart of radical relativism: anything goes. There is a god behind whatever happens. All analogies drawn from an image are equally valid. Nothing objective to hold to; no "true" truths because there are many truths. Ultimately, nothing presented in an image or stated about an image is better or worse than anything else. The imagistic approach is not only relativist; it is cynical and nihilist.

The Icelandic proverb is important. It says that what we do with dreams comes true somehow, somewhere, and unless we can work out the difference between a right interpretation and wrong ones, wrong things will come true.

PROTESTOR: *You seem at last to be holding out hope for practical guidelines so that we can tell when we are making a good or right interpretation. Until now, each time I have pressed you for clear-cut indications, you have danced out of the corner, demonstrating less what to do than your own fancy footwork.*

Maybe that footwork demonstrates the tactical way to answer general kinds of questions. It exhibits two main principles: *parry strategic questions with a tactical operation* and *stick to the image.* You know, it's not altogether what we say in this inquiry but equally how we behave that shows our methods. So in regard to the radical relativism of interpretation, let's operate with a dream. Patricia Berry has already given us an excellent occasion. Her essay opens with a woman patient's short dream:

> I was lying on a bed in a room, alone apparently but with the feeling of turmoil around me. A middle-aged woman enters and hands me

> a key. Later, a man enters, helps me out of bed, and leads me upstairs to an unknown room.[30]

Then follow seven different interpretations of it, any of which could be convincing, valid perspectives of radical relativism. However, Berry's concern is not with the right-or-wrong of these interpretations. She is concerned more with the supposition: of the interpreter than with the accuracy of the interpretation. She is interested in the insight afforded the interpreter by recognizing which particular line he or she takes for approaching the dream.

PROTESTOR: *What about the patient who had the dream?*

We have to see our suppositions about the dream in order to see the patient who is in the dream. The patient doesn't exist independent of the dream or of our suppositions about it.

PROTESTOR: *The patient can correct your suppositions. I know when an interpretation is right because it clicks.*

We'll come to that "click" in a moment. But first let's make clear what Berry's paper did. It made us realize that even a simple dream has polysemic possibilities, which show in the seven different interpretations.

PROTESTOR: *Even if all seven are right, surely some are closer to the truth, better analogies, or more right than others.*

"Right, closer to the truth, better"—this begs a question. Let me show you what I mean: Let's say that the dream of the woman is the beginning of an Icelandic fairy tale. The woman dreamer sets off upon seven different paths, one after another, coming to seven different modes of the dream coming true. The "right interpretation" would then be the one that leads the woman furthest in accordance with whatever goals she wants to "come true" in her life. If her goal, say, is spiritual development by means of introversion, then the right interpretation is the one that says that by facing inner turmoil in seclusion she receives aid from her inner femininity and is let to a higher level by her inner guiding spirit (*animus*) (Interpretation #5). If we imagine the patient's goal to be feeling relationship, then the right interpretation is the one that says that when the patient is cut off and isolated, she is in turmoil, passive to what happens,

30 Berry, "An Approach to the Dream," 56.

and easily led into upper stories by an unknown (unconscious) *animus* (Interpretation #2).

If, however, she is working on her transference relationship with her analyst, then the dream can be saying that she is lying in a half-conscious sexual position on a bed, filled with the turmoil of half-repressed desires. Then fantasy solutions enter: a) a phallic mother figure with a key that the dreamer takes in her hand, and b) a faceless man who lead her step by step to an ascending climax. Either way, depending on the gender of the analyst, the dream refers to projections on the analyst as savior (Interpretation #3).

PROTESTOR: *I couldn't agree more! It's what I've always believed: we can only interpret a dream in relation to the context of the patient's life. We have to know the patient and what the problem is before we can say a word about the dream. Interpretation #5 makes sense only for a patient for whom #2 would be definitely wrong, and vice versa.*

But I don't agree. Your conclusion to this demonstration is not at all what I had intended. You are saying that the dream fits into the patient's picture of the problem and her wishes for resolving it. Thus a right interpretation serves the ego personality and its central wishes. A dream comes true when it clicks with these wishes. This language of "coming true" belongs to the wishful world of fairy tale.

"Right interpretation" belongs in that world too. Let's try instead to see *what the dream says*—without suppositions about the patient's problem, wishes for resolving it, or interpretations that click so that the dream comes true.

The dream has its dreamer "lying on a bed." What happens, happens to her as "lying-on-a-bed-I"—a situation that may stand for supine passivity, receptivity, quietude, horizontality, Yin, etc., but that I feel is best left in its own words. A key handed to this bedded "I," and only to this specific I position, by a middle-aged woman. The key, the lying on a bed and the middle-aged woman are an interconnected image. No lying down, no key; no middle-aged woman, no key. To be a lying-down woman on a bed is how to receive a middle-aged woman with a key.

The key is handed (in contrast to given, passed, offered), so that handing is the way she gets a key, and may be a key. However, the key is not what takes her upstairs. She does not go up by being keyed up but by being helped and led. Between the woman who enters and the man who enters is the key that is in her hands.

The woman enters while the dream ego is embedded in lying down. Is this the only way middle age can enter her space? When the middle-aged woman enters, there is a feeling of turmoil. Turmoil is not in her but around her; not around in the room but around her in feeling. This is precisely where the middle-aged woman enters with the key, interconnecting her feeling of being alone and in turmoil with the personification of middle age. Might we say that the key she is handed is precisely being bedded down inside a feeling of turmoil, for that is where the dream-image places her so that she can receive the middle-aged key woman?

When she is alone, she is with her feeling. She is with her feeling even if apparently alone. There is a disjunction between her aloneness and her turmoil, signaled by the word "but." Does she expect something else when alone on a bed rather than turmoil?

Although being led upstairs by a man can be interpreted in many ways from orgasmic climax to paranoid isolation, these are projective suppositions of the interpreter. Partly they may be evoked in the interpreter by the "unknown room" to which the man leads. As interpreter I must watch out lest I fill her unknown room with furnishings from my own head.

The dream itself says only that lying on a bed leads upstairs, that the room above is unknown (her unknown space is above her lying down space, and to get there, she takes steps), that upstairs helps her out of bed, that "out of bed" equals help, and that the dream proceeds from past to present, moving from "was lying" to "helps me out" and "leads me." We note a hiatus marked by the word "later," so that the distinction between the parts of the image is announced by a temporal adverb, an action in the language of time; the image itself suggests a story with steps.

We also note the curious realization within the dream that when apparently alone, she is evidently not alone, that "alone" constellates kinds of reality, for then she is entered by both a woman and a man, even though apparently she is alone.

From this recapitulation of the dream, much in the manner of our previous demonstrations, we see that Berry's alternative Interpretations #5, #2, and #3 each apply equally well or unwell. Instead of envisioning the seven alternatives as differing paths, one of which is right or true, let us take them as seven aspects of the same image. They are each right inasmuch as they analogize with it; but they are each wrong insofar as they leave the dream speech.

If all seven are "images of the image," then there is no right path (perspective), no need for a click to tell us the way, no right key to the dream. The dream is enclosed in its combination of images and we must twirl all the tumblers. Moreover, each bit is inherently related and necessary to all the other bits. *A wrong path into the dream occurs when we take one path only.*

PROTESTOR: *So this is how a polytheistic psychology works in practice?*

Yes. Wrongness now means singleness. The constructs of right and wrong imply an either/or world, not the polysemous, polyvalent one of dreams and images. When we realize the inherent multiplicity of meaning in the image itself, we cannot force the dream into any single truth.

When I restate the dream close to its own speech, I have not taken any of the seven paths toward any of the seven goals of her conscious life. Nor have I tried to fit the dream into her or my notions of her context and problem. Yet all of the seven have been implied by the image, even though none of them has been supposed by the interpreter. I have stuck with the image...

PROTESTOR: *...but not interpreted the dream!*

That is an open question. I believe I have interpreted the dream, inasmuch, the dream is its own best interpretation. By this I mean that translation relocates the dream directly into her life by suppositions about her life. Instead of translating it as supposing it into one or another meaning, I have amplified it by letting it speak in multiple restatements. Restatement serves it best because the image is usually not full enough to our untrained ears that miss undertones and overtones. We don't usually hear the metaphors until the dream is restated. For instance, the "upper stories" to which the dreamer is led suggest higher physical levels, a superior place, and also a narrative (story) that is more metaphysical or intellectual.

Restatement also synchronously relates the dream to many parts of that larger image that is her life. So, I am neither taking the dream out of her life, nor opposing it to her life, nor translating it wholly into her life. Rather, my interpretation works in deepening that life by means of its metaphorical analogies with the dream. This may make possible an imagination of life that restores to it its dream.

PROTESTOR: *So then there is no right interpretation, and the dream comes true in multiple ways. I understand that this happens because your method does not translate from the speech of the dream (middle-aged, later, upstairs, apparently) into the language of psychology (passivity, isolated, inner femininity,* animus*). But still, how do you know when to stop? I asked you that before. Analogizing can go on and on; more and more complexity. Don't we still need a click that indicates when the dream has come home?*

Not at all! The click is a sign of singleness of meaning and, indeed, stops the analogizing process, ending it with a literalism: "Aha, this is what the dream truly means." But we have to ask: means to whom, to what? And the answer will be to the ego or another strong complex that wants a meaning that it can use for a key. I am suspicious of interpretations that click because they imply an already made mechanism into which the dream fits. A good interpretation does not click but ferments, stains, illumines, or wounds. The only clicks that refer to dream interpretation are those when-then connections that show us where the dream holds itself together and how it inheres in our psychic life. It's the click of the dream with itself, its interlocking necessity, that is important, not the click of it into the patient's mental set.

Besides, if the value of an interpretation is determined wholly by its effect on the patient, then a cheap conversion works as well as a subtle insight, a magical suggestion is no different from a careful feeling, a demagogic cliché equal to a home truth. Or as Berry herself has put it:

> [The click] opens the way to an aspect of psychotherapy little different from charlatanism, syntonic transference neurosis, hysterical suggestion, doctrinal compliance, religious conversion and political brainwashing. For these, too, "click" and in these, too, the subject feels himself changed for the better on the basis of insights revealed.[31]

To wrap up this chapter in a few plain statements. A dream interpretation clicks into a single meaning; if there is no singleness of meaning, there is no click. Analogizing does not come to a stop, for it is a process of deepening the image, and the depth of an image, like that of a psyche, is endless. A well-interpreted dream therefore *goes on being dreamt* in restatement even more fully and vividly than in its original nighttime appearance. Interpretation is an imaginative revisioning that enhances and amplifies the dream. The way in which a dream comes true is the

31 Ibid., 57.

way truths come from the dream—by means of analogizing. If the analogizing process goes on long and deeply, the truths that come are many, are radical, and are always relative to the dream's images.

PROTESTOR: *I am not convinced, but I did enjoy watching you parry a strategic question with a tactical operation.*

You are not supposed to become convinced. The game of inquiry would be over if the Protestor ceased his protesting.

9

IMAGE-WORDS: CONCEPTS VS. IMAGES

PROTESTOR: *Let's go back to the arrow and the cave (Chapter 1). As you examined the image of the arrow ringing through its verbal changes, it became clearer that they all could be included under the concept of aggression. So, what is the advantage of speaking of arrowly and arrowing rather than of aggressivity? Why invent words like caving and cavernity instead of saying capacity for depth (or for receptivity, silence, or inner space)? Why replace the standard traits of character psychology with these oddly twisted verbal images?*

First, images evoke, and so they carry more unconsciousness with them. They speak to the unconscious, whereas concepts address the conscious—to use those classical terms. Second, imagistic speech is more therapeutic because it allows for wider analogies, suggests more implications. One begins to feel arrows and arrowing happening in many ways through one's life.

PROTESTOR: *Aggression has many dimensions too. You may be verbally or sexually aggressive, use aggression in defense, be aggressive especially toward women, etc. A concept like aggression has an additional value. We can collect under its head various instances of it, like aggressive dreams. These would extend way beyond arrow dreams. Your image approach doesn't allow even for comparing two different arrow dreams.*

It certainly doesn't. I am not doing science, in the old sense of it. A collection of arrow dreams takes us back to approaching dreams conceptually, back to symbols, back to nouns. You see, I am not attempting an empirical study of "arrow dreams" but inquiring pragmatically into what your arrow is doing in your dream. What arrows do elsewhere in a sample of arrow dreams may become relevant when the information can be used for a therapeutic analogy. Scientific facts become psychological information when they have therapeutic bearing. And this they can have only where the facts, too, have become images. Your question continues to treat the arrow image as a concept.

The difference between images and concepts has been laid out often enough and by better hands. But still, let's listen to the difference between aggression and arrow: He is aggressive versus he comes on like an arrow. She is so full of aggression versus she has quiver full of arrows. We hear a further advantage of the image in that it speaks just as the world speaks, concretely, and as dreams speak, sensately. We can't see or touch aggression; we can certainly see and touch arrows. Images bring body and concepts remove body. Aggression presents itself only by means of an image, as clenched fists or teeth, with a sneer, a needle, or a wallop in the balls—or arrowly.

Where arrow particularizes and yet spreads its significance through resonance, aggression generalizes without serving communication. For what you, Protestor, conceive with "aggression," and the fantasies that the word evokes in your mind may be quite other than my notions of it. That is why people who talk in concepts must define their terms in order to talk sensibly. Because aggression is second-level, an abstraction from an image, in therapy we have to locate it precisely in an image, even return aggression to its actual usage, the phenomenon as it appears. So why use the concept aggression at all in therapy? Why not just stick to the image from which the concept was derived?

But the most important difference between images and concepts is their mode of signifying. Now I will not be comparing arrow and aggression but be making a contrast between two ways of using arrow. As a *concept,* arrow signifies or refers to a thing, a noun—some arrow in your mind, in your bow, or in a sentence. As an image, it signifies itself, and its signification emerges less from its ability to refer to an arrow outside the word than from how the word works in its context. The more work we can get the word to do by inventing (*inventio* in classical rhetoric) implications, the more significant the arrow becomes.

I am saying that what we do with the images of dreams, dances, and paintings is all invention. Interpretation belongs to the ancient art of rhetoric, *peitho,* persuasion. We persuade a dream into a meaning by the skillful use of imagination. The images before us release imaginative responses that discover (*inventio*) more and more about the image, increasing its inventory. *Inventio* was the Latin term for the Greek *heuresis,* the "heuristic principle," as Jung (*CW*7: 139, 216) called his way of working, which simply means discovering as you go along ways that persuade the patient by giving the feeling of meaningful explanations of what is happening. This is an art, specifically the art of persuasion, just as dream images, themselves artful formations, follow principles of *poesis,* as Freud said: condensation, symbolization, displacement, depiction, etc.

It is crucial to remember this rhetorical background to work with dreams, else we lapse into belief. We become convinced by what we say—which is precisely what rhetoric is supposed to do. It intends to persuade, and so we get caught in our own art. The language that most persuades our Northern-Western minds is that of concepts: transitional objects, ego, negative mother, repressed desire, recovery, journey, defense mechanism, and of course, aggression.

When we replace image-words with concepts, arrow with aggression, then they take their significance from what they refer to. If these referents are high-powered words like the symbols we examined in Chapter 3 (baby, pearl, river), then these substantives become the focus of our attention. Our attention moves from the dream to the referents, amplifying the meaning of baby, pearl, and river abstracted from the dream. But when dream words are regarded as images, then a big word is no more powerful than little words like "just then," "comes by," "I guess," etc. (Berry's "full democracy of the image").[32] We saw this in the example of the sister-Chevy-phone dream where we treated the words wholly imagistically (Chapter 4). There the dream words took their signification from the image, its tension and implications. We did not regard beer or curb as substantial things or as nominatives that name substantial things and refer to them. Instead, we explored the inhesion of these words in the image, the chords of response their placing and sounding evoked as analogies with psychological behavior. When we look at dreams as images, then we have to look at the dream's words doubly carefully because there is nowhere else to look to find their significance.

This distinction between words as concepts and as images is also the basis for the difference between the scientific and the poetic understanding of dreams. In scientific discourse, words gain their significance from what they refer to. Science works in concepts, and even its images are used conceptually. And the scientific view reads the words in dreams as descriptions of objective correlatives: the dream text is a secondary elaboration upon a primary process in nature that is invisible or unknowable and only represented by the dream.

---

32 Berry, "An Approach to the Dream," 61.

In contrast, a poetic understanding does not consider the dream as a report or message giving information about something other than, or prior to, the dream. Rather, the dream is like a poem or a painting that is not about anything, not even about the poet or the painter. The painted lemons on the plate must not refer to the lemons on a plate the painter used as model; the painted lemons can be experienced altogether without reference to those lemons, or lemons anywhere. (Nor do they refer to an invisible archetypal essence of lemons—lemonhood, lemonness; they refer neither to physical lemons nor to metaphysical ones.) They may analogize with and evoke all sorts of lemony experiences, but the image transcends such referent evocation—that is, we might buy the painting not because it so well represents lemons on a plate but because it speaks so well to and of our soul.

So, too, with the lemon in a dream. The poetic view does not need to posit an objective psyche to which the lemon refers and from which it is a message. The psyche is there in the lemon, located nowhere else than in the actual presented image. Psyche is image, as Jung said. We stick to the image because the psyche itself sticks there.

Hitherto, like other analysts, I tended to take dream words conceptually, as referring to psychic contents. A cat in a dream indicated catness, animality, instinct, *anima,* pussy, Bastet, self-reliance, etc. In order to feel the image of the "cat," I had to go outside the dream, either to symbolism or personal association or to other dreams. But by playing with the dream word in its context, running it through analogies, puns, and changes as we did in earlier chapters, the particular cat emerges in its own image and in the echo of the image, the other dreams, the personal association, and the symbolic cat all reverberate.

For a long time I felt dissatisfied with this conceptual approach to an image and would remind myself that I didn't really know to what the cat referred since it is a symbol. I remembered Jung said that "cat" was not a sign referring to a known thing (Bastet, witch, self-centeredness) but "the best possible formulation of a relatively unknown thing" (*CW*6: 815).

Now, however, I can see that this "symbolic view," so essential to my "being a Jungian," *still treats the dream word as a concept.* Whether the referent is known or unknown, it remains a thing. The symbolic view indeed does require nouns, concepts, substances. Even if we declare them to be unknown, then we have not dissolved the conceptualizing move that makes for literalism and for all the theological, scientific, and metaphysical snarls of analytical psychology's view of dreams.

PROTESTOR: *The move that dissolves nouns and says that dream words do not mainly refer to anything outside their context is self-destructive. Do you know what you are doing? You are now de-literalizing one of archetypal psychology's own favorite and basic moves, personifying. Your dissolving acid has got out of hand!*

I am doing away not with personifying but with the literal notion of these persons as agents in the psyche: complexes, gods, archetypes—and other figures of speech that are taken literally because they are presented as nouns. Even when these figures are experienced in visions or as voices, and thus as nominative agents, we must remember that we hear them *only in an image,* as an image, and that they are inseparable from their imagistic appearance. Therefore, they must be approached in accordance with the image in which they inhere, otherwise we tend to abstract them from their context, mood, and specificity, turning them into enduring hypostases that give literal messages.

PROTESTOR: *So there are no gods? What about them as premises of your polytheistic psychology?*

Take the gods, too, as adjectives and adverbs, as modes of qualifying and styling our perspectives. This is rather like the ancient Greek and the Japanese way of speaking about gods, not as things to which the word "god" refers but as a sort of adverbial suffix that can be attached to other words, divinizing and sacralizing them. The theological problem in psychology arises when we take our words as concepts that refer to something outside or beyond, to something else signified by the word.

When we use words as tokens that point to real, objective contents that the words signify and gain their meaning from, then dream words are not worth attention for themselves. They are mere stand-ins for the real actors. Whereas we have been demonstrating that the way the dream is presented is the way it is acting, and that it does not gain its meaning from what is not in the dream.

You know, we empty out each dream and the miracle of its presentation when we refer a dream outside itself. Analytical interpretations of dreams into empirical life—our past history, present problems or future prospects—arise from treating the dream words as concepts that signify something not in the dream. This analytical signification does not even have to be symbolistic, e.g., swan signifies *anima,* or Apollo, or death. Just the fact that the dream swan must be referred to some sort of swan somewhere kills the bird as an image.

Images don't stand for anything. They gain their sense from where, when, and which way they stand. We can get meaning out of the sister/Chevy/phone dream (Chapter 4), a significance that analogizes many ways through my experiences, without those nouns having to refer to my sister, my Chevy, and my phone.

PROTESTOR: *You mean they don't refer to the outer things but to inner objects... your inner* anima, *your drive, and your communicating apparatus as internal images?*

No, not that either. An internal object is still a noun, still a thing, even if now placed "inside." Internal objects don't differ in their logic from external ones: both entail that images be regarded as derivatives of referents. But an image is not an image of an object. It images itself. It imagines; and, in its imagining, objects, wherever they are—lemons on a plate, sister in a Chevy—become imaginational, parts of the image, as if painted, as if dreamt.

Internal objects are further analogies of the image. These analogies come into awareness only because of the image. Actually, the idea of my internal sister or car comes after the event of the dream, so that the internal object is an idea derived from this or that particular image, not the other way around. The concept of an internal object is a theoretical construct used to account for the image, though actually it is a result of the image. Unfortunately, we have all come to believe in these constructs as real things to which the images refer.

PROTESTOR: *But you yourself still use "thing words"—all those hyped-up Neoplatonic terms: gods, archetypes,* daimones. *What's the value of doing that?*

You can hear the value. Instead of speaking of sexual attraction, or the eros principle, archetypal psychology may conjure with Aphrodite or the Venusian perspective. As we already said, this way of speaking in archetypes is a mode of valuing, a way of giving volume, depth, necessity, universality to an experience. These imaginal figures give dignity, culture, mystery, beauty, mythical fantasy, but they cannot be taken for literal realities. Their actuality is wholly imaginal and any explanation of human behavior that rests on them rests on fantasy. They are by definition metaphors, and their main value is that they keep us in an imagistic perspective, which conceptual language cannot do.

You see, psychology really does believe in the literal reality of ego, aggression, and sexual desire. They are held to account for our behavior, and psychology says they can even be measured. But no one can take Mars and Venus in this literal way (except perhaps an astrologer). And that's just the beauty of Mars and Venus; they are gods, but they do not operate as gods. A god, after all, is defined not only by what theology says. Operationally, any word becomes a god when it posits itself as a dominating substantive or when we operate with the word as a literalized dominant with the power to cause behavior. Religion isn't going to take over psychology because of Mars and Venus. Religion is already in psychology, in its pantheon of words that do not let us see through them. Aggression is only one of hundreds of these demons; ego is probably their king and feeling his consort. And these verbal gods are protected by a psychological priesthood that makes its daily obeisance by rituals that no one has ever seen and are held to account for human behavior.

PROTESTOR: *Now you are saying that there are no psychic contents whatsoever. Words, just words—and words that do not refer to anything. If Venus isn't a divine person, the arrow not related to arrows I can put in my bowstring, and my sister not even an internal psychic object, then what is the psyche composed of? If the arrow and my sister aren't factors in me that make me do things, factors that persist over time like a complex, how can I work on my arrow problem or my sister problem? How can I relate to it, talk to it in active imagination, watch its process by means of dreams? How can it be transformed?*

Now your fear of the image is finally coming out—but your fear is justified. By deliteralizing symbols and the thingness of psychic contents, we are also deliteralizing their transformation. Our acid is eating into an old tenet of therapeutic faith: transformation of the personality. You have pointed out that psychodynamics depends on symbolized concepts, psychic agents that do things to other things, an entire literalized system of nouns: types, functions, instincts, censors, archetypes, superegos, energies—and symbols. This is metaphysics, cosmology, theology—not psyche. The symbolic, conceptual view goes hand in hand with the development fantasy, i.e., the notion that we have inside ourselves fixed things that are subject to transformation. We can then watch the process of transformation by observing the development of these fixed things. The Chevy moves through alchemical stages from black to white to red, indicating a transformation of the symbol of my driving vehicle. So if there is no Chevy as an inner psychic thing...

PROTESTOR: ... *then there is no alchemy, and no transformation!*

You make me feel like Hume, but unless we see transformation or development *in actu,* we ought not use the word. We interpret dreams by means of the idea of transformation, but only rarely do we see a dream itself saying, "The bug transformed into a little girl," or "I then became the criminal whom the police were chasing." I prefer to speak of transformation only when I can point at its actually happening.

The story of black-to-white-to-red is imposed upon a series of dreams from outside the dreams. It is a scientific hypothesis or a theological tenet of faith, based on symbols. This is the symbolic view of dreams, and I have been pointing out its danger even though I use it as a tool myself.

We can still work with the idea of transformation in another way. When we shift the dream words around, letting them play other parts of speech, transformation takes place right in our ears. A dream is itself transformational because it transforms its own statements through polyvalence of its images. A dream is always deepening and differentiating itself. We do not need to go beyond the dream for a developmental or energetic theory of psychic transformation.

But to release this transformative effect, we must lift the dream words from the Procrustean bed of syntax and grammar, and allow words a Protean freedom to shape themselves imagistically. We must break free of the notion that a dream is using its words in the referring, indicating, signifying sense. Here we return to Freud's view that a dream is a self-satisfying narcissistic event. Because dream words are not concepts that refer, no dream can be interpretatively translated to other referents. A dream can only be interpretatively re-imagined as one does with a piece of any other *poiesis.*

This leads to a further thought about soul-making. If an image does not have to refer beyond itself to gain significance, neither does our therapy that works with and from images. Soul-making needs no external referent. The activity of therapy receives its meaning and value from the activity itself. We go to therapy for the sake of therapy, not for development, adjustment, healing, or individuation—processes to which therapy has been generally referred for its significance just as the image has been referred to external objects. If psyche is image, then psychological work or soul-making is image work, image-making, *poiesis,* and the goal of therapy cannot be distinguished from the way it is performed.

10

IMAGES AS PERCEPTS: AN ANALOGY WITH PAINTING

My friend Howard McConeghey who paints, teaches both studio painting and art therapy, and also has written about all three activities,[33] told me that when a student asks him, "Show me how to draw an eye," McConeghey says, he can't. He can't because there is no "one eye" to draw. Sure, you can learn to make an eye in the manner of graphic arts or academic painting–horizontal arcs, almond shapes, black dots, glints. And you can learn to draw eyes in a semiotic manner, that is learn how to transmit a certain recognition by means of a conventional gestalt, say, an open eye as an airport sign pointing the way to the observation deck. But drawing those sorts of eyes is not what the student asks to learn and not what McConeghey wants to teach because he is interested in images.

For McConeghey, as I understand him, there are at least four different kinds of eyes: ideational, perceptual, memorial, and crafted. The first is the one I carry in mind; the second I see in the mirror; the third I recall from a dream, a face, or a Picasso portrait; and the fourth is that one the hand actually draws.

These other eyes impinge on the one I try to draw. It's as if you, Protestor, were over my shoulder, saying, "That's not an eye; there aren't any lashes, and its drawn like a rectangle instead of an oval." The idea of eye, like an eye from memory, affects my hand's movement just as much as does the eye of a model I may be looking at in a life drawing class.

You know how long it takes a student in a life drawing class trying to draw a nude model, to see the actual body rather than his or her ideas of it? Any time you have tried to rid yourself of an idea, or change one, you surely have felt how *hard* it was, how obstinately an idea can return as if endowed with its own power. The French use terms like *idée fixe* and *idées*

---

33 See H. McConeghey, *Art and Soul* (Thompson, Conn.: Spring Publications, 2017).

forces, recognizing just how tough they are to play with. As I've said, ideas we don't know we have, have us.

PROTESTOR: *Then we go to a life drawing class to empty our minds of ideas and memories so that we can really perceive an eye as it is and reproduce it on paper?*

Of course not! A life drawing class is like analysis: we go to both for the sake of imagination. A life drawing class is a place where the movement between idealism and empiricism continually shifts back and forth. The hand tries to copy what's there accurately and thereby feels the inhibiting and informing power of ideas, while the ideas are continually being corrected by the facts of what's actually there. The whole exercise aims to separate ideas and percepts, so that finally the hand is given back its native crafting ability to imagine, no longer enslaved to either ideas or percepts.

Images that the hand makes include and transcend both percepts and ideas, just as imagination is a way out of the idealism-empiricism alternatives. Let's take a Japanese master of painting. For years, he looks at (perceives) natural bugs and branches, and traditional paintings of bugs and branches, and he meditates in his mind on bugs and branches. From all of this is formed a complete and differentiated idea of bugs and branches. When he paints, he retreats away from all these bugs, all these branches, and tradition, too, so as to paint a bug on a branch that condenses and leaves behind perceptions, memories, and ideational distillations. He paints an essential or archetypal bug and branch—an image.

PROTESTOR: *Back again to that word! I know what a perception of a bug on a branch is, and I know what one looks like in my memory. I also have an idea of a bug and a branch that I could try to draw. So what else is there that you refer to as image?*

Let's follow McConeghey again. He turns this question on its head. Image is not what's left over but was there *from the start* and is always there, making the percept, the memory, and the idea possible in the first place. Actually, McConeghey would say that imagination presents us with a bug on a branch just as nature does. We paint what is imagined, even the untrained hand when it concentrates intently. We paint a particular image, only this one and not some other, an image disguised in as well as informed by and infiltrated with percepts, memories, ideas. To the degree that we credit these modes with more reality than the psychic image (which curiously seems to lose itself in these disguises), we will forget that our actual start with our actual hand was a movement of imagination.

It is because the image hides in these other modes that we value so highly that Japanese master of bugs and branches, and Van Gogh for his paintings of chairs, shoes, and apple blossoms. They seem so real—but what is real is not the accurate reproduction of perception, memory, or idea but the invisible image laid bare. They let us see beauty bare, the essential image at the heart of things, what Michelangelo called "l'immagine del cuor." If we follow McConeghey right out to the edge, I think we could hear him saying that even our usual sense perceptions are images. He wouldn't for a moment accept the naive-realist view that my hand copies the eye I "see" in the face of my model, because that view doesn't recognize that an image, unconscious to me, is actually guiding my hand. The way my hand shapes the model's eye, and even the way my own eye perceives her face out there, is an imaginative process. No perception without image, no sight without vision. McConeghey follows Jung who says, "image is psyche," and for the psyche to "see" anything at all, to shape anything at all with its hands, it must begin in an image. There are no naive perceptions, mechanical and simple: photographers, too, have taught us that. Whatever we perceive, conceive, recall, even photograph goes by means of psychic images. These images that ceaselessly, ever-freshly stream through our psychic blood are the very vitality of the soul. Imagining is vitalizing and image-making, soul-making. How does Yeats say it?

> Those images that yet
> Fresh images beget,
> That dolphin-torn, that gong-tormented sea.[34]

Wallace Stevens says,

> . . . the study of his images
> Is the study of man . . .
> It is, we are.[35]

Images are simultaneous with psychic life; they *are* psychic life. So theories of perception that try to reduce imagination back to some sort of plain, naive, optical impact are setting up optical illusions. There ain't no such thing as a thing seen as itself. If the baseball umpire can say, "There

---

34 "Byzantium," in *The Collected Works of W.B. Yeats,* Vol. 1: *The Poems,* ed. R.J. Finneran (New York: Scribner, 1989), 253.

35 "Study of Images, I" in *The Collected Poems of Wallace Stevens* (New York: Vintage Books, 1990), 463.

ain't no play til I call it," McConeghey might say, "there ain't no eye til I draw it."

Furthermore, the manners in which I see and draw an eye are determined—not so much by previous eyes I have witnessed or ideas about eyes held in the mind—but by imaginal structures that archetypal psychology calls mythical fantasies and gods. How my hand moves is governed by psychic patterns within my individual "style" and "touch." These patterns produce eyes that show striking similarities even between different geographies, times, and cultures—Egyptian eyes, Coptic, Mexican, Cretan, Dravidian. We do not have to substantiate this claim by accumulating comparative evidence, nor do we have to argue about free will, historical context and archetypal determinism. We do, however, need only bear in mind that gods have hands and have a hand in what we do.

In fact, McConeghey would say still further that *we* do not see an eye at all in any literal photographic replicating sense (unless that be the mode of imagining, e.g., trompe l'oeil, surreal precision, pop-art verisimilitude). A god, so to speak, sees an eye through us, composing percepts into images—or, even better—imagines the eye that we believe we see and that we paint.

PROTESTOR: *If I get you right, you are saying that McConeghey cannot tell a student how to draw an eye because there is no eye until he draws it. And, to believe there is an eye before he draws it, is to be deluded. He can only tell his student to get going, letting the image teach him how it wishes to be drawn. I hope you will allow McConeghey to instruct his student how to improve his hand, make his images more effective and accomplished?*

I'd like to say, "of course," but McConeghey won't admit even this. The hand may acquire skills (shortcuts) from teachers, but the image (the form or *eidos* to use Platonic language) is the real and true teacher, and if faithfully followed, instructs the hand to make real eyes, true eyes.

Plotinus says that what artists do is no different from what nature does. Both shape their material according to an innate image:

> In the case of workers in such arts there must be something locked within themselves, an efficacy not going out from them and yet guiding their hands in all their creation... this indwelling efficacy... must exist in Nature, no less than in the craftsman.[36]

36 Plotinus, *Ennead*, III.8.2 (trans. Stephen MacKenna).

So the technique that our imaginary McConeghey is encouraging is actually "only natural." He is relying on our innate capacity to shape—what Plotinus calls "contemplation."

A principle is beginning to emerge from our distinctions between image and percept, imagination and perception. They are each styles of regard. No longer has the difference between an image and a visual percept anything to do with what we are looking at actual things like bugs on branches; or where we are looking—back in memory or out in nature; or into fantasies and dreams. Our eyes may be staring or shut. *Percepts may be experienced imaginatively, and images may be experienced perceptually*—that is the principle.

No matter what the image, we may experience it as if it were a perception insisting that it came from actual sense events. This is the way in which a positive scientist imagines, and also the way of the hallucinator, the realist and surrealist, and the Thomist psychologist (nothing in imagination that is not first in sense). They see images and construct a world that presents images in this style.

Contrariwise, no matter what the percept, we can experience it imagistically. This is the way of the traditional landscape painter whose perceptual cows and hills are all context, mood, and scene—an inscape; or of the traditional still-life painter whose dead fish with lemons have become a living stillness, a mute presence echoing and analogizing far beyond the perceptual representation. This might also be the way of the pop-art painter who can make a two-dimensional soup can or freight car so vividly imagined that we can never again perceive such objects as simple perceptual events. They have been moved to the imagination, their image essence revealed.

PROTESTOR: *The argument between perception and imagination has been around a long time. What else could be going on here? Isn't there something archetypal "behind" their opposition? Isn't it possibly just a difference between introversion (imagination) and extraversion (perception), or intuition versus sensation? Or, using your terms,* metaphor versus literalism.

These terms don't really solve anything. They just reduce the problem into another pair of opposites and leave them there as unresolved givens. So we have to go on inquiring. First, to recapitulate, percepts are based on images; perception, on imagination. Then we said that as percepts are a kind of psychic image, so perceptions are one of the modalities of imagination. We have been claiming imagination to be the psyche's basic activity, what it cannot help itself from doing; even if numbed, deaf, dumb, and blind, fantasies flow forth. Some of these fantasies are conceived as *memories* (fantasies with a sense of past time attached, as Augustine said), as *ideation* (imagining with sensuous content abstracted), and as *perception* (fantasies that are immediately present in sense). It is this last we shall have to fix on.

By reducing perception to imagination as I am now doing, I am saying that a percept is *a certain sort of image*—the sort of image that does not carry with it the fantasy feel of imagination. Somehow, a percept gets cut loose, sheds its sense of image, feels to be utterly concrete, objectively there, impinging directly on my tongue or skin or eyeball. This style of imagining feels itself attached to a sensed object that it believes itself to be faithfully perceiving. Its faith is in its attachment to a fantasy of objective thingness and to the correlation between the physical senses and this thingness. (That's why it finds hallucinations so disturbing and must call them crazy. Hallucinations attest to the utter reality of images freed altogether from the necessity of arising from objects.) This style of imagining believes in seeing, naively, directly, literally. It believes itself to be an instant camera copy of the things it sees; and to be virtuous and sane, it would be the truest, most faithful copy.

The perceptual imagination believes quite humbly that it is merely the result of input, of data, of what is given through the doors of the senses, which may make occasional mechanical mistakes (owing to tricks of light and memory) but cannot lie because the senses obey mechanistic physiological laws. This style is also an imagination of the commonwealth whose images may all be shared in open and public demonstration. The theory was first presented most clearly by John Locke, a founding father of democracy.

What is called "perception" demonstrates its fantasy of itself by pointing at things and at other persons' images that are always nearly identical. What you see and what I see (unless an emotional event like a car crash) are quite alike—so therefore the Lockeins would say we "can't be imagining." Since all us rational citizens see the fish on the plate with lemons "just as it is," we are not imagining; we are perceiving. Imagining and perceiving become implacable antagonists—even Bachelard says this.

Moreover, since perceiving is declared to be rational, unemotional, and objective, imagining must be irrational, moody, and private. Perceiving becomes accurate and truthful registration; imagining, sheer fantasy. As the notion of percepts as copies neglects the images that make experience possible in the first place, so the theory of perception regards imagination only as a weak sister (the crazy woman in the attic, as the French called her) in hand-me-down clothes, subjective, irreal. She exists, so says the belief, only by the negative virtue of gumming things up or twisting the accurate reproduction of objects into dreams—even if this waywardness is sometimes lauded as "creative."

Yes, this is literalism at its roots. It springs from a faith codified into a theory of perception—an epistemology. That is confirmed by each perceptual experience. Each time we "see" something, we feel certain in our belief in a world of literalities literally out there, exactly as they appear to our objectivity registering minds. The faith says: this I know is so—not because I believe it is so—but because I see it is so. The faith of literalism always argues as if it were speaking from experience (empiricism) and not from belief.

Look what this faith does to the soul! It declares the soul capable only of receiving impressions, like a wax tablet, without innate images or innate activity. Activity has to come from the will. When theory does not permit imagination its native formative activity (Coleridge's esemplastic power of imagining), then the will, like an oversized Herculean muscle, must do the job. The personification within our dominant Western theory of perception is none other than the passive aggressive heroic ego.

The worst part of all this, today, is less what literalism of perception does to the imagination of the arts and therapy than what it does to the ecological world. Percepts that are so devoted to objects as stubborn out-there facts, so dependent on them for their objectivity, holds them to be without imagination. (Imagination is only subjective.) The reality reproduced by our perceptions becomes utterly unimaginational, soulless, lifeless. Perceptual literalism doesn't just kill the spirit, as the old saw says; it actually kills the soul of the world.

PROTESTOR: *There must be something about imagination that wants to imagine in this literal way. If imagination is the ground of memory, ideas, and perceptions, as you say, then why does it choose to conceal itself in these disguises? What's it getting by calling itself perception; what's the* telos *of the perceptual mode; how does the perceptual imagination serve the psyche?*

Right. It's time we find something good about perceptions! Once we begin to imagine them beyond their own theory, we see that the perceptual mode confirms that images are not merely mental figments and aesthetic fantasies but real, objective, in the world. That images have an independent being and show themselves as natural things like rocks and trees, like winds, ghosts, visions—this is common to animistic peoples. When they address natural things, animistic peoples respect things as ensouled (animated) subjects. The autonomy of the image apart from themselves doesn't give them a philosophical headache. Their imagination is comfortably perceptual, and they do not need to distinguish between perception and imagination: what they see is what is there, whether it is there or not; and it is always there, whether they see it or not.

For us, it is different. We can recognize the independence of imagination and the autonomy of images only by literalizing, that is, only by objectifying the image as a perceptual object. Our Western theory of knowledge—if you allow me to read John Locke's tradition in my imaginative way—actually affirms the objective reality of imagination. How? By insisting that imagination requires perceptions of the actual world, so that images always refer back to the world as their source. This is a backhand way of keeping images both "real" and inseparable from world. This means that our Western theory of perception serves the psyche because the theory affirms the *anima mundi*: that the world is animated by imagination, ensouled, affording to our animal senses a constant stream of imagistic effluences that we call information or perceptions.

It's so hard for us to allow the objectivity and autonomy of images without literalizing them into objects. I suspect we are so hung up on hanging paintings, and give them more worship (high price equals high value in our economic religion), because they confirm the objectivity of images. Look! See that plate with fish and lemons, that lovely scene of clouds and cows—well, that's really only a painted two-dimensional illusion, merely an image—yet its worth twenty million dollars! And it is worth that in our civilization, for by means of that painting we are convinced in the utter objective autonomous reality of the image. We have to literalize imagination into painted images to accept their facticity. As Descartes invented litter with his theory of matter as mere dead extension, so Locke is responsible for the inflated art market.

PROTESTOR: *But you still haven't accounted for literalism itself? What or who makes us? What god or goddess, mythical demon, or hero makes us forget imagination? Why does it get neglected, forgotten, disguised, as you say? What is the mythical ground of literalism?*

If I could answer that, beyond simply repeating what I've said too often: the Heroic ego who must have his literal cattle to steal and enemies to kill; if I could dig into the roots of the hero myth itself and uncover its psychological and cultural necessity, then this entire inquiry into image would be largely superfluous. A full answer to your question would tell us much about our civilization, its philosophy, its patterns of action, its science, and what it holds to be truth, health, consciousness, and reality. This answer would also tell us something about why, in our culture, images have to hide lest they release the fury of iconoclasm. Let's not forget what rage can be mustered by a single image, whether in a Jew, Muslim, Christian, or in Jesse Helms. Could we fully answer your question, we would learn something profound about one concomitant of neglecting images, that is, our civilization's loss of soul, that collective neurosis to which this inquiry is addressed; and we would then begin to grasp why McConeghey has such endless trouble trying to teach that process of concrete imagining called "painting." Also we would discover why I have the same difficulty in trying to teach dream interpretation so that the dream, like the painting, stands free of its disguises in memories, ideas, and perceptions, enabling it to reveal through the craft of our response to it the essential and irreducible power of its beauty.

11

IMAGES AND PICTURES

PROTESTOR: *Why do we talk about images as if they were pictures? Is this mix-up just one of easy talk? Or are images really mental pictures?*

More likely, there is something inherent about the mix-up. The German word *Bild* means both image and picture, even painting. A *Bildhauer* (sculptor) is an image hewer, and a *Bildmaler* (painter) is an image marker. This confusion of images with pictures also results from sensationist psychology that understands images and imagination to be leftovers of actual things seen, like decayed or weathered photocopies.

PROTESTOR: *You better clear this up, because when you use the word "image," I can't tell whether you mean a fantasy or a picture.*

You have both a fantasy of your mother and a mental picture of your mother. Both enter into an image. Usually, we don't know that we have a fantasy unless we see it as a mental picture. In fact, therapy spends a good deal of time trying to separate fantasies of mother from mental pictures of mother (like memories), and these in turn from the actual mother. But what gives the most trouble in therapy is the muddling of image and picture: patients think that they have to see pictures in their minds in order to have an image. If I ask them for an image of what is going on in a problem (of family, of sexual relations, of anger), they try to see something, and when they don't find anything to see, they say they have no image, no fantasy.

The confusion gives trouble to theory too. People accuse imagistic therapy of being mainly visual, hence optical and intellectually distant, hence gutless.

Are images flat, two-dimensional mental things that I look at? Let's turn to dreams to inquire.

When I look at a dream in the morning, recording it for my dream book, it is like a picture. I try to see it as it was, picture it in my mind. I may even squint my eye as I try to get the details of the image; it is very visual.

But when I am in the dream at night it is like a scene; and when I am pervaded by the dream during the day, it is like a mood. Here the dream is the constant, and whether it becomes a pictured event that I look at depends on my approach to it. An image perceived as a picture can tend to become optical and intellectual and distanced; it is there, we are here. But imagined as a scene, I can get into it; and when imaged as a mood, it gets into me. This shows again the usefulness of referring to an image as context, mood, and scene (Chapter 1). When considered in this light, an image cannot be something only set before my eyeballs, or even before my mind's eye, since it is also something into which I enter and by which I am embraced. Images hold us; we can be in the grip of an image. Indeed, they can be gutsy.

So the complaint that imagistic therapy is gutless is the complaint of a consciousness that pictures its images and regards them optically. It is a consciousness that hasn't got into the image as a body. Maybe the complaint is a fear of these very guts and defends itself against the image-body by insisting images are pictures only, only mental things seen, hallucinations, phantasms.

PROTESTOR: *Still, the same word,* Bild, *is used in German for "image" and "picture"; and in English we use the same verb, "to see," with both.*

But no longer exclusively. The word "image" is nowadays breaking free of optical seeing. People say: "I get the image"; "That's not my image"; "He's ruined his image." Here "image" does not refer to a picture in the sense of a photographic likeness of a person. Rather, "image" is a complex notion of a person imagined by the mind. It is as much choreographic as photographic. We get and are an image with our whole body.

But you are on the right track, Protestor, even if you are getting off one station too soon. The similarity goes further than the two senses of "see," perception and vision. What makes pictures and images alike is their presentational quality. An image presents itself, and pictures do this too; in fact, this is what pictures do best. They fill the field of vision with their presence, drawing us more and more into their space. What makes images like pictures is just this independent presence of the image that seems to stand still, or at least stands me still before it, as does a picture. So it is not that the image is a picture but that the image is like a picture. The analogy has been mistaken for an identity, much as the vision with which one "sees" an image has been mistaken as identical with visual, optical sight.

As the eye watching a picture both concentrates and darts, so the mind confronted with an image starts racing even as it stands still. This double action discloses levels and builds complexities without ever leaving the scene, without ever going beyond the dumb object with which it is presented. Like a picture, an image, too, has borders. It sticks to itself, inheres within itself. It doesn't lead somewhere else, as does a story. Thus the mind's activity can find nowhere to go but more deeply into the image.

Time doesn't enter pictures. When one looks at a painting, it doesn't matter where the artist first put his brush or what he painted last. One can't say that his last stroke resolves the picture and was its lysis. All the parts are happening at once. Their "mutual modification," in I.A. Richards's phrase,[37] is also mutual temporality, synchronous. When a dream is written out as a story, the end comes after the beginning and is its result. But when we take the same dream as an image, then the last sentence can be heard in terms of the first (or any other) and can result in the first (or any other). The connections between the parts of a life, including its end in death, can also be taken as the interrelated images of a larger image, and not only as a story through time. Picasso, who was a painter, understood his life as multiple self-portraits in facing mirrors, images of himself that did not narrate a story through time. He said: "I don't develop. I am."[38]

And we might add: I am only within the limits of the image: our possibilities are limited to the dimensions of each particular frame.

---

37 [I.A. Richards, *Coleridge on Imagination*, ed. J. Constable (London and New York: Routledge 2001), 74: "This mutual modification, did it occur—most readings exercise only Fancy—would be Imagination...In Imagination, as I have taken it, the joint effect...ensues only through and after a reciprocal stressing, one by another of the parts as they develop together, so that, in the ideal case, all the possible characters of any part are elicited and a place found for them, consentaneous with the rest."—Ed.]

38 ["I often hear the word evolution. Repeatedly I am asked to explain how my paintings evolved. To me there is no past or future in art...The several manners I have used in my art must not be considered as an evolution, or as steps toward an unknown ideal of painting. All I have ever made was made for the present." "Picasso Speaks: A Statement by the Artist," *The Arts* (May 1923).—Ed.]

The confusion of image with picture has now been clarified as an analogy between them. And this analogy with pictures may teach us something about how to look at an image. Certainly we learn that there is nowhere else to look but further at or into the image. It holds our attention—and what is attention but a primary definition of consciousness? And our attention is held in the present; an image makes us present to ourselves, convocates consciousness to be all present and at attention. This implies that attending to images makes for a precise presence of consciousness. (No wonder we get so tired in galleries and museums or in doing active imagination.)

Exhaustion overcomes us, not only because there are so many images, gallery after gallery, but because the images, encrusted in frames and statically stuck on the wall, are nonetheless each inexhaustible, coming to no stop. Our thoughts, however, stuck in their sentences do stop with that tiny omnipotent dot. Period. It's all over. Proceed to the next. By thinking about images in sentences, we are caught in the ideology of progress, forward movement, marching the image heroically toward a conclusion. The allegories and dogmatisms that I have accused therapeutic theories of interpreting into images may begin not in the theories themselves but simply in the sentence structure in which the theories are cast. Roland Barthes says, "Any completed utterance runs the risk of being ideological," here reversing a statement from Julia Kristeva that "every ideological activity is presented in the form of compositionally completed utterances."[39] It is as if we cannot think of images except in a manner unjust to them. (Paul Valéry: "One does not think words, one thinks only sentences."[40]) So, of course, we try to remove punctuation, especially that dot, try to chant the image, try to respond with further images, and to imagine images as pictures to escape the sentence and the ideological judge who resides there.

And another thing: the muteness of an image is essential for altering our habitual mind's way of experiencing in language, that is, in stories made up of sentences, strung out in time, based on words and letters. As a picture stops our syntax, so an image stops our clock. People often talk about "eternal images," but now we are removing the metaphysics from

39 R. Barthes, *The Pleasure of the Text,* trans. R. Miller (New York: Hill and Wang, 1975), 50.

40 Quoted by Barthes in ibid.

that idea, returning it to operational experience. The imagistic view eternalizes (Chapter 14) in that it moves us out of a temporal way of regarding things. It's not that images are eternal (in an archetypal realm of the gods) but, rather, that images, like paintings, have all their parts going or, concurrently, simultaneously. There is no before and after, and so the image is always going on, eternally present. To get out of time, one makes images. (Is this why so many painters live so long?)

These similarities in what we do, feel, and think when in the presence of images and pictures make them akin, justifying the German word *Bild* for both. This kinship in response makes me believe it rather a fortunate thing to confuse the two, providing we keep their kinship as analogy, remembering to distinguish between two analogous senses of "seeing." When we look at each dream as a picture of ourselves, it will then be less a message that helps program our lives and more a self-portrait in the frames of whose silent testimony we stand reflecting further and further into our nature.

12

IMAGE AS IDOL: ANALOGIES WITH RELIGION

PROTESTOR: *Aren't you getting a little religious? Instead of simply regarding images by standing back and looking at them like pictures, you are now saying that we are inside their moods, that they embrace us, that they provide silent testimony to our natures. You are giving them a lot of power beyond the definition of context, scene, and mood, beyond the components of fantasy and mental picture. I detect the odor of sanctity rather than the disinfectant of inquiry.*

Could this power reside in image itself and not be merely my inflation of it or projection on to it? Let us suppose that an inquiry, by drawing us ever further into the nature of our subject, is revealing something essential about the nature of images: that they are fascinating, that they take us out of ourselves and into a kind of devotion. Our speech must become "religious" to do them justice—and, we can begin to see why religions the world over focus on images or are counterphobic about images. The centuries of wars over images in the Catholic church and the Puritan destruction of images, to say nothing of Jewish and Muslim iconoclasm, attest to this religious power that you accuse me of letting slip into this inquiry. It has to come in because there is a power in our subject. Our inquiry would remain inadequate if it were to it refuse to recognize this fact.

Therefore, the maxim "stick to the image" is less a moral commandment than the result of the image's effect. An image sticks to itself and sticks us to it, in it. This is its power. I call this "sticking to itself," *inhesion*: all parts necessary, intrarelated, simultaneous, reversible. The necessary quality makes us feel caught by it, yoked to it, fateful. Jung: "The effect of these unconscious images has something fateful about it... Perhaps images are what men mean by fate."

So we are bound by, bound to, the limitations—depressing and pathologizing and fateful—of this inhesion of the image. Like a picture, an image arrests, yet, owing to its reverberations, it releases itself from fixation. An image acts as a *temenos* (Greek for sacred precinct). Sticking to it is an act that conforms with the power of the image, an act that is therapeutic, scientific, and religious at once. Staying there, enduring the image, is therapeutic because we have to attend to and care for the immediate psychic given, the actual state of the soul; scientific because observations derive from the datum of the image; religious because this devotion places the entire psychic business within the *temenos* of the image. Images are the foci of that psychological, scientific, and religious ritual called psychotherapy. We give over to the image's inhesion. Yet this religious analogy can be stated without such power words as "sacrifice" and "numinosum tremendum." We have not invoked powers beyond the image, outside the *temenos.*

This notion of *temenos* returns that sense of special space to the image. Instead of images of the *temenos* (city squares, courtyards, mandalas), we recognize the temenosity within any image. An image offers protection, refuge, sanctuary for the soul because it holds the soul where it actually is, where we are psychologically. It affords a "where." Where therapy takes place, then, is less on a couch or a chair, in a group or a room, or even in a relationship but in an image, by its images. And, the exploration of these images is an entry into sacred space; our activities with images, a ritual.

PROTESTOR: *I still recoil when religion gets into psychology. I think your claims for images turns them into idols. You attribute powers of healing to them and demand they be attended to devotedly. Isn't this the beginnings of idolatry?*

For me, idolatry is simply freezing an image into a representation of something. For example, when I read a Russian novel, I construct houses, scenery, faces, even clothing in my mind's eye. One day the novel becomes a film made by a brilliant director who depicts the book in such a marvelously concrete form, with all the period props, that the shadings and overtones of my imaginings disappear. Better one's idiosyncratic fantasies of the horrible Mr. Hyde than see him acted in the movies into a fixed form. That fixity is the idol, not the psychic image.

PROTESTOR: *But earlier you said that filling in details helps image-making. The rather vague image of bag, baby, and pearl (Chapter 3) took on weight and power when the flowers became narcissi; the baby, a sitting boy; and the river, blue. After all, the basic reason patients want to depict their psychic life in crayons and paints is to make their images more developed and expressed. Now you're saying this depiction makes images into idols.*

Something is gained in depiction—and something is lost: analogy. Let's use a simple example. When "cat-and-mouse" as proverbial phrase or as a scene played out on my kitchen floor become depicted in a Tom-and-Jerry cartoon, a snapshot, or any particular visible configuration, then the metaphor "cat-and-mouse" no longer as widely analogizes with office life, married life, selling cars, or the games people play in arguments. Instead of the metaphor, I have a static figured object—a cartoon, or photo I can put on my refrigerator door. And I will need a new act of imagination to hear that figure speak. Its power to suggest requires new fantasies.

This happens every day. The objects we buy, like posters and little sculptures, tend to lose their ability to speak the longer they hang about the walls and sit around on shelves. Some months ago I bought a postcard of a frog because it so vividly depicted an emotion and a dream. Then the frog slowly grayed and died from neglect. What maintains the psychological freshness of an image is its suggestiveness and not that it clicks directly with an experience. Not that it corresponds exactly with a particular event in my life. When the postcard I bought represents something (the reason I bought it), then it has become an idol. As the ink (or paint or emulsion) dries, the image solidifies into a literal meaning. It has been transformed into an allegorical symbol: frog equals my hopes for change, a green redemption into a better state. The image is lost in its graven meaning. Frog as idol. Analogy as allegory.

I find it curious how objects lose their voices as images and tend to speak as fetishes: "I carved this little stone during the worst depression, and I turn to it again and again for strength." Or they speak as allegories: "That Gothic crucifix tells the whole story of what I am going through." Or as mementos: "We bought this on our honeymoon, and so it hangs over the fireplace." Depiction can turn images into these kinds of symbolic idols. On the one hand, images become more rich and solid; on the other, they solidify at the expense of suggestiveness.

PROTESTOR: *Then asking a patient to paint concrete figures of his inner life is not psychological, not therapeutic?*

Anything can favor or hinder the therapy's progress. Your question is too large to have an answer. The point here has to do with religion, with the fact that all images can become idols, thereby engaging us in a magical work with sandplay toys, with poems in calligraphy, with fetishes and fixed meanings, *if*... A big if: if we do not allow the image to dissolve into the multiple analogies of its context, which we saw (in Chapter 2) extends far beyond personal meanings or any known meanings and emotions.

So I am not ducking the question of religion. Rather, I am exposing that my notion of image is rather Hebraic! It analogizes with the *deus absconditus,* the hidden God, who cannot be represented. This doesn't mean we are not supposed to depict imagination; it means only that we are not supposed to allow imagination to represent something already imagined. An idol points only backward to a meaning; as such, an idol—to stay in Hebraic language—is the enemy of a living image whose nature is always kinetic, that is, self-moving (*primum mobile*), evocative, calling forth, an unclosed gestalt.

PROTESTOR: *Aren't you now dividing images and idols, calling images good and idols bad? A more psychological approach would surely try to find out why the psyche makes these supposedly "bad" moves like making idols of images.*

Why does the psyche idolize? That is a magnificent question. It has been around ever since Moses and the golden calf, ever since the Vedas, since Mohammed. Let's go at it by following from what we've already said earlier rather than making a larger theological excursion on idolatry and its existential relevance for offering security in an uncertain, dread-filled universe.

As we saw, the idol fixes the image into singleness of representation and meaning. Even if we give Shiva eight arms and legs and the raven innumerable meanings, we still have by no means captured the wealth of implication in the raven in a dream or Shiva in any of the texts where he appears; the idol holds onto sameness. Sameness is one of Aristotle's major categories; it's necessary for anything to be what it is and not dissolve into something different. Idols provide concrete stability, singleness, sameness. And the psyche, which is endlessly deep and always flowing, seems to need islands in the stream, banks to the river, and roots for its floating lotuses. We know this from our own fantasies and dreams; they seem able to go on endlessly, like the thoughts in this book. Idols put a stop to images; they fixate. That's their virtue, their necessity.

The alchemists understood this process by means of their motto, *solve et coagula* (dissolve and coagulate). Whatever is endlessly suggestive and unfolding (images) needs to coagulate; whatever is solidified and defined (idols) needs to dissolve. May we conclude that images need idolatry and idols imagination?

13

POIESIS: WORDPLAY

PROTESTOR: *Something fishy is going on. On the one hand, you speak about images and pictures. But on the other hand, what you are doing is not pictorial and instead is highly verbal. Why all this interest in speech when you have just praised the image for its "muteness"?*

Take care here, Protestor. Don't get too literal about muteness as dumb, nonverbal simplistics. The muteness of the image, I said, is necessary realization for altering our habitual way of experiencing in language, our habitual way of telling our dreams. Our usual ways of speech may keep us from hearing what the image is saying. And a main determinant of the volume of an image resides in the multiple implications of its *words.* To get at this volume, this amplification, we have to break through the roles assigned to words by grammar and syntax; we must break the literalism of the parts of speech. For we have been sentenced by our sentences (including the very one I am writing and you are reading). In grammar and syntax are lodged the fundament of our collective unconsciousness and its nonimaginal singleness of mind. We are unconscious in the very instrument of our consciousness: our speech.

To work with images, we need more than symbology, more than psychology in its psychodynamic analytical sense, and more than archetypology. We are forced toward the field of those who are specialists in images—in the field of aesthetics in its broadest sense and also in one of its narrowings, the scrutiny of the verbal imagination, poetics.

This move toward aesthetics seems an inevitable consequence of Jung having based psychic reality upon fantasy images, a term that he said he took from poetic usage (*CW*6: 743). His theory of images announced a poetic basis of mind, and active imagination put it in practice, even while Jung went on using scientific and theological language for his explanations. Part of what archetypal psychology is trying to do is follow Jung consequently along lines he opened but did not pursue himself. One of these lines is poetics: the exploration of image-making in words. Let us inquire into how this is done.

Did you notice that the words of a dream that one takes to be symbols, the words one looks up to amplify, are nouns, e.g., arrow, cave, swan, leg, or adjectives used as nouns, like numbers and colors. One way of breaking out of the symbolic mode and returning to the freshness of the image would be to modify these symbols so that they could no longer be looked up. We can qualify swan, knee, or arrow, moving them back from general terms to the particularized nouns that appeared in the image: cave swan, wobbly knee, five arrows. We can stick even more closely to the image by speaking of breasted arrows, many-angled arrows, for that is how the arrows were actually presented by the dream.

Noun combinations of this sort recall the imaging language we find in Native American names: Sitting Bull, Crazy Horse, Black Elk; and also in nicknames: Slim Jim, Big Red, Mac the Knife. The Greeks, too, spoke of the gods and goddesses in this way. Athene or Poseidon require epithets, like gray-eyed Athene, Gorgon-bearing Athene, earth-shaking Poseidon, sea-maned Poseidon. We have to remember that the way our monotheistic consciousness conceives the gods, as distinct abstractions that can be organized in a dictionary, is not how these figures appear to a polytheistic imagination. The Greeks had no index, not even a mythology book.

We have now made an advance by qualifying the nouns more specifically with adjectives. But still the nouns are the *Hauptwörter* (chief words) who carry the burden, and the adjectives are secondary, only adjected or thrown onto the nouns.

We may go further still, following Berry[41] and the idea of the *reversibility* of the image. If the various parts of an image are reversible, then why not the parts of its speech? Let us imagine a blue arrow in a dream. "The arrow is blue" can also be stated as "The blue is arrow-like," "arrowly," "arrowish," or "arrowing."

Not only does your arrow—and I am addressing the dreamer—take you into the blue, come from out of the blue, bring the blues, seem true blue, and so on. But also, in reverse, your blueness comes from an arrow shape, straight as an arrow, arrowing sharply. You have an arrowy blue-

41 Berry, "An Approach to the Dream," 66–67.

ness, and the nature of blue in you, according to this dream, is pointed, swift, shafting, feathered, straight, airborne, flying, aimed...

And to take another example: "black snake" can state both that your snake is black and also that your black is snakey: creepy, hidden, reptilian, ancestral—and whatever other adjectives we need to give a snake quality to black.

Principle: Not only can images be reversed; the act of reversing is a step in making images.

Warning: Reversals sometimes can be helped by *punning*. Puns spin a word into another sense: swan in a cave, a caved swan, a caved-in swan. There are puns, and puns—some puns are veritable shafts of illumination in which the play on words unpacks depth and builds intensity. *Poiesis*. Similar to puns are elliptical collapses: Your arrow is your oyster—you can open it like a bluepoint. Joyce was the master of this imagistic wordplay. But we are mostly not masters, and instead of following Joyce, we follow his daughter's schizzy *anima*-ish play words that do not make an image but skitter away from it sideways, an elliptical jump over the shadow, what Jung called *Klangassoziationen*, an amusement without body.

These examples—caved-in swan, bluepoint oyster, amusement—don't make an image or help with the ones we have. Possibly, in another context, in another writer's or dreamer's hands, they could be important because they would resonate. But here these puns have worked surrealistically, in keeping with a Dadaistic sense of the image, a startle without soul, the dream world without its underworld sense. They keep us only to the words (not the images) by means of irrelevant associations, such as oysters. These associations then command attention for themselves so that soon we have left the blue arrow in search of pearls, cabbages, and kings. Words have magic. They can inflate, take us on manic flights, invent worlds to inhabit—all defenses against the image. We protect ourselves from the attractive pull of words by "sticking to the image." By means of this maxim we can test the value of any pun.

Let's look again at what we did with that blue arrow. At first it seemed as if a *blue* arrow was less a symbol and more an image than arrow alone. But actually, by keeping to usual grammar where nouns carry adjectives, the adding of blue to the arrow gave the noun even more weight and substance. We did make a move, but not far enough. For though the arrow got more precisely qualified, it also became more fixed, more substantial. Actually, its nominative power increased by virtue of the adjective, blue.

So we reversed the grammar. We freed the noun from its fixity, the arrow from having to be so sharply stuck in its own substantiality. It, too, can be a qualifier, even present itself in multiple modes—adjective, adverb, or verb (to arrow, is arrowing, arrowed). We dissolved the nominative substance (the arrow as naming a thing) into metaphor (the arrow as a shifting action and many-faceted qualification). Since this verbal action and adjectival qualification always also bears its nominative substance (the noun, arrow), metaphor echoes right in the word itself. It sounds as several parts of speech, playing several roles, at any given moment. We no longer hear it make only one kind of sense.

Another principle: Where the symbolic view tends to *substantiate* (make nouns of) even adjectives and verbs, the imagistic view tends to *dissolve* nouns themselves into qualities and actions. *The chief words in an image do not depend on their grammar.* We are working toward what Rudolf Ritsema has called a "syntax of the imaginal,"[42] the parts of speech freed from their narrational obligations that link them into time sequences for storytelling.

The imagistic view of words frees them from having to submit to logical reason and operational definition. No word would be restricted to mean only one thing according to its operational usage. Instead, the full extension of any word, all its meanings, and all its grammatical possibilities could be brought into any context in which the word appears. Freed from the chains of grammatical usage, words would no longer implicate us in causal readings of dreams. (This caused that, subjects acting upon objects, helped by adverbs and adjectives, prepositions and conjunctions.) We would be able to read a dream as we read a metaphysical or lyric poem, as an imagistic statement. The words in the dream, like those in a poem, would not be responsible to any semantic principles above and beyond the image, principles that would dictate what words mean and how they must fit together independent of their appearance.

Instead of grammar and syntax determining what is meant in the dream, the dream's words would gain their sense from their inherent intelligibility (the angel in the word) and from the help of their friends, the community or context of the image in which the words inhere. And the first move in this dissolution of grammar is letting go of nouns.

---

42 R. Ritsema, "On the Syntax of the Imaginal," *Spring: An Annual of Archetypal Psychology and Jungian Thought* (1976): 191–94.

If we can effectively let go of our reliance on nouns we will have taken an important step away from the symbolic perspective. It needs nouns, and turns other parts of speech into them. For example, the adjective *red* must become the nominative, redness, in order for it to be amplified as a universal concept. Red moves from a staining, emotional qualifier to a quality that can stand alone as a symbolic abstraction. Therefore, one can discuss the symbolic meaning of redness apart from any image in which it appears. This conceptual move of adjectives into nouns is also done to verbs. The verb "to hunt," to the symbolic perspective, becomes the general motif of hunting, a concept that we can look up in a dictionary of folklore, primitive art, or in an anthropological cross-index. The symbolic view requires concepts, and so it starts with nouns. They are the *Hauptwörter.*

But to the imagistic perspective, nouns themselves lose their exclusively substantive and substantiating function. This function, in fact, is viewed as only one of the many modes in which a word can function, so that each and any word becomes multiple and may be heard as a metaphor. If in Chapter 3 we broke up our usual dream reading habits by removing punctuation, here we are breaking up another usual habit that identifies words with their grammatical roles. Nouns are not restricted to playing the parts of subjects and objects of actions, bearers of qualifiers, namers of things. An arrow may arrow, be arrowly, arrowize. This desubstantiation aids deliteralizing.

PROTESTOR: *I can't see why you have to destroy normal speech in order to deliteralize it. Surely you can make a metaphor just by the way you* hear *a word. That verb, "to hunt," when used by a scholar in a library who is tracking down an obscure reference, or by an analyst who is on the spoor of a hidden anxiety or a camouflaged meaning, is already metaphorical. No need to talk in terms of their being hunty or huntly searching to build an image or hear a metaphor.*

Quite right. It isn't necessary to twist words—if one can hear them resonate. You heard the metaphor to begin with or you could not have transposed into your image of the scholar and the analyst such words from the hunt as tracking, spoor, and camouflage.

Usually, we don't hear and can't build an image. This is especially true with verbs. Some can be looked up as symbols: hunt, dance, steal, pray, plow, bake. These are motifs of folklore and religion. But what about to turn, to swim, to hurry, to look, and hundreds more that commonly appear in dreams? We tend to take them at face value without listening for a metaphorical, deliteralizing echo. Instead of resonating, they fade away as our attention notices "bigger" words. We need aids that amplify these ordinary verbs.

Dance and theater are not necessarily privileged. They, too, can fall into the same literal pits of allegory, symbolism, conceptualism, and meaning that we have decried all along. Only when we think of dance and theater as founded on or presenting images so that the image performs the performance rather than the dancer or the actor, and the performance escapes the sentences of the author's text and director's designs, releasing multiple resonances, then, I would say, dance and theater become exercises in the poetics of verbs, providing an analogy like painting.

The very first step—notice right here my use of the word "step," a verbal noun, a metaphor of action—for imaging a verb is to keep it attached to an adverb: *hurry desperately, turn away, quietly leave.* Already an image is forming. Next, if we reverse the verb/adverb roles, we have: to despair hurriedly, to quiet leavingly. We gain insight into the behavior of the dream ego who hurries his desperation, whose mode of quieting is to leave or whose away-moves are in the form of turns. Also, we can gain therapeutic insights from the verb image of a specific mechanism—"turning," for instance. We would be on the watch in the analytical conversation for the patient's turns of phrase, of topic, of interest, for these would reflect his absenting or manner of avoidance, his being away.

Verbs combined with adverbs and verbs reversed into adverbs can't be looked up as symbols. One can study the symbolic meaning of smiling (the smile of the gods) or combing (the fairy-tale comb) as universal motifs, but one cannot look up *smiling sheepishly* or *combing languidly.* Just as the living image begins to show, amplification fails utterly. No research into the meanings of smile and sheep can catch the image.

14

GADGETS, OR IMAGISTIC MECHANICS

When/Then. The one universal wrench that opens any image and also serves to fasten its connections has already been exhibited in Chapters 1 and 3. I refer to the when/then move called by Patricia Berry "simultaneity."[43] All the events of an image occur together. Simultaneity contrasts with the sequential reading of narrative in which events follow one after the other.

Look now at this difference between simultaneity ("When I go for daylight, then I twist my knee; and when I twist my knee, then I go for daylight") and sequentiality ("First I twist my knee, and next I go for daylight"). The first reads the image as an intralocked mechanism with reciprocal action between its parts, back and forth, between twisting the knee and going for daylight. The second reading implies that which comes first in time is the cause of that which comes next. What follows results from what precedes, i.e., because I twist my knee, I go for (escape, flee, return) daylight. To read imagistically, in fact to live imaginatively, requires the when/then sense of things. Then we recognize the complexity of constellations, their all-thereness-at-once, and that what comes first in telling about an image is actually inconsequential to what is actually going on now within it.

Paintings show this simultaneity most clearly. In a landscape by John Constable, the cart, ditch, hedgerow, nestled village, trees and bushes, clouds and steeple are all present at once. To know whether the painter put the cart in last as an afterthought to fill a space, or the village to make more variety in the tangle of shrubs, whether he began with browns or blues or with a sky of clouds or the earthy ditch makes no difference at all to the completed painting (even if the sequence of events might serve for a narrative reading of Constable's psycho-biography and the "origins"

43 Berry, "An Approach to the Dream," 60–61.

of his art). When there is a cart, then there is a steeple, and when there are clouds, then there are a ditch, a hedgerow, a steeple, etc. All always present, timeless, and everything there is necessary to everything else.

The sequential reading, however, turns an image into a story. Narratives require a series of events, one after the other. They are linked like a chain. Whereas an image is woven, like a web, a net, or an electronic chip: all is there at once. Simultaneity makes us think more spatially and mechanistically. All the parts clickety-clack and interdependent. Sequentiality makes us think more temporally and dynamically. Things lead or grow and develop from one phase into the next: beginning, middle, end. When we tell images into stories, we are led back to earlier moments in the chain, and these earlier moments are given the power of origins. Probably the entire house of cards of developmental psychology is built upon the reading of images in terms of sequence. Simultaneity does not imply equality; as if all colors, strokes, areas, surfaces are of equal value. A painting, and a dream image too, relegates some bits to the foreground, others to the background; some to detailed polish, others to sketch hints; some to darkness, some to light. Emphasis, focus, variations of intensity are not blotted out by simultaneity, which, as I said, simply means that all is there at once.

Eternalizing. As is the Mercurial wont, a word slipped into an earlier section that was not adequately introduced. I said that one way "archetypal" implies value is by intimating "eternity."

We don't want to get too almighty with that term; no metaphysics of eternity is intended here. I mean something operational, something we can actually do with an image to increase its volume.

Taking the when/then statement, let us change "when" to "whenever." The sentence at once becomes immensely amplified, right out of a single time and into eternity.

Let's use the same example: "I turn toward daylight, and my knee twists." First let's put this into the when/then construction of the image: "When I turn toward daylight, then my knee twists." Or in reverse: "When my knee twists, then I turn toward daylight." Now, let's carry it further by eternalizing: "Whenever I turn toward daylight, then my knee twists" and "Whenever my knee twists, then I turn toward daylight."

This bit of gadgetry, the attachment of an "-ever" suffix, eternalizes a connection that might too easily be passed over. It strengthens the hidden harmony (when/then) by making me feel that a particular connection in a dream is *always* going on in my life, a kind of eternal mechanism. My reaction to twisting my knee, to my weakness and pain and wobbly underpinning, is *ever* to turn to daylight. Whenever I am lame or limp, then I go for daylight. My eternal turn toward daylight twists my knee, has a self-inflicted wound in it, is at the necessary cost of an unhinged connective joint that may no longer be able to bend (genuflect) or give generative support. That little "ever" makes one feel that the connection is necessary, unavoidable. If it could be going on always, I will more likely watch for its analogies as habits, thereby spotting my habitual mechanisms in more places (always as all ways). And if a mechanism feels necessary, I may also become more tolerant of its pathological implications, for they, too, are necessary.

One can go further and eternalize a whole dream. Then we say to the dreamer: "Suppose this were the only dream you *ever* had, ever were to have. Never any other dream than this one." At once the dream is lifted into a cosmological myth; the whole revelation of the psyche and its fate now there in this one dream. Its depth could never be plumbed, and one would give it endless time, intelligence, and love.

Eternalizing is a move of value, not a statement of fact. "Ever" is "only a metaphor" and does not mean that a dream connection is always and everywhere literally going on. But it might be—and this metaphorical possibility tunes one in to listen for it. Besides, eternalizing adds more substance to the when/then connections, giving them the feeling of being fixed, interlocking mechanisms, a permanent synchronicity in the image stating an unchanging pattern in the soul. It is like saying that this is your eternal dream, so have an extra good look at what's going on here.

Contrasting. A dreamer says: "I have no idea in the world why I dreamt of Aunt Ella in a blue blouse. She was one of my mother's three older sisters. I never met any of them. I like blue. I have two blue blouses, but not in the same shade as in the dream."

In working with this sort of image and this sort of response to it, I find it useful to start a fantasy of contrasting. Images that are closed because they are so familiar, or so freakish, often block fantasy so that the fantasy of contrast helps start it up again.

Why does the dream single out Aunt Ella, and not Aunt Eva, Emma, or Etta? Where is Ella different from her sisters? Then we find that she never married, lived the longest, or most resembled mother. Why does the dream bother to dress her precisely in a blue blouse that is unlike the dreamer's own, and yet is not mauve or maroon? Then we find that blue is a uniform color like at camp or school or feels comfortable and goes with her eyes or really belongs to older women. And so on with blouses over against shirts, halters, tops, dresses, etc.

Contrasting differs from associating, which edges off into personal reminiscences even in the face of a highly symbolic image like the moon. When I say, "So why the moon in this dream?" the dreamer may associate something about blue cheese, an article read yesterday on space-shots, or a feeling of irrational mystery. Then we would have to work on these associations as images and would have left the actual dream far behind.

Contrasting differs also from amplifying, which, as we already have discussed, moves away from the image in another direction—toward universal symbolism. In this case, the dreamer might respond to "Why the moon?" with something culled from alchemy, myth, or folklore.

But if we understand the question by means of contrasting, then we ask, "Why the moon and not the sun, not the earth, not a light in the night?" This move, unlike associating and amplifying, keeps us in the speech of images. We hold up *one image against another.* We stay in the genre of the dream, in the imagination. Our move may fetch images from afar, but we do not go astray by switching tracks into either personal associations or symbolic knowledge. Instead, we press the dreamer toward imagining a difference, asking for some specifics inhering in his or her moon image.

Then we get something like this: "It couldn't be the sun because the moon is cool; not the earth because the moon is so far away; not a light in the night because the moon was only a thin crescent." These three easy contrasts have increased the volume of the moon for this dreamer, telling us that his or her dream moon is particularized as a cool, remote, and thin-crescent image. Its particular feeling as an image begins to emerge, and contrasting has helped bring this out.

Singularizing. We can bring out particularity in another way. This way is similar to eternalizing, except that we now introduce the word "only" into the when/then construction.

"*Only* when you leave the cave, then you twist your knee" or "When you leave the cave, then *only* do you twist your knee." At first, this move seems a radical restriction of the dream statement. Indeed, the dreamer may twist his knee on many other occasions in many other dreams. But since each dream is unique, whatever inheres in it is also unique, occurring as such only in this particular image. We can then say quite legitimately that the intraconnection of my image occurs only in the way it is stated in that particular image.

The value of singularizing is that it specifies the occasion of that knee twist. We can say to the dreamer: It happens only when you go toward daylight, turn your back on the cave, hurry. Only leave that cave and, bang, your knee twists. Twisting your leg, losing your standpoint, finding your understanding wobbly—whatever that knee twist analogizes with—happens only at that singular instant of turning from cave to brilliance. We have been able to pinpoint a pathologizing instant; the only has allowed us to see a singular mechanism at work, allowed an insight into his singularity, individuality.

The restrictive value of "only" is especially helpful when a dreamer becomes contaminated by the symbolic effect of his images. Then they spread universally all through his consciousness: "I'm a mess. There's nothing left for me. My swan is shot down and dead—and with it my hopes for something really beautiful coming out of my work."

Here we may singularize the dead swan as occurring *only* in the cave within the specific context, scene, and mood of his downward and backward deeper darkness and his reactions to it. The swan may still beat its great wings in his heart in other contexts. It is shot down and dead only in this single image. "Only" here helps keep us to the image, therapeutically preventing the dream from becoming symbolized into a message for his entire life, work, soul. An image is only an image.

Balancing. Therapy tends to understand balance too narrowly. It tends to rely on the image of the scale from which the word "balance" derives (*bilanx,* two flat pans). The two pans become opposites. Put something in one and balance it by compensation with the other. Then, we look at images in terms of one-sidedness and try to add a balancing factor.

If, for instance, the dream has no women in it, like fairytales sometimes have no mother, princess, or females at all, then we ask for the missing gender. The dream or tale is "unbalanced," patriarchal, etc. If the right side of a painting is carefully done, but the left side darker and rougher, then it is out of "balance." If a geometric abstraction builds on triangles, then where is the fourth that would bring it into balanced completion?

There are other notions of balance beside the two-panned scale: There are balanced wheels, balanced accounts, balancing acts by acrobats, a life may hang in the balance, as the balance may be the remainder that is left over and doesn't fit it. The root idea in all notions of balance, including the flat-pan scale, is disposition of weight. Balance refers to gravity, being in the right relation with gravity. To balance an image therefore doesn't mean to compensate it with an opposite but, rather, it means to find the vertical pull within an image, its downward hang, sinking toward rest.

The balancing point of an image may be the fulcrum around which it all turns, a central focus, a vivid point, a crucial phrase or metaphor. It may also be discovered by asking little questions like "What's left over if the whole thing collapses? What keeps the image turning in your mind? What does your mind go around and come back to? Where does this image give you a sinking feeling? Where does it come to rest or where does your eye rest? What in the image gives you aesthetic pleasure or the feeling of proportion?"

These questions don't lead away from what is there toward compensation with what is not there, i.e., "the painting has no vivid colors and the entire upper part is blank, so it is unbalanced, and therefore you have a problem and need more attention to the bright and the high." We have left the idea of "in balance" and "out of balance" and inferences about right and wrong, sick and sound. Also, we are not reading the internal relations in a painting or dream in terms of compensatory pairs (upper/lower, beginning/end, masculine/feminine, father/mother, etc.), a reading that never fails to show imbalances, since the scales of justice always tip if ever so lightly, thereby making each image when weighed in those flat pans somewhere unjust, incomplete, requiring a therapist to set it straight and justifying his or her endless correctives. Let it hang. It will find its own balance.

Sexualizing and Familiarizing. We may pass quickly by these gadgets since they are such common tools, sometimes the only tools, which therapists use regularly. In fact, we have been applying these gadgets to images for so long that we don't recognize them as practical instruments for making analogies, believing them instead to be literal truths. Ever since Freud, we have applied the gadget of sexuality to every cave, hollow, shoe, purse, entrance, spherical fruit, slippery surface, bowl, waste-basket...giving to these images the simple single value of female; to every crafting manipulation, from shaping a pot, playing the piano, flipping the leaves of a magazine or opening an umbrella...giving these acts the value of foreplay; to every tall, expandable, long, ejaculating, or headed thing whether grease gun or guided missile...the equivalence of penis. And so on with coitus, anus, testicles, masturbation, breasts, pubic hair, birth canals...The gadget of sexuality has charged images with eroticism, flushing them with excitement, adding to their body, intensifying our voyeuristic curiousity, so that we want to dream on and explore images further for their libidinal possibilities. A little like pornography.

The interpretation of every older man as father and woman as mother, of every peer as rivalrous sister or competitive brother, has been successful for keeping images close. Instead of strangers, ghosts, and shadows inhabiting my imagination, everyone is a relative. It's all in the family. So this gadget has made images more tolerable, more related and less alien. Nonetheless, both sexualizing and familiarizing are simply pragmatic tools. The utility of the first is to incite libidinal interest by giving genitalia to the image, and the second, to make the image more familiar.

Tolerating. This gadget is sort of Taoist. It's a doing by not doing. Letting be. If it were as simple as that, we wouldn't need a gadget, but the truth is: images are intolerable.

I am referring to something in any and every image that makes us want to escape it. Is this "something" the inhesion—all the parts intricately interlaced like a spider's web? Is it the mood that embraces us in its clutches? Is it the compelling fascination of the *temenos* that keeps the psyche arrested and constrained? Is it the shock waves of realizations that seismographically reverberate and unsettle my fixed positions? These traits give rise to claustrophobia. So we share the dream, show it to a mate, an analyst, forget the image, associate away, amplify, prophesize, symbolize, intellectualize—anything to escape.

Tolerating an image is like seeing a painting in a museum and neither judging it nor comparing it with another on the same wall, nor reading who painted it and when. We don't need to study it closely. We don't even need to like it—or hate it. I simply allow it to be there and admit that the main feeling it produces is discomfort. Toleration is easy enough if you don't feel uncomfortable. Tolerating an image is a successful gadget only when there is an acute or chronic feeling of discomfort brought by the image.

However–we tolerate an image not so the discomfort goes away but, rather, to become more savvy about the intolerable. What aspect, quality, detail, juxtaposition specifically produces this discomfort: Is it that I keep on dreaming of the same old boyfriend, my mother, the cellar stairs where I get frightened? Is it that I hate sickly yellow, or spiders and roaches? Or has the intolerable to do with the fact that my images are so fast and chaotic and don't make any sense? That they feel like they have nothing to do with me at all? Then, with the more precise specification of the intolerable, the work of entering the image begins.

Thickening. Dreams do vanish into thin air, while scrawls, drawings, and even sand-play scenes for all the emotion they express soon become sheer fantasies in retrospect. What can we do to make images more substantial?

a) We can add ingredients from our bottled knowledge: symbolic amplifications, personal associations, recollections. We can take down books from the shelves to show comparative motifs; bring illustrations from folklore and ritual; refer to movie themes and theater figures. By this we add exotic spice and flavor, thereby thickening with added material what seems at first to be transparently thin.

b) We can intensify the heat by challenging the lukewarm lassitude with which the images are displayed. What analysis has called "resistance" often comes dressed in an attitude of nonchalant negligence, a shrug saying, "This is of no importance"; "I haven't a clue what I was drawing–it's just a doodle"; "same old dream–always this odd dog in my backyard." Nothing works better for turning up the heat than a transference remark for thickening the soup in which patient and therapist both find themselves: "That figure in the doodle looks like me with glasses and extra ears"; "Who do you suppose that dog is who keeps coming back?"

c) In several chapters above we examined reduction. There is also an alchemical reduction: coagulation, distillation, evaporation. We allow the image to blow off steam (emotional moisture that clouds and befogs), so as to get at the stubborn essence of what will not reduce further. By allowing the enthusiasm and optimistic fantasies to bubble up and boil over, an image begins to shrink, cool, congeal, condensing into its essential salt, something in it that endures as a substantial value with a long-lasting power to bite and burn as an inner truth.

d) Thickening also takes place by layering, like building up an oil painting, a patina, or a rich glaze through several firings. Another analogy would be a chord of music. We layer by letting several tones interfuse, several levels of understanding illumine each other. We also layer by moving closer and closer toward the inner intimacy of body habits and body memories. Sexual interpretations of an image move too quickly in this direction. They feel like assaults not only because they expose but mainly because they rip off the slow work of layering, which is a discovering, uncovering, and covering process all at once. The moves therapists make toward childhood are often successful attempts at layering. However, let's not forget that this success depends not on uncovering an "inner child" but upon the therapy's developmental model, which identifies this child with the deepest layers of the unconscious psyche, its deepest tissue fascia.

e) We can thicken by shadowing. By underlining with blues, browns, and grays, we give to salient images more poise and weight. Of course, these sombre colorings are metaphors; we don't actually introduce colors into someone's dream, poem, or sketch. We can, however, introduce these blues, browns, and grays by shadowing the mood in the room and the conversation itself with ummh, hmmm, and deeper breaths and sighs. All too often shadowing has meant pointing to projections and prejudices, as if someone gets better by becoming more guilty. Shadowing here means simply becoming a bit slow-witted, stupid, dense—less bright. It is an act of restraint, slowing and quieting, adding *gravitas* to the given.

f) We can thicken also with pleasure. Alchemical psychology considers sulfur to be that component that gives oil, fat, and joy to the work. On the one hand, sulfur easily catches fire—a surge of desire. On the other hand, sulfur acts like a gummy glue that makes the material hold together as a body. Take pleasure in the image; find some bit of it that is sensual; roll around in it, wallow, and stay there until it becomes fat.

g) Finally, thickening is what we have been doing in this inquiry all along: working poetically, *poiesis,* creating in words, elaborating the poetic basis of mind. In German, a poem is a *Dichtung* (Thick-ing), a poet is a *Dichter* (Thick-er). Why? Because the poet knows the art of condensation, and condensation is one of the psyche's native activities occurring in the dream work every night, according to Freud. Thickening, condensing, *poiesis,* is an activity the imagination achieves *sui generis.* When we thicken, we follow the psyche's own nature. We are doing what imagination itself wants to do: to reach the condition of poetry, each image a poem.

Longing. Ask this question of yourself, of your patient: "Is there anything in that image that you long for, long to have or do or be? Even if the image be as plebeian as the Chevy at the curb and the sister at the kitchen sink, the question of longing lifts the dream to the stars and the heart with it. Yes, I long to make up with my sister after all these years"; "Yes, all my life I wanted a convertible, to drive with the top down, red leather"; "Do you know the kinds of desires you have when you're really poor and haven't got a dime?"; "I long for you to love me even with dumb, lousy images like this one."

If the imagination resides in the heart, or speaks to and from the heart, then each image will awaken the heart's desire. Advertising knows this only too well. Because images have the power to remind us of our longing and because our longing comes in images, spiritual disciplines decry images or attempt to manipulate them into allegories of their doctrine. To control images—whether as the Church has done for centuries, as censors of art and literature attempt, as puritan enemies of TV and pornography insist—is to manage the soul's longings. These longings are more than wishes; they are, as the Romantics said, the revelations of our true natures. Tell me what you long for, and I will tell you who you are, said the Romantics. (They did not ask about your income or what your childhood was like, about your sociological background or psychological profile.) You are your longing, and your longing resides in your images. This Romantic vision encourages us to call forth from each image its impacted inherent desire. More than what the patient needs, or even wants, is what the image itself longs for, its reach toward the impossible, its innate song.

Keeping Images. We often encourage the patient in analysis to hang in, whatever the trouble, wherever it is. This therapeutic prescription derives partly from Freud. He made it a tenet of practice that no essential changes in a person's life—marriage, divorce, job, etc.—be undertaken during the analysis because such moves would likely be displacements of neurotic conflicts. The prescription can also be derived from Jung's notion of the sealed alchemical vessel in which the psychic process of transformation takes place. One's soul stuff mustn't leak out and mustn't contaminate others.

But from the imagistic point of view, there is another reason for keeping, and a reason that may be less morally prescriptive. Images so often start off in an opaque, obscure, private condition. Paintings, poems, and dreams need to be cracked open so as to enjoy their pathology and necessity, feel their essential value, their claim. But another mode of clearing their opacity is by keeping them. Rather than an imagery of walnuts, let's imagine them in terms of wine.

Often I receive a dream in analysis and haven't anything to say to it; there seems nothing I can do with it—or it seems just too hard to crack; I haven't the strength. I leave it behind, skip over it, go to the next. That's the usual move. But, instead, I can keep the image (and tell the patient to keep it) around for a while, like standing a bottle of wine upright on the table in plain sight in the middle of my living space, letting it warm to room temperature. And sure enough, a sedimentation occurs; it begins to clear; it loses opacity; its specific quality lightens through the glass. It's ready to be appreciated, its subtleties disclosing themselves without heavy work.

After thirty minutes of waiting and watching the images of a dream or a series of paintings, the concoction begins to clear. And one has done nothing more than just keep the images present with peripheral vision, an oblique awareness that accords them value without forcing too hard.

There are other ways of keeping images. Alchemy tells us to let matters cool, like keeping a dream in the refrigerator in a steady state, unusable, uncombinable, but letting it look at you every time you open the door, making you wonder what can be done with it, what it goes with. Or one keeps seedlings that show no specific leafage—are they weeds, vegetables, flowers?—until they sprout of their own *vis naturalis.* Also, there is the backburner, a gentle heat, a slow brewing that encourages a fermentation of a dream throughout other dreams and images, like yeast moving through the whole psyche. Or one can keep an image as a baby is toted over the hip, at the breast, on the back—the image as a weight, a nonverbal demand, that requires tiny attentiveness, little shifts of worry through the day, listening and smelling. Heraclitus says that the souls in the underworld perceive by smell: a subtle mode of sniffing the spirit that goes on in cooking, baby care, wine, soil, telling us about time and changes.

Whatever fantasy we use for keeping—and there are many more that would have other purposes than clearing and differentiating, that have rather to do with coagulating or with storing up in reserve—*keeping is for the sake of the image.* It is a way of attending to a living thing, like a wine, a dish of food, a sprout, a baby. Its aesthetic inutility in its primary state, that closedness that makes it feel such a bother, is met with the fantasy of the artisan or craftsman. (Plato's god was a craftsman, by the way, not a "creator.") No moral "should" here in regard to the wine. No prescription but a desire to enjoy the wine when it clears. Attention is paid, credit given, not for the sake of consciousness, the duty of analysis, but because you take delight in watching the behavior of psychic processes, the enjoyment of recognitions and insights as things disclose themselves, which they do if kept like gardeners, cooks, nurses, and oenophiles "keep." Again, a model of doing and making in regard to psyche.

The Hiatus in the Image. Robert Grinnell in a pathbreaking paper noticed that there is a moment in a dream, a "hiatus which at once divides and unites the two portions of the dream" and "acts as the fulcrum and the turning point."[44] He understands the hiatus to be where the mystery of the conjunction occurs. It is the arcane substance of the image itself as well as the arcane activity at work in and on that substance. It is non-representable, but indicated by a gap. In this gap, a great deal is going on, says Grinnell.

There is not only an intended comparison with Jung's notion of the turning point in the dramatic structure of the dream. There is a further analogy with an idea mentioned twice by Freud in *The Interpretation of Dreams* where he refers to the "dream's navel, the spot where it reaches down into the unknown" and from where the image itself seems to emerge "like a mushroom out of its mycelium."[45]

The "navel" suits the hiatus very well. It can be discovered in small, ordinary, and very common words in the very belly of an image. Look particularly to adverbs and conjunctions, some of which we have already drawn attention to: *suddenly, then, until, however, only, nevertheless, later,* and, most commonly, *but.* When these occur in the midst of an image they announce a hiatus in the hidden connections that may be signifying a hidden disconnection, a juxtaposition that makes the spark of consciousness leap across empty space.

---

44 R. Grinnell, "Reflections on the Archetype of Consciousness," *Spring: An Annual of Archetypal Psychology and Jungian Thought* (1970): 24, 29.

45 *SE5*: 525.

Whether the disconnection is "merely" a formulation in the morning by the dreamer's mind that cannot tolerate the juxtapositions of seemingly nonsequential, and thus for him nonsensical, images so that he must turn the tension of the image into a disjunctive break in the written story; or whether the disjunction is "truly intrinsic" to the image, this we cannot know for sure. But these small words reveal a nodal point and, if explored, can mushroom into considerable complexity. They may be of more importance at getting to the root of a problem (Freud's earth image), into the primal lacuna of our consciousness (Grinnell's hiatus image), than are the visible images and connections themselves. For I suspect that in the little hiatus, absconding Mercurius hides.

15

AESTHETICISM

PROTESTOR: *Images can make troubles too—particularly for therapy. If the symbolic approach can make analysts into priests of traditional knowledge, the imagistic approach may make them into poetizers. If you build a psychology upon the "fantasy-image" from poetic usage*[46] *and draw your analogies and models from the arts, then sooner or later aestheticism will raise its pretty head. Dilettantism, sensationalism, and effetism will get into therapy.*

In the arts, aestheticism refers to the position that a work of art must be sharply distinguished from and may not be reduced to pleasure, to personal emotion, to social communication, to political change, or to utility, morality, raising consciousness, natural reality, or to conceptual knowledge. In a nutshell, aestheticism is art for art's sake.

In psychotherapy, aestheticism refers to an attitude in the patient that is superficial, diffident, and sensationalist—highs and lows. Life is experienced provisionally, vicariously. Psychic work never gets in deep and takes hold but is valued by aesthetic constructs, such as beauty or excitement or dispassionate contemplation. The dreamer's relation to his dreams is characterized by "wows," by ennui and petulance, by expectations of sublime individuation symbols, and by a diffidence toward everyday "working through." Missing is a sense of psychological importance. The dreamer seems not involved in the imagery. Images are out there, objects of report, fascination, theoretical speculation, but soulless.

PROTESTOR: *Jung connects aestheticism with sensation and intuition types, who haven't developed their feeling and thinking functions.*

46 Jung, *CW*6: 743: "When I speak of 'image'... I do not mean the psychic reflection of an external object but a concept derived from poetic usage, namely, a figure of fancy or *fantasy-image*."

Aestheticism has also been connected with various psychopathologies: adolescent neurasthenia; hysteria; psychopathic feeling disorder (superficiality, asociality, sensationalist impulsiveness); different modes of narcissism. We could also trace aestheticism to a variety of archetypal constellations, for example, *puer* romanticism; the Adonis-Tammuz postures of the mother's beautiful son; Venus herself; Apollonic-Orphic worship of the Muses and the artistic; a fascination with the maiden-*anima*; or a lunar consciousness, the moony sleepiness of Endymion. These archetypal backgrounds could be said to account for the neurotic foreground of aestheticism in some personalities or in phases and aspects of any of us.

PROTESTOR: *Isn't it so that if one connects with the beauty of an image, one fails to feel the morality of the image, its psychological necessity and claim?*

A long tradition would agree with you. Kierkegaard, Schiller, and Jung set up an opposition between the aesthetic and the moral. We need to look very closely at this supposed opposition because it affects therapy every day. If the aesthetic attitude keeps the image from entering your patient's psychological life, then you will try to drive the dream home with moral suasion. You will interpret the dream into social responsiblities and practical realities. You will try to convert lunar or *puer* aestheticism into heroic morality.

Here we would be making a move in our practices that has already been made in the history of aesthetics. By opposing the aesthetic with the moral and interpreting a dream into social usefulness, therapy recapitulates the movement from Baudelaire, say, to the realism of Zola; or from Pater to the socialism of Shaw.

This move jumps over the psychological. When countering aestheticism with moralism, it's one "ism" against another, and the psychological is left out. When an antitheseis is set up between the aesthetic and the moral (as if beauty had no moral goodness, and moral goodness no beauty), we are pushed into one or the other opposite, forgetting the psychology of the image and that the image always presents both: an aesthetic experience and a moral claim.

To locate the aesthetic problem in an "attitude"—even one backed by Apollo, *puer,* Luna, or a Venusian *anima*—does not really save us or the phenomena of aestheticism from moralistic corrections. In analytical practice, archetypal influences eventually become "ego" problems. The patient needs to become aware of his "problem" and begin to "work" on it (hardly a Venusian approach). The appeal is to the reason and the will, or what we now imagine as that figure called "ego." Let me show you how this happens.

Let's say that the Venus perspective takes events from their aesthetic side. It looks at dreams, fantasies, even relationships in terms of sensuous beauty and appearance. It doesn't dig deep or seek conflict. What then happens in practice? Don't therapists try to promote in the patient a change of "attitude" that goes deeper than mere pleasure and appearance? We may see through behavior to the Venusian quality in this aestheticism, but soon enough we leave her by addressing the patient's "ego." The gods may be brought in, but in the end everything returns to that scapegoat, the ego, who must make changes, learn, grow, become aware, etc. (Sometimes I am led to think that the entire ego fiction was invented to carry responsibility for whatever is "wrong" with psyche.) We always turn to the ego for our psychic faults, whether psychotic, neurotic, or aesthetic. Once morality is placed there, then, of course, we can't dispose of the ego. We have to keep an ego in the system to keep the system moral. This further divides conscious moral ego from unconscious aesthetic image, leading Jung sometimes to declare that images are without moral intention (the old Christian anxiety about pagan delight in images). No wonder that the scare of amorality arises when archetypal psychology places the ego in brackets and returns morality to the image suggesting that images do make a moral claim.[47]

PROTESTOR: *Images make a moral claim? How so? I thought that one of your main points all along was that images are free of good and bad judgements and that the worst thing you can do to an image is approach it with moral categories.*

Please keep clear the distinction between the morality you use to judge an image and the morality inherent in the image itself. What do you think makes you write down your dreams so carefully? What makes you correct a word, saying to yourself, "Nope, it wasn't brown; it was reddish-brown, more like rust." What makes an artist try to get a line right, a color true; or a poet find just the right rhythm or break? There is a morality of crafting that steers the eye, the hand, and the voice, and the feet in dancing, beyond any imposed principles of morality. And this sense of getting

47 See J. Hillman, "Pandaemonium of Images," in *Healing Fiction* (Putnam, Conn.: Spring Publications, 2009), 51–81, for a discussion of the morality of images.

things right, correcting yourself, making it honest, sincere, good, so that the finished product works—all this comes from the image. The morality of the image claims that you obey its governance. Preachers and moral philosophers don't have a corner on the moral market; potters and drummers are responding responsibly to their images in each moment as they try to get it right. The rectitude of a craft.

PROTESTOR: *All right; so let's drop the idea of gods or the fiction of an ego attitude for explaining what is "behind" the problem of aestheticism. Let's drop the idea of an attitude altogether. Could there be something about the image itself that is the ground of aestheticism? Could it be that images have a special beauty? Or as you said before, the special sacred power of religious fascination (Chapters 7 and 12)—what you call* temenos*?*

To say yes would be to literalize the aesthetic in overt beauty (whatever our criteria for beauty might be). This move would also be naive, neglecting the historical sophistication of aestheticism itself from the 1830s (Théophile Gautier) to the 1890s (Oscar Wilde, Audrey Beardsley) and into the shocking and brutal aestheticism of today (Jean Genet, William Burroughs, Francis Bacon, Ken Russell, Brian de Palma), where the beast stands in for beauty. The historical development within aestheticism itself has at least removed from it its former identification with beauty. Beauty is no longer the way we recognize the aesthetic. A film, a short story, or a painting can still be regarded as fully aesthetic even where there is neither beauty nor beast, only a hunk of gloppy plastic or words listing the junky content of a discount shelf or language poems that have no common sense. If anything, these art objects, neither ugly nor beautiful, are most open to the charge of aestheticism.

Let's examine as our working text a trashy image, and with nothing either beautiful or beastly, in order to discover in what might lie the inherent aestheticism of an image, and thus what in the image itself might give rise to the aesthetic attitude. A variation of the curb-beer-sink dream that we used in Chapter 4, just as plain as plain can be:

> I drive my Chevy up against the curb. Stuck. Need to phone my sister to bring a dime so I can phone. I see her like usual with a beer at the kitchen sink, looking out the window.

This is a most uninteresting image—no swans, no symptoms and, as we said earlier, no symbols either. A lousy "as usual" dream with nothing much to offer. No big individuation process here. Endless examples of similar dreams come to therapy, where the patient says (and the analyst agrees): "I don't have interesting dreams"; "The only fantasies I ever get are about usual things—things I do all day, the people I'm usually with." These statements are often said with a diffident lassitude and a nostalgia for the marvelous that is characteristic of an aestheticism that separates sordid life from fantastic image.

Yet this image is just right for representing what Kant considered to be aesthetic. He held that aesthetic contemplation was "disinterested," *indifferent to the reality and utility of the contemplated object.* The aesthetic for Kant was wholly self-sufficient, without reference beyond itself.[48]

Here the diffidence, the disinterestedness, is in the dream itself. It is an indifferent image, nothing much happens, nothing much matters, all is as usual. It feels useless (without utility). And it is indifferent even to its own reality: it does not notice that its own logic is faulty. It says: I need my sister to bring me a dime so that I can telephone her. I need to telephone for help but have no dime to telephone—and yet I do telephone. This is a vicious circle, a boggling paradox, which the dream simply states without a care. Much as it states that though he is calling to his sister at a distance, he nonetheless sees his sister. The dream makes no issue of the odd difference between his seeing and his calling. The dream accepts without a qualm that its reality is irreal. We are in an autonomously imaginary world, purely aesthetic, because it pays no attention to the object world of common sense.

And yet the dream seems perfectly to imitate the everyday world. Like a *trompe l'oeil,* this dream is a mirror held up to life but does not easily let us notice that it is not life, and the dream seems utterly unconcerned in pointing this out. It makes no attempt to startle or to raise a doubt. No "suddenlys," "buts," or "thoughs."

So this dream fulfills another basic criterion of the aesthetic: self-sufficiency. It makes no call on the dreamer, and the dream ego performs satisfactorily within the irreality of the image as if it were in an everyday universe. Here we have an a moral image making no claim, without utility value, imparting no immediate message other than banality. Like a bit of day residue, it seems wholly reporter's prose without poetics. It could be compared with the poetry of the Imagists against whom the charge of aestheticism and trivial amorality was also leveled. Like imagist poems,

48 On Kant's aestheticism, see "Immanuel Kant's Aesthetic and Criticism," in R. Wellek, *Discriminations* (New Haven: Yale University Press, 1970).

this dream is a bare, concrete, and everyday scene with little narration and no high-blown language or emotion. The dreamer is tempted by the dream to skip over it in his therapy, letting it be just a statement of itself for itself like a piece of art for art's sake.

The response that the image evokes in the dreamer is precisely the aesthetic attitude: an indifference to the dream, treating it as if it were an object on its own without social or moral utility. My disinterestedness in it reflects its apparent disinterest; and my self-sufficiency of being able to get along quite well without it reflects its self-enclosed sufficiency. Furthermore, the justifications I use for my disinterest tend to be stated in aesthetic terms or to suppose aesthetic values: the dream is purposeless; it is prosaic, mundane, trivial; it is without expressive or affective importance, presented with no rhetorical persuasiveness; it is noncommunicative, nonallegorical, and certainly not sublime. All the qualities that psychology attributes to the aesthetic attitude and locates in a disengaged amoral ego *are in the dream itself* or result from the dream.

A principle is emerging: that psychological scalawag, aestheticism or the purely aesthetic attitude toward images, derives from an image that is too self sufficient to be heard or seen except as it presents itself. The image appears to be only in its own terms, offering nothing further than its appearance. Does this not indicate that aestheticism is another mode of literalism? A literalism of the image itself. It is sheerly what it is. No resonance or implications. It provokes no supposings (Chapter 2). What Kantian aesthetics and Jungian psychology consider the self-sufficiency of an attitude we now see as the self-sufficiency of the image.

This sort of image both cries out for interpretation and just as adamantly defies it. In practice, these petty dreams give us the most trouble. Now we know why—they are images of aestheticism. They are so closed in on themselves, such marvelous pieces of artfulness. It would be easy enough to detect aestheticism in Gothic horror nightmares or in decadent dreams—those with swans or with flowers by blue rivers. But now our criterion of aestheticism has changed *from beauty to self-sufficiency*, similar to what psychoanalysis calls narcissism: an image that has no echo and so does not "relate." Without echo it makes no metaphor of its mirroring, and so we cannot hear it tell anything. It does not "matter" to any "body."

What we usually do with images of this sort is pass them by, or pass them off in various ways. We might say this dream *arose from* my phone call yesterday to my sister about selling her car or parking her car; or it *belongs* to my actual sister (on the objective level) and her problem of drinking and driving; or it *corrects* a conscious attitude of "bad" driving coupled with *anima*-cheapness; or *reflects* the relation with the analyst as soul sister; or it *warns* about an accident that might be impending.

These moves into usefulness result from the opacity of the dream. The fact that the dream is so self-enclosed makes us want to find social and moral import for it, setting off a series of counter-reactions into direct, practical interpretations, *none of which* are psychological...

PROTESTOR: ... *because these moves are moral. They are instructions to do this or that, and they leave the image. So a clue to recognizing aestheticism may not be the beauty or ugliness of an image but, rather, a moralizing reaction to the image, wanting to do something, explaining it, put it into action, make it useful.*

If you leave the image, you leave the psyche, which is the first thing the psychotherapist is not permitted. This means that the old opposition between the aesthetic and the moral results in malpractice!

Because contemplating (sticking with) the image threatens us with aestheticism, we want instead to put the image into practice somewhere, somehow. We rush it into life before we have heard it out. So it is especially the aesthetic image that is conducive to the five unpsychological moves I sketched above:

a) simplistic reduction (the dream arose from)—let's get at what was going on in that phone call to my sister.

b) projective repression (the dream belongs to)—I will tell my sister about this dream.

c) analytical moralizing (the dream corrects)—I need to pay attention to my beer drinking and my shadow habits of cruising around and spending money.

d) transference intensifying (the dream reflects)—I'm stuck in my analysis because my soul is distant and daydreaming.

e) spiritualizing magic (the dream warns about)—take care right now in situations with my car, my sister, and particularly when parking, phoning, and even in the kitchen.

When we catch ourselves making these sorts of moves, we may realize how little we have psychologically entered the image and that we are using the dream to fit a theory.

These moves also further the provisionalism always associated with the aesthetic attitude. Because the dream seems not to involve the dreamer psychologically (only externally as a moral corrective or magical warning, etc.); he waits for a more important dream bearing on his soul, his inner life, his big self. Disinterestedness increases, and partly as a sensible defense against the simplistic and moralistic reductions.

Therapy of aestheticism, then, is not necessarily a critique of ego attitudes, of developing a moral counterpole, or a therapy of the *puer* or *anima,* of Narcissus or Venus, etc. It begins with the image, cracking open the hard shell of its self-sufficiency, getting it to echo much as we have been demonstrating.

For instance: The dream shows precisely where the dreamer is "stuck": directly between "curb" and "need" (inhibition and desire?). When his drive is curbed he calls for his sister. Calling, voicing (phoning) is his way of seeing. And when he calls for her, he doesn't even have a dime—that silver sliver, the thin moon coin of liberty. And this shows him how and when he is stuck. Maybe, even further, he is stuck because he sees his sister as usual (just as he sees this dream as usual), while she is looking out the window—gazing elsewhere, beyond the kitchen sink and the beer. *He* sees her with beer, even though *her* look is out the window, and perhaps he is stuck in the usual, curbed by the limits of an everyday street notion of reality just because of this kitchen-sink perception of his sister, his soul, from whom he needs the disc of silver, needs to call, to get out of his Chevy drive that is anyway curbed.

PROTESTOR: *Don't you think you came down far too hard on those five "simplistic and moralistic" interpretations? When all are taken together, they serve a purpose beyond demonstrating wrong moves. Each of the five alone is a naive therapeutic reduction, as you say, suiting the interpreter's theory more than the image. But together, they explore the implications in the dream and broaden its range of suppositions and inferences.*

Okay. Just so long as they are not taken literally, which means monotheistically. You need all five, maybe more, annulling the possibility that any single one of them tells what the dream is about. The dream's own narcissistic aestheticism, its perplexing inward-turning on itself, fortunately keeps the suppositions multiple and flowing. So you see, the aestheticism of the image helps prevent singleness of meaning.

This leads to a final point. Our method that is so iconic, so respectful of each image as such apart from its therapeutic value, from interpretative theory, from denotative referents and symbolic meanings could too be condemned as an aestheticism. What keeps our entire endeavor from being but another vain exercise in aestheticism is the conviction that image demonstrates soul and the passionate engagement with image furthers the making of soul. This means that any image is aesthetic in its first appearance as long as it remains closed into its self-sufficient autoerotic independence. Only our love can break into its love for itself. Any image whose inherent implications are not unfurled fosters aestheticism.

16

IMAGE-BODY, OR ACTING-OUT

Now I want to inquire into the body of the image. I want to meet the charge that images are mental and therefore gutless. This charge also implies that, since images are psyche, psyche too is gutless.

PROTESTOR: *Does image work evade body or generate a body problem? Don't therapists encourage imagining in order to take the pressure out of actions that could be rash, foolish projections? Doesn't image work intend to put the brakes on acting out?*

"Acting-out"—what is it really? Freud introduces the term by opposing it to remembering. When a patient starts reproducing his past, and when past events become activated by analysis, the job for the therapist, says Freud, is "to be prepared for a perpetual struggle with his patient to keep in the psychical sphere all the impulses that the patient would like to direct into the motor sphere; and he celebrates it as a triumph for the treatment if he can bring it about that something that the patient wishes to discharge in action is disposed of through then work of remembering."[49]

Since Freud's time, "remembering" has become more sophisticated.[50] Heidegger and others, by playing with the words *er-innern* (re-membering), as well as Freud himself, have led us to consider "remembering" to mean re-connecting (or re-collecting) fantasy images that have the atmosphere of having "really happened" in "past time." But we no longer take that "really happened" or "past time" literally. We are less concerned with reconstructing the "real" past time. We are interested in the fantasy image that has disguised itself in historical dress. *The problem of remembering has become one of fantasy imaging.* The Freudian formulaic opposition between remembering and acting out has now become one between *doing*

49 S. Freud, "Remembering, Repeating, and Working-Through," in *SE* 12.

50 Cf. E. S. Casey, *Remembering: A Phenomenological Study* (Bloomington and Indianapolis: Indiana University Press, 2000).

and *imagining*. Or, in the words of Anna Freud, "acting out of primitive impulses versus their verbalization."[51] Doing things instead of telling things. Imaging is further specified as the use of words, speech, rhetoric—the very theme engaging us in this inquiry.

We need to divert here for a moment to think about the concepts used by the two Freuds when they discuss acting out: "discharge in action," "motor sphere," "primitive impulses." Might these terms indicate particular images for acting out—motors, trains, trucks, engines; the descriptions of sulfur in alchemy; vivid colors like bright purple, fuschia, red-orange; with driving and being driven; with uncivilized places, animals, dances; specific body parts and motions like fists, thighs, heels, jaws, and pelvic thrusts? Are there images that analogize with the concepts, a rhetoric in dreams and paintings that indicates doing or acting out primitive impulses in the motor sphere?

I want to suggest, and then leave it at that, the possibility that convincing concepts may be "visible" as images in imaginative works like dreams and paintings.

To go on, we ought to go back to Greek ideas of remembering. Remembering, in the Platonic view and probably earlier (Orphic), meant a musing reminiscence in relation with Mnemosyne (Mother-Memory) who mothers all kinds of musing as she was the mother of the Muses.[52] Musing here would refer to the various arts and studies, each a way of forming images. According to the tradition we inherit from the Greeks, to remember we must be able to muse, to imagine. Remembering *is* image-making.

Forgetting (Lesmosyne, Lethe) meant just flowing through like a river, just running on or seeping out through a porous vessel, a leaky sieve (as in Plato's *Gorgias* myth). The psyche of those in the underworld just leaks out, and so these souls are always thirsting.

Underworld myths tell us what could be going on under our usual world, beneath our usual consciousness. This forgetting, this leaking and running on impelled by a thirst for life[53] is precisely the not-remembering

---

51 A. Freud, *Research at the Hampstead Child-Therapy Clinic, and Other Papers, 1956-1965*, in *The Writings of Anna Freud*, vol. 5 (New York: International Universities Press, 1967), 14.

52 Cf. G. Paris, *Pagan Grace: Dionysos, Hermes, and Goddess Memory in Daily Life*, trans. G. Moore (Thompson, Conn.: Spring Publications, 2018).

53 K. Kerényi, *The Gods of the Greeks* (New York: Thames & Hudson, 1980), 89.

of Freud, the acting out in life of the images that we have forgotten (let slip through our porous souls).

Plato's leaking vessel as an image for acting out reappears in various other mythological modes as in Pandora's opening the jar (box) and Psyche opening hers. Both "forgot" and were caught in the "motor sphere." The alchemical vessel of Jung allegorizes the same moral warning. The spirit in the bottle must stay stoppered if it is to be transformed (*CW*9.1: 400ff.).

PROTESTOR: *That sounds moralistic. Repression. Count to ten, put a cork in the bottle. Isn't there a psychological question here: Why did Pandora and Psyche "forget," and why have we these leaky vessels so that it is a "perpetual struggle" to keep impulses in the "psychical sphere"? Why do the jars and bottles open up, promises break, and secrets leak out? Why does the stuff want to come out? Tightening the lid with moral remonstrations seems not enough.*

Again to Greece. Heraclitus made this remark: "It is hard to fight against impulse (*thymos*); whatever it wishes, it buys at the cost of soul (*psyche*)."[54] The root *thym* still appears in psychiatry where it means drive, affect, or desire. Originally, *thymos* referred to the emotional "blood soul," the seat of passionate willing, a kind of striving angry desire of blood located in the heart or the chest.[55]

Jung (*CW*8: 414, 420) might call *thymos* the infrared end of the archetypal spectrum where instinctual behavior reigns, that impulsive, compulsive acting out in the "motor sphere." Alchemy uses similar imagery. Mercurius the wily rogue as *multi flores* (many flowers) lives in the swollen blood vessels from where he urges us into the world of sensation, go forth and multiply, redden the world. All argue that to go with the body is unconscious action: leaking (Plato), costs soul (Heraclitus), makes psychization impossible (the Freuds, *père et fille*). The very notion of "acting out" is tied to our Northern-Western "body problem."

To cap this historical excursion let us look at the Grail, the legendary cup that holds Christ's blood. Some of Northern-Western man's greatest exploits in the "motor sphere" were performed in its name. The passion to find and have that cup, a silvered soul symbol par excellence, drove the crusading fantasy to redden the world literally by spilling blood.

54 Heraclitus, fr. 85 (trans. Philip Wheelwright).

55 R. B. Onians, *The Origins of European Thought: About the Body, the Mind, the Soul, the World* (Cambridge: Cambridge University Press, 1951), 44.

Christians, Mohammedans, children, animals–blood spilled for centuries. The blood could not help but be spilled, for the cup was not to be had. Hence, a vicious circle: the more desperate the search for the grail, the more blood was spilled; and the more spilled blood, the more desperate the need for the vessel. The grail that the Christians sought was, of course, an image–an imaginal mode of containing their compulsive acting out. The grail was each Crusader's personal myth. Each Christian was (and maybe still is) looking for a vessel to hold the blood of the myth that is driving him. Jesus, the personal Lord and Savior, lives in the slaughtered lamb, the bleeding heart, the sacred blood wine, and pours out through the wound in the side a compassion for others and through stigmata in the hands and feet actions toward them.

Like its Nordic configuration, Baldur, and like those young Levantine beauties Adonis, Attis, and Tammuz, the Christian god bleeds. Not only does divine *thymos* flow into the world, but *thymos* itself is divine, the very substance of the god. This passion assures redemption, celebrated in communal ritual by drinking in the blood soul of the god. "See, see where Christ's blood streams in the firmament," says Marlowe's Faustus, "one drop would save my soul, half a drop!"[56] The Christian cult of blood sanctifies the streaming leak, the open vessel. Christian myth blesses with the person of its god and the ritual of its faith that problem of acting out set by Heraclitus and the Freuds. (Attempts to close the lid, seal the flow by means of Christian pietism and asceticism only accentuate the problem by repression. Ascetic practices always focus on the motor sphere, the primitive impulses; just say no.)

By ennobling the urgent wishes of *thymos* into the missions of compassion, the Christianized psyche spends its images in acts. The Acts of the Apostles; mission, conversion, spreading the Good News. The *imitatio Christi* means following faithfully the mission of the blood soul. "Do unto others," where do is the operative verb and *others,* the major concern. The images that lie behind and within the "doing" and the fantasies about the "others" drown in the red tide of urgency. Christ's blood streams in the firmament, the Grail still not found, the sieve leaks in Hell, and Northern-Western *thymos* pushes its mission, its motoric projection of bloody enterprises at the cost of its imaginal soul. Yes, acting out, because it is blessed

56 C. Marlowe, *Doctor Faustus,* Scene 14.

by the Christian myth, makes analysis a perpetual struggle according to Freud, just as religion makes analysis impossible according to Lacan. This because they are one and the same, acting out is our Northern-Western religion.

PROTESTOR: *That's your peculiar reading of Christianity, but what has it to do with psychotherapy?*

Psychotherapy devotes itself to reflections and subjectivity, to remembering. So in a Christian culture it must become a heretical enterprise (as it was at the beginning with the Freudian circle). In order to counter the collective drive to act out, psychotherapy is driven to the narcissistic mirror of self-study. Doing to others is projection. Go inward, not outward. By standing fervidly at the blue end of the spectrum, psychotherapy seems to be evading body. Unfortunately, it is caught in the very trap it seeks to evade, for by locating images only in a person's subjective interior, therapy leaves the world out there to Caesar's legions, to *thymos,* as if images were not in the world, as if image had no body, sheer reflection in a silvered looking-glass, optical not material.

PROTESTOR: *But Jung doesn't treat images this way. He says they have a sensation aspect and that they are actually the pictures or representations of instinct. So they must have some relation with body. Even his term "active imagination" shows this.*

Jung's model goes beyond the usual pairings that are standard in psychology: thought versus action, imaging versus doing, cognition versus behavior. Jung's model keeps the two ends, *psyche* and *thymos* (blue and red, or archetypal image and instinctual urge) from becoming contraries (*CW*8: 414). Jung's theory says: no instinct without archetypal image that patterns it; no archetypal image without compelling power of instinct. Fantasies are always being behaved, and behavior is always enacting fantasy.[57] Images have guts because images are the formal aspect (the patterns) of the blood soul or *thymos*—"instinct" we now call it. All behavior, no matter how wild and driven, presents a pattern of imagination. Acting out may therefore no longer be conceived as simply forgetting images at the cost of soul. Rather, acting out must be considered *as a mode of doing imagination.*

57 See J. Hillman, *Pan and the Nightmare* (Putnam, Conn.: Spring Publications, 2007).

PROTESTOR: *Jung's model looks very different, then, from that of the Freuds, and also from Heraclitus.*

Very different! They say: the more blood, the less soul; the more impulse, the less psyche; the more forgetting, the less remembering. Anna Freud is quoted to have said that the patient who acts out exclusively cannot be analyzed. They are also saying: the more psyche, the less blood; the more image, the less action; the more analysis, the less acting out. Here are the grounds of that charge we have been trying to meet in this chapter: image work is gutless.

Still, if we look more carefully at Freud, he does offer a way out of his conundrum. He says that acting out is based on fantasy images. It is a re-enactment of something in the past, an unconscious repetition of a memory image. In other words, acting out is *an attempt at remembering.* When a patient acts out or a Christian crusades, the intention is to give body and blood to a fantasy image. He is bringing his body to the image that is driving his body. *His bodily action in the motor sphere is where his soul is actually remembering.*

PROTESTOR: *You have turned it all around! Now you are saying that acting out is "good" because it brings the unconscious into life. Particularly the blood soul, the instinctual body.*

I am saying that acting out is a style of remembering that reconnects us with what the culture itself has repressed and forgotten. I am saying that so long as we condemn acting out rather than try to see through it, we stay stuck in our Northern-Western repression of *thymos,* the blood soul. And since the repressed returns, as Freud said, we will be forced to act out ever more furiously.

I am saying even more: Acting out is a desperate search to resolve that giant historical problem it defends against. After all, the Freuds call it a "defense mechanism." Defense against what? They say: it defends against the psychic sphere. I think it can take us to the psychic sphere. We are driven by a fantasy in search of a physical person, concrete place, material thing that is the cup, jar, box, body that can keep, be keeper of, my blood soul. Some person, place, or thing to hold the bloody drive of *thymos.* Acting out makes me recognize how intensely passionate is the imagination and that I live inside its appetites. To act out is not to run amok—as if that fantasy of fantasy-less actions were even possible. Even the rabid maniac who shoots down a school class has definite intentions and patterns in his motoric sphere. Each rush is specifically patterned because the red end entails the blue. The archetypal structures the instinctual; they are aspects of each other. No, they *are* each other. In each drive there is a dream. Acting out is modern man in search of a body.

And that is why we had to take that excursion into Christian myth, because acting out both defends against and resolves the Christian separation of body and psyche, perpetuated in Freudian theory as motor-driven body versus verbal psychic image. The problem of acting out is the problem of Christianity.

PROTESTOR: *And images? How do images fit in? Evidently they may no longer be called gutless.*

The image is the crucial factor because it combines physical body and verbal psyche. Imagistic religions make no separations here and do not value the word over the flesh. From the viewpoint of the image, body is always enacting the imagination of soul, and soul is always behaving imagination in body. As long as we stick to the image, body and psyche don't come apart, and images don't have to be set off somewhere in a nonphysical realm. Instead, we may conceive them as we feel them: day and night coursing through our blood soul as phenomena of the *thymos*—sudden fears, sexual delights, strange cravings, glorious feats, hate-filled assaults, grievous memories. These images are pictured emotions; drive and pattern together (no drive without pattern, said Jung). Images are the self-perception of instinct, presenting the motor sphere as fantasies. This means that the more imagination we have, the more instinct too—not the old idea that active imagination quieted emotion by transforming it into words and pictures. No, imagining makes us instinctual, gives body and words both, enables us to contain ever more emotion. The more blue, the more red, and vice versa.

Even when we are most intellectual, turning for instance to dictionaries to amplify an image, even then we are driven and thirsting for understanding. Yes, on the one hand, we are escaping the direct confrontation with the image as such; but on the other hand, the turn to amplify attempts to find more body in the image, gather material to substantiate, and uncover its weight, strength, and power—its full extension and long durability over time. Amplification may be both a defensive intellectualization against the image and an acting out in its behalf. We amplify to revive the image and regain the feeling of imagination as a big living animal, that we live inside this animal, see its shapes as we peer about. Our offering is the tribute that gives it satisfaction: further animals, further images.

Finally and in general, acting out occurs and must occur when we neglect the animal nature of images, when we neglect their blood soul. Tribal peoples, and high literate cultures too, slaughtered animals as gifts to their divine images. They knew that those archetypal fantasies named gods require remembrance at the red end, not at only the blue end. They want dance, drum, fruit, fire, and smoke–and animal blood. For me, the true meaning of forgetting the image is more than a lapse of memory or a simple neglect. Forgetting the image means severing it from the body of its instinct.

17

IMAGE-SENSE

Our usual language for perceiving dreams is curiously imprecise. We *listen* to the dream to see what it is *telling* us or we *look* at what it says. We *see* through it in order to *hear* its message.

The quick movements back and forth between seeing and hearing seem to prevent either from being the privileged sense for image work. We cannot assume that understanding images is simply a matter of seeing by means of images or hearing by means of metaphors. It is as if the psyche mixes these two modalities to remind us of its complexity: that at least two senses are needed for grasping an image.

There is something more here: I think we are also being told that we can't get an image at all by sense perception, taken in the usual Aristotelian or empirical view of it. Images are not the same as optical pictures, even if they are like pictures. Nor are they actual physical sounds. We do not literally see images or hear metaphors; we perform an operation of insight that is a seeing through or hearing into. The sense words *see* and *hear* themselves become metaphors because, at one and the same time, we are using our senses and also not using them as we may believe we are. By appearing together in the single psychological act of studying an image, seeing and hearing relativize each other. We see through our hearing and listen into our seeing.

By confusing our usual sense language, images and dreams are also retraining our senses. They are being freed from the conceptual constraints that decide how they must perform and what their proper objects are. So a dream is indeed a derangement of the senses as was said long ago by both rationalists and romantics.

Perhaps the key to the training of dream workers is this retraining of the senses by the image. Perhaps the reason for collecting our dreams so faithfully, amplifying them with symbols and studying cultural imageries, is not mainly to learn archetypal patterns of content but to train our eye and ear out of their habitual modes of sense perceiving so that we can "read an image" (Rafael López-Pedraza) and "hear psyche speaking" (Robert Sardello).

Unfortunately, so long as we go at our training in terms of knowing about images (symbolizing) rather than sensing images (imagining), we may never let the image derange us enough to retrain us. Much of what we learn to do with images in therapy-training institutes defends against the derangement of the senses.

I suppose that is why these places are called "training" rather than "retraining" institutes. The senses and the mode of consciousness based on them are taken for granted; they are given new kinds of content to work with, but the mode of perceiving the content is left unquestioned. It is as if one could read the dream of William Blake with the mind of John Locke; whereas Blake's intention is precisely to break Locke's notion of consciousness based upon sensation. So it seems to me that a primary purpose of the dream is not to redress the balance of consciousness but to retrain the senses, our simplistic belief in them, by means of the dream. Dreams, after all, are incursions of imagination into the usual world of sense that we pretentiously call "consciousness." In this world, dreams don't make sense because sense doesn't make dreams. Dreams are images, made of imagination.

PROTESTOR: *Are you doubting our notion of consciousness—that it is a* waking *consciousness and implicates us in a sense-perceived world?*

I am doubting this notion of consciousness now only in regard to images and dreams. For this notion is not adequate to imagination—whether the images of dreams, insanities, or the arts. To go at imagination with straight-on sense perception creates insanity. It forces the image into hallucination (experienced as perceptually "real"—material, objective, true) or loses it as illusion (experienced as perceptually "unreal"—immaterial, subjective, false). We sense images and make some sense of them without having to sense them in the simple perceptual meaning of sensation.

There is probably something still more perplexing being said by this mixture of sense. It suggests that *imagination has no sense language of its own.* Maybe it has no language *at all* of its own. Even those words that are most appropriate for discussing imaginative products—tension, inhesion, vision, voice, expression, authenticity, surface, spontaneity, fecundity, structure, maturity, integrity, creativity—are concepts that do not present themselves as images or have images as their first reference. They are equally valid for other sorts of events. The language of poetics (stylistics, rhetoric, aesthetics) and the technical terms of each art are only tenuously connected to the imagination as it presents itself in images. The dream comes in its own terms, images—just like life.

Now you may see better why I have been trying to use the actual words of the image for grasping its significances. I have been very literal about "sticking to the image," even sticking literally to its language, so that the image can tell us about itself in its own words. I have been experimenting—probably too literally, obsessively—in hopes of showing that imagination can speak of itself without borrowed terms, that concepts are neither sufficient nor necessary for making sense of dreams.

It is not to be bemoaned that imagination has no conventional language of its own (except the word play of the image), for imagination seems to turn this weakness into an amazing grace. Its borrowings from the language of sense perception are also transformations of that language. When we speak of "hearing a metaphor" or "seeing an implication," we have twisted hearing and seeing from their common-sense meanings, for we do not hear a metaphor as we hear a bumblebee buzz by. Seeing and hearing are deliteralized, having lost their *sense* sense. One of the major accomplishments of our dreaming is precisely this re-sensing and re-visioning usual scenes and events, forcing us not only to train our sense in a new way but also our language sense of words.

Gaston Bachelard[58] saw this deforming-transforming capacity of imagination better than anyone. But then he came on the heels of a nineteenth-century French tradition that insisted upon shocking the senses, deranging them thoroughly out of their accepted paths in order to awaken the sensibility to images. We, however, come to our dreams via Locke and Freud, the empirical tradition that starts with sensation as the fundamental criterion of reality. Our public-and-palpable ontology insists that what is ultimately real is what the senses perceive. That is why the spontaneous confusion of the senses when speaking of dreams is so very important: it shakes our foundations.

58 See G. Bachelard, *On Poetic Imagination and Reverie,* trans. C. Gaudin (Putnam, Conn.: Spring Publications, 2014).

Both aesthetics and psychology have tried to deal with the confusion of the two senses in terms of "synesthesia" and the relation between poetry and painting (*ut pictura poesis*). Synesthesia is not only a puzzling quirk in certain sensitive persons for whom numbers are colors, colors taste on the tongue, or musical tones present sculptural forms. Synesthesia—confusion, interpenetration of one sense with another—goes on all the time in our common speech when we talk imaginatively or of imagining. Evidently, synesthesia is how imagination imagines. What this does is transform the singleness of any one sense out of its literalness. It brings us to a new sense of the senses, making metaphor of sense perception itself. Consequently, synesthesia plays a special role in the arts because it helps art's own intention—metaphorical insight, awakening of sensibility freeing it from depiction and representation.

My point here is that when imagination does use usual language—and that is about all it has to use—then it must twist this usual language into a second sense. "Running" is merely abstract until we can hear the word visually, as a faucet running, flat-footedly running. A curb is but a curb until we can hear other senses in that granite-hard edge, its further potentials. And any word, every word in a dream can reveal a second sense, especially when we play with it as we have shown in earlier chapters.

PROTESTOR: *If imagination has no language of its own, then how can we claim it to be a faculty? Other faculties have their languages: feeling, thinking, the moral faculty, and the will, each has a string of terms describing its modes and concerns.*

Granted—imagination is not a faculty! The claim that it is a faculty has been precisely what has deceived us most about imagination. We have considered it one function among others; whereas it may be essentially different from thinking, willing, believing, etc. Rather than an independent operation or place, it is more likely an operation that works within the others and a place that is found only through the others—(is it their ground?) So we never seem to catch imagination operating on its own, and we never can circumscribe its place because it works *through, behind, within, upon, below* our faculties. An overtone and undersense: is imagination prepositional?

Let's look for a moment at prepositions. I want to show what I mean by the "preposition of images" as an essential factor in imagination. If, in a dream, "I am walking with my wife," this is an image not only of walking and of wife. The image is prepositioned by *with,* and the components of the image—"wife" and "walking-I"—are ligated by this *with*, so that the persons and the actions are prepositioned, governed by, this "with-scene," a "with-walking" of the I who is in a compound, combine, or complex with the wife. Does this further imply compliance, even complicity? And may we read whatever else occurs in this dream in terms of the relations specified by this preposition? You see, I could also have been walking behind, or across from, past, toward my wife. Or the dream could have said, "My wife and I are walking," no preposition at all; simply the conjuncted walking, a pair in tandem, no inference of unconscious complicity.

I said at the beginning of this inquiry that an image is a specific mood and scene and that what definitively determines the context (mode of weave) are the prepositions. They specify the mode of relations, the structure of events. They are the subtle joints that articulate the internal positioning of the image, how it knits together. "Subtle," by the way, probably derives from *sub-toile*: the underlying canvas, weave, texture, the invisible network.

Symbols are held in the subtle net of an image. They can be discovered in substantial things (nouns like redbirds, hags, pearls) or in actions (verbs like fly, grow, sleep). But it is the prepositions that subtilize symbols by dissolving their substantial university into a specific pattern, an image. This shift of noticing—from *what* is seen and heard to *the way in which* it inheres—is sensing an image. Here I am explicating Edward Casey's useful dictum that an image is not what you see but the way you see.[59] Imagination might here be defined more closely as the subtle sensing of the prepositional relations among events. Of course, these prepositions don't have to be written out as words. They are also there in melodies, in sculptures, in a walk down the street ("up" the street, "through" the street). So we sense the subtlety of images by means of prepositions: their overtones and undersense; looking into and behind; listening for and hearing through. The sense of images is a composite of the gross sensations of nouns and verbs, adjectives and adverbs, and the subtle sensations of their relations; the composition is performed by the prepositions.

59 See above, 91n5.

PROTESTOR: *I believe you are pulling a fast one on me. This subtle sensing of invisibles, these little prepositions that make for whole patterns—this is the intuitive function, the very opposite of sensation. Your second sense and subtle sense is nothing other than what Jung describes as intuition.*

Jung's model cuts the double sense in two (sensation and intuition), opposing them to each other. In that system, sensation perceives consciously and intuition, unconsciously. They are laid out across from each other and supposedly cross each other up.

The problem that this model causes for sensation is much like what that cross does to thinking and feeling. They are forced into diametric opposition. However, common speech, which betrays common experience, employs terms like "thoughtfulness," "consideration," and "attentiveness" equally for thinking and feeling. Psychological functions are not inherently opposed; we make them so with our conceptual models. An image begins to make sense as we intuit its significance. (Jung himself has indicated this, holding that the careful aesthetic elaboration of a psychic event is its meaning (*CW*8: 402). Only when we leave the actual image do the two ways divide into sensation and intuition, aesthetics and meanings (*CW*8: 172-76).

Listen to Jung: "Fantasy is just as much feeling as thinking; as much intuition as sensation. There is no psychic function that, through fantasy, is not inextricably bound up with the other psychic functions" (*CW*6: 78); "All the functions that are active in the psyche converge in fantasy" (*CW*7: 490). When we stay with the imagining mind in its engagement with an image, then all functions take place together and throughout. The four functions are irrelevant to imagining, so that too much concern with the functions is anti-imaginal, even anti-psychological.

I am also trying to deliteralize the sensation function from its narrow definition based upon physiological sensations. I want to give sensation back its intuitive power, its second sensing of archetypal invisibles. I am also trying to return sensing to intuition, giving it back its precise appreciation of significant detail. And my way of doing this is by "sticking to the image" (a very sensation sort of idea). For an image offers a way off the cross of typological oppositions.

It follows that our usual talk about certain images, that they refer to the sensation function or that they are more concrete, sensuous, and gutsy than others, is not to be taken literally. Van Gogh's shoes, Zola's whores, and a dream of emptied bowels and rock drills do not show more sensation than images of wee elves in leas forlorn, or primary numbers and bare ideas, or images presenting highly qualified feelings. To consider some images sensate and others not, deprives some images of their sense and literalizes sense into the narrowed meaning of grossly earthly. Bachelard would hold that each and all these examples are images but bespeaking different realms of imagination: one group presenting the poetics of earth; the other, the poetics of air. It is all *poetics.* And all involves the senses—though a sense beyond sense, a second sense of sense, a sensibility of the sensuous, not the sensuous as such.

PROTESTOR: *Now what in the world is that? Is it in the world at all, or have you left it for something mystical, like second sight, twice-born man or third eyes and ears, subtle bodies?*

It has something to do with those mystical expressions, though they put second sense into a metaphysical mystery, while I am trying merely to show that imagination remains in the world of sense and takes this same world from a different angle. I think we can keep to our double understanding of the simple word "sense," which means both concrete, physical, directly tangible, and also, meaning, significance, direction, invisibly mental. When you "lose your senses" or get "some sense knocked into you," an undersense of the word begins to emerge.

Here, Protestor, I am really on your side. I am trying to deliteralize the high-powered language that generates a metaphysics of imagination—or leave this to the mystics. To speak about "subtle bodies" and "second sight" does not mean to posit such things as things. Metaphorical insight does not require a paraworld of its own, over, under, and beyond. We do not have to take our preposition as literal positions. Imagination takes place wherever we are, as we are. We do not need to substantiate the imaginative perspective by means of visionary witnesses; we do not need to measure auras and perceive astral bodies. The metaphysical mode again separates imagination into a faculty or a realm of reality, hypostatizing it and returning it to literal sense perception, straight-on seeing and hearing, the witness of film and tape. I am trying, however, to keep imagination close at hand, prepositionally, as the way in which things appear, imagining it as a permeating ether that dissolves the very possibilities of separate faculties, functions, and realms. Yet, curiously, whenever one tries to deliteralize the senses, one finds oneself using such words as "ether" and one is soon enmeshed in spiritism and spookiness, as if our habitual minds cannot stick with an *imagination within the senses* but must phosphorize it into an epiphanic marvel.

So let us return to what we do. Let's examine more closely how this second sense works in one of the dreams that we have been using: the image of the swan in the cave from Chapter 1.

The dream begins: "In some kind of a cave, a dark cavern. The whole place slopes backward and downward from where I'm standing." This seems a simple presentation of optical vision. I can see myself standing, and behind me, as on a stage set or in a photograph, the ground and walls sloping backward and down. Then, as I stay there *looking* at the image, I begin *hearing* "backward" and "downward" in a second sense. (Perhaps this resounding of the image is an effect of this image itself, its echoing cavernous resonance.) The scene is no longer a simple descriptive reproduction; now it has a second sense of implications. Metaphorical insight emerges through hearing while seeing.

Insight occurred largely because I slowed my reading of the image from narrational sequence (what happened next? and then, and then?) to poetic imagistic reading. In narrational reading, the sense emerges at the end, whereas in imagistic reading there is sense throughout. Most poetry (not the heroic epic, of course) is printed on the page in a form that forces the eye to slow itself to the cadence of the images.

Now, the second level of "backward and downward" is given with the first, and not added to it as an interpretation. The classical gestalt psychology of Wolfgang Köhler and Kurt Koffka would consider the menacing pull of the dark cavern to be as important as the speleological description. For them, description is always physiognomy. We do not project the second sense into the first, since the quality of depth is immediately presented to the senses by the scene itself, that it slopes back and down, that it is a cave, that it is dark.

Freud might have gone yet further, saying that the primary level of the dream scene is the latent meaning of "sloping backward and downward" (regression towards the mother), which the dream manifests in a speleological metaphor. I think a trained psychological mind works the way in which I am here imagining Freud. Such a person would not have to look at the scene first as a photograph; he would start right off hearing the image with metaphorical insight. He would see the sense in it even while sense-perceiving it—or even before. A second sense would be immediately intuited and felt as present whatever the situation. I wonder whether Freud's idea of latent meaning needs to be taken so literally. Perhaps, "latency" (in childhood, in dream content, in psychosis) merely intends to remind us not to stay in manifest position. It is a sign that says: "keep digging." Have I made myself clearer?

PROTESTOR: *Clearer but not less mystical. You have put the second sense first, as a sudden apprehension or intuition of significance "whatever the situation." You have extended your claim beyond gestalt and Freud, declaring that this world, like Prospero the magician said, is a dream, that everything is imagery, that the very geology of the earth and how we stand on it is the expression of hidden significance, meanings everywhere. You are giving us the old "doctrine of signatures"—the handwriting of gods everywhere, whatever the situation. It sounds paranoic to me, and the best protection against it is sound common sense, leaving some things as sense data, just as they present themselves to the eyes, ears, and nose—our animal sensing.*

I admit to extending my claim to sensing images everywhere, not only in dreams, and I admit to an affinity with the old doctrine of signatures. I can go even further. I can agree with Plotinus who held that the soul perceives *only* this second sense and cannot perceive what you call "sense data." Psychological perception is always of intangibilities, forms—what we would nowadays speak of as pure intuition, or as the apperception of physiognomic gestalten. For Plotinus, the soul is affected by sense data only because the soul is located in a body. When you split sense data from meanings, you not only split sensation from intuition, you split body and soul. Only a soulless body, or a soulless psychology, can speak of sense data apart from the image in which the data is presented. You see, the Greeks, too, had trouble with the word "sense" (*aisthesis*), which meant both sensation and perception. Neoplatonic thought resolved the problem of two senses of sense much as we are doing: by radically distinguishing the two, yet maintaining them together in a single act. So, yes, there is a second sensing going on wherever and whenever your simple "animal" sensing goes on. Both at once.

But let's examine your charge of paranoic. Certainly, this second sense suggests a "hermeneutic of suspicion." One may not impugn to things an only natural, or face, value; this has been condemned as the "naturalistic fallacy." So, inasmuch as every thing manifest is suspect, our second-seeing is paranoic ("suspect" = "below-looking"). It is paranoic, too, in that the activity of sensing implications is basic to image-making: we can hardly point to something as an image unless we mean that some thing *implies.* Indeed, we do build images out of naive events by paranoic means: suspecting, supposing, implying.

But in a far more essential way, the act of second-sensing or metaphorical insight is not paranoic. The act does not dissolve what is there in the image, into what is not there, a meaning. The cave is not transformed but remains a cave, sloping backward and downward. We hear the implications of standing in this cavern, feeling its gravitation into depth and backwardness, sensing the inclination in the ground of our stance. This significance emerges without exchanging the image for a hermeneutic about "the ground of being," "regression," "the mother's womb," "the unconscious," or even into phenomenological "caveness." We are not putting the cave into any symbol system—for that is where the truly paranoic begins. In fact, by keeping the significance right within the "sense data" of the image, the second sense embedded in the first, we avoid the paranoic literalization of meaning as a plan or plot at which the image hints. Our kind of sensing is a precautionary therapy against a more severe kind of paranoia: systematic interpretation. Like takes care of like.

Those literary critics who are "anti-metaphor" are probably worried by this same paranoic question that you have raised. They, too, protest that since poems consist of images, why read them for metaphors. Why paraphrase a poem into meaning: paraphrase = paranoiding, systematic fallacies of one sort or another. Poems don't mean; they are. However, the anti-metaphor campaign has taken metaphor too literally, as if a metaphor really does transfer images into meanings on another plane, whereas I understand metaphor as enhancing the image by hearing and seeing more sense in it. We can amplify an image from within itself simply by attending to it more sensitively, tuning in, focusing.

PROTESTOR: *What about what I said: leaving some things as sheer sense data, just as they present themselves to the eyes, ears, and nose—our animal perception. What about sound common sense?*

This again splits the word "sense" into two meanings: psychic and natural. Whereas I am insisting that the two are contemporaneous and even correlative. We get more sense (significance) from an image the more we note its sense (data), and the more it signifies, the more it affects us sensuously, sensately, sensitively.

You connect the natural sense to animal perception, the nose. Yet even smell makes a metaphor of itself, for we can stink from foul clothes and from moral turpitude; we can both smell a fish and something fishy. The modern way of handling this double sense is to explain that the second is transferred from the first. However, the alchemical way, like my way, holds them together: alchemical *putrefactio* is a rotting substance, both natural and psychic at once.

The sense of smell alone may be a better analogy for image sensing than both seeing and hearing together because smell is both more concrete, and less. Heraclitus, for instance, considered smell to be *the* mode of psychic perception (a proposition treated more fully in *The Dream and the Underworld*). When Heraclitus further implies that the nostrils are the most discriminating of the sense organs, and that the gods distinguish by means of aroma (frs. 7, 67, 98), he is referring to invisible perception or the perception of invisibles. Like perceives like: the invisible, intangible, inaudible psyche perceives invisible, inaudible, intangible essences. Sensate intuition or intuitive sensation.

Even the word "essence" has a double sense: both a highly volatilized substance like a perfume and a primary principle, seed idea, form. Smell involves us in whatever is most sensate and most subtle; primitive and primordial in one and the same sense. I do believe that the divine mode of the gods or the underworld mode of souls is not so far apart from what you call our "animal sensing."

PROTESTOR: *You mean to say that we smell images!*

I mean to say that smelling is the best sense analogy for imagining for these reasons: first, we commonly hold smell to be more gutsy than sight and sound. So the sense of smell gives a sense of body depth to whatever is smelled. By smelling an image, I am implying the image has body.

Second, smell is held to be the most parasitical sense, that is, it has hardly any language of its own—something we have already discovered about imagination. Smells, like images, are "reflections," "effluvia": the odor of a rose, the scent of burnt toast, the stench of a refinery. Odor, scent, and stench have no smell of their own, no content without a particular body. Smells cannot stand alone. They must be linked to an image: rose odor, toast scent, refinery stench. On the analogy with smell, therefore, the sense of an image inherently "sticks to the image" and cannot leave the image without losing its sense.

It follows, third, that a smell refers to a particular image in which the smell adheres. It conjures a unique event and favors discrimination among unique events. If we want to understand an image for itself, we must smell it out. We need a good nose for differences, *diakrisis* of the spirits, the imaginative precision that is the main aim of the imaginal method.

Fourth, smelling images guards us against optical illusions about seeing images. If an image is not *what* you see but the *way* you see, then smell reminds us that we don't have to see an image to sense it. In fact, smell reminds us that we can't see them; it keeps them deliteralized, like the old definition of archetype: nonpresentable form. So by "smelling" images we keep the archetypal as an actual sensation in the image, without having to exaggerate this sensation by calling it numinous or tremendous.

PROTESTOR: *All these sensation details, it's like Wundt's laboratory revisioned. Are you sure you're not a sensation type—or is this the compulsion of your inferior function?*

We are all sensation types as soon as we are seized by an image. Can anyone image without sensing? The moment you leave sensing out of imagining, it is imagining that becomes an interior function: sheer fantasy, mere imaginings, only a dream. Let me go on.

Fifth, smells are there at once, like images. There is no beginning, middle, and end, like in stories. We are less likely to read images narratively.

Sixth, unlike the words of our other senses (touch, see, etc.), smell has a "bad" connotation. Something negative, offensive, is carried along with the sense, so that smell reminds us of our native aversion to images. We shy from them. Iconoclasm is inherent to the image itself. The cult and worship of images requires flowers and incense, as if to sweeten (as Adolf Guggenbühl says[60]) what is inherently obnoxious. As said above, there is an intolerable aspect to *every* image as image. Its habitation in the undersense of things is their underworld and "death." An image as a simulacrum is but a shadow of life and the death of concretistic faith. Imagining implies the death of the natural, organic view of life, and this repels our common sense. Hence the underworld stinks; dung and corpses; brimstone. Images are demonic, of the very devil; keep a distance. Have a keen nose.

Seventh, the cognition of smell is like a recognition. Smells bring the remembrance of Platonic recollection together with an instinctual

60 A. Guggenbühl, *The Old Man and the Corruption of Myth*, trans. D. Wilson (Putman, Conn.: Spring Publications, 2006), 93.

reaction. Lured by musk, swayed by damp honeysuckle, we respond to the Aphroditic evocation and recognize love arising without previous learning. Reflex and reflection together. The smelled image is both immediate and remembered, both animal and memorial.

Eighth, smells cannot be summoned. Though they may evoke remembrance of things past, we cannot willfully recollect them as we can a room or a tune. We are subject to them, assailed by them, translated into their world; with one whiff of mixed lavender, cedar, and camphor, I become a little boy excitedly hiding in a chest—imagination utterly beyond control of will. The egoless spontaneity of smell is similar to that of imagining.

Ninth, this spontaneity beyond control of will, however, is not beyond limit. It does not imply imagination as flight into pure possibility, as if one could imagine anything. No, smell is always of something, so imagining is always held within the bounds of a specific image—this image, right here, under your nose. This is what I mean by "the body of the image": its particular limits, which are its shape and its way of working. If, as Jung says, psychic reality is simply that which works in the psyche, then what does this working, and always in a specifically patterned way, is the body of the image. Images don't work for us when we cannot sense their body. And it is our nose that reminds us that images have bodies, are animals.

PROTESTOR: *If I take you seriously, it would mean that images are actually perceived by an animal nose at an intellectual level, and that they must have, in some sense or another, an animal body. Aren't you merely elaborating what Jung always insisted upon: that images and instincts are inseparable?*

Let's leave it right there: images as instincts, perceived instinctually; the image, a subtle animal; the imagination, a great beast, a subtle body with ourselves inseparably lodged in its belly; imagination, an *animal mundi* and an *anima mundi,* both diaphanous and passionate, unerring in its patterns in all ways necessary, the necessary angel that makes brute necessity angelic; imagination, a moving heaven of theriomorphic gods in bestial constellations, stirring without external stimulation within our animal sense as it images its life in our world.

PROTESTOR: *Preposterous! Must you go so far out?*

Not far out—here and now. Don't you see that I am protesting against all notions of "mere" sense, as if the scenes were inferior, chaining us to a concrete, literal, mundane world, a physical world without spirit, a body without soul. Descartes. I am also trying to restore to us the animal of "sheer" sense who has been banned to the laboratory and jungle, leaving us without imagination. To restore our earth to a ground in creative imagination we must re-imagine the creation. To recover imagination we must restore the preposterous sea monsters and every winged fowl and everything that creepeth. Only the animal can answer Descartes. Imagine—the subtle body is our brute awareness; and angelology, a logos of animals.

This chapter has been so difficult because we have been working within the region of the *opus major,* the grand conjunction of body, soul, and spirit. What holds that conjunction of concrete sensation, psychic image, and spiritual meaning is *aisthesis,* which denotes originally both breathing in (smelling) and perceiving. I am saying that when we walk through the world aesthetically, we experience images like breath through the nostrils, a reflex consciousness on which life depends. Instead of the search for meanings, the perceptive sensitive response which transforms events into images. This *via aesthetica* would be what is meant by "living psychologically": the undersense returned from symbolism and from paranoic meanings to the significance of the senses. A significant life does not have to "find meaning" because significance is given directly with reality; all things as images make sense.

The old dictum—nothing in mind that is not first in the senses—can be affirmed as it is deliteralized. For it means that the mind is primarily aesthetic. As well as Apollonic reflection (leaning back and away, distancing), there is another sort of attention, moving closer to sniff, discrimination with the eyes closed as in music and prayer and kissing, as in remembering. Close noticing.[61] This approach to living psychologically reconnects us to the ancient meaning of *psyche* as a breath soul of the head whose passages were the nostrils.

Does this not rekindle your animal faith in the image? To our animal faith, the image is simply there, living, moving like the airs we breathe, whether we believe in it or not, whether it numinously nods or not, whether we understand it or not. Release from *pistis*: "I don't believe in

61 Persephone's reaching toward the fragrant flower when Hades suddenly irrupts can be read as her move into deepening the senses, which brings him forth. It is her movement toward the underworld mode of perception, smell, a delight in the discrimination of essences. The aesthetic, too, opens into the underworld.

these things; fantasies only; I make them up myself." Release from symbolic hermeneutics: "I must find out what the image means; interpretation, understanding." Instead, aesthetics as the "mythical realism" of Charles Boer and Peter Kugler.[62] It seems that aesthetics is the *via regia* if we would restore our life in images and work out the appropriate method for the poetic basis of mind—a mind based in fantasy images.

62 C. Boer and P. Kugler, "Archetypal Psychology Is Mythical Realism," *Spring: An Annual of Archetypal Psychology and Jungian Thought* (1977): 131–52.

18

PROTESTOR'S LAST STAND

PROTESTOR: *All through this inquiry you have elaborated a method, but I want, finally, a theory to which the method belongs. Unless you give me a theory, I don't know why I should apply the method. What holds it all together, brings the insights into line? Without an overarching theory there is no coherent weave, leaving ideas in fragments and practical gaps. Most importantly, you made no mention of two critical issues: the mundane one of time and the transcendent one of value.*

Do you make better images through time? Does imagination improve as we go along? What about development, progress, getting better? Does soul-making proceed through time since, certainly, life proceeds through time?

Second, you offer no values beyond insight or awareness. Is your method good for the patient? Is it good in itself? What is the value of soul-making with images? Why learn it unless it offers something that other artistic and psychological methods don't offer. In short, why bother?

Beyond the clarification of terms and procedures, beyond the many distinctions and examples, and the packet of useful gadgets, I want to know what objective you are pursuing with the psyche. How do you justify what you do in terms of working with an actual client's dream, dance, or artwork?

Let me put to you why I work on my *dreams and make clay figures and paint my emotional states, why I go to therapy and belief in Jungian-style analysis. First off, I accept fully the idea of the unconscious psyche and its implications: my ego awareness is limited, but there is a deeper self-steering awareness below. Since I cannot fully know or feel what I am doing, I turn to my dreams and fantasies to discover what the rest of me, the main strength of me, is doing and what it intends. This material gives me self-confidence and self-knowledge, and I am able to act with more awareness.*

Second, I accept fully the idea of a self beyond my ego and the idea that unconscious imagery (dreams, drawings, dances, fantasies) are ways the self reveals its intentions. Following this imagery allows me to comply better with my unconscious nature and live in accord with this self. You see, I accept the idea that this self is a spark of the unknown divine presence in my nature, which is my particular destiny asking to be lived as my "life."

By doing my level best to interpret my images and follow their messages, I am best able to keep in tune with his self, be conscious, and therefore less destructive to myself and fellows, and so more valuable to the world. Interpretations of this unconscious material requires knowledge of symbols and myths because, following Jung, the self expresses its natural movements in age-old patterns described in myths, rituals, fairy tales, and religious symbols. So knowledge of symbols is crucial for becoming the better person that becoming conscious implies.

My approach affirms that I am serving a higher principle, the self or an unknown god in the psyche, and, moreover, that this unknown god urges me to do just what I am doing. In other words, being psychological in the way I am describing it is actually a vocation. This means that working on dreams and other images has a wider purpose, a transcendental aspect. It is part of a Lebensphilosophie *or way of life. I feel myself on rational grounds with empirical evidence in a social adaptation and with a religious purpose. The way I work with images shows the reason in my life and keeps me on a path.*

You don't offer this. I see neither a casual nor a final viewpoint in what you do with images. It seems to be an operation only, and has a secular, surgical feel to it. I see no deeper reason why *I should discover this or that analogy, move the images around, pay close attention, except that these operations makes my perceptions more precise, more intense, and more suggestive so that I discover aspects of my experiences that I might otherwise have missed.*

But these perceptions remain isolated. Pearls of insight, maybe, but unstrung, without the thread of a theory such as the Self or Individuation Process.

Sometimes you mention Zen, as if comparing your method with Zen, or with various teaching styles of people like Krishnamurti who bring awareness not by a doctrine that they impart but by regarding consciousness itself, regarding the regard as you call it. Seeing through the seer. Inasmuch as your method does do this, I understand how it works. But—you neglect one thing: these teachers place their method within a wider philosophy about the nature of reality and the nature of human beings within that reality. Zen is not only a method; it's a Buddhism. Those teachings offer a telos *to what they are doing. The method is part of a theory of the cosmos. One undertakes the method and submits to it because of the theory.*

Even if the theory is never fully realized, remaining but a hope or an indication—like cure, or like individuation in Jungian analysis—it is always for the sake of the goals expressed in the theory that one suffers the method.

I'm even willing to admit that the goal or theory is only that—a hopeful promise. It may even be illusory. Maybe cure or individuation is a delusion. Maybe, as Jung himself says, the self is never realized and cannot even be known. Nevertheless, I need the illusions or delusions in order to follow the vocation of becoming conscious. I am willing to admit that these unattainable goals serve my process. I need an overarching value in order to undergo a method.

The Jungian theory of individuation offers what I want. It clearly relates a method, the moves I make with an image to the contents revealed by the moves. Theory is realized in practice. When I interpret an image of a tricky carpet merchant as a Mercurial shadow and a seductive female as a Venusian anima, *this method of archetypal reduction reveals the deepest content in the image and gives it a meaning within an overall system. By looking at images in terms of symbols, myths, and cultural history and fitting them together with the theory of ego, shadow, archetypes, self, and the tension of opposites and types, I discover more and more meaning in the images. I don't mind admitting that I take Jungian theory of an individuating self, which is also the unknown god within, together with its archetypal components as a modern theology. It gives meaning and hope, importance and adventure to the methodical work with images. Moreover, Jungian theory connects outward to the main history of our civilization, Christianity, so that I can feel my work linked to a very old and broad stream. I am given structures of knowledge and patterns of understanding so that I can know where I am and where the patient is in his or her journey. The very act of knowing, his gnosis, is part of the change of being as I proceed on my way.*

I am not speaking as a Jungian for Jungianism. My charge against you is wider. All the schools of interpretive psychology structure a world. The conceptual structures that your inquiry demolished are part and parcel of a comprehensive theory of the psyche and a mode of comprehending life itself. In exchange for my Jungian theory of opposites and compensation, of development and transformation, of inner and outer, positive and negative, symbols and meanings, you present no conceptual structures at all. You leave me in a nihilism of unstructured images, a radical relativism of values, where each and every thing is valid because it can be operated upon, scrutinized, and thereby take on archetypal significance. This is pure immanence, even a kind of pantheism, all things ensouled, but there is no transcendent outward impetus. You have taken away the philosophical and spiritual grounding of the work with images, even though you purport to be merely inquiring into words and operations. Instead of depth, you offer only practice; instead of meaning, only method.

Either you are perpetrating a kind of existential situationalism and radical relativism—no quotes, no truth, no standards so that nothing is better or worse than anything else just so long as you do not stray from the image here and now. Or you are merely using this relativism as a critical tool only to pry lose literalisms and uncover dogmas because all along your basic script is Jung's theory of the psyche and an unacknowledged adherence to its practice as therapy.

If the former is the case, if you really have no theory behind all your maneuvering, then you must meet my charge of emptiness; if the latter is the case, then your whole endeavor really rests on Jung's premises, and you are begging a primary question by not admitting that you, too, are tacitly following Indian theory.

Now I'm going to sum up my position by laying the following accusation on you. The sophistication of your mind, the elegance of your style, and the empathetic feeling you bring to images cannot conceal a nihilism, even a despair, about soul work, maybe about the meaning of life. For you, all is fantasy—ideas, experiences, convictions, sufferings. The acid of your skepticism offers no philosophy of what is real, true, and good, and so we can never know what is unreal, false, and bad. You do not even posit the gods and goddesses as real. In the guise of broad and supportive affirmations, you're actually undoing the foundations, and so I fear a deeply demonic and distractive negativity in your method.

Suppose you laid your argument on a poet or a painter (I turn to image-makers for my first reply because I am trying to respond from my poetic basis of mind in order to stay within the context of this inquiry). I imagine a painter saying, "I paint. That's what I do and why I do it." He or she makes paintings, and the *why* of his or her actions is performed in the action. The purpose of painting is both the act of painting itself and the resultant picture. To go outside that statement in search of justifications, such as expressing the self, becoming more conscious or more useful to others, interferes with the act of painting by introducing a program that forces my image-making and the resultant picture to comply with this theory. I'm into a program instead of a painting. I would be measuring my work daily against whether I was becoming more conscious, following the self, etc., and I would be looking at my pictures for symbols or asking about their social value, or their relation to my dreams—all this rather than examining the painting itself in its own imagistic terms such as we have collaborated in this inquiry.

PROTESTOR: *So soul-making is like painting? It has no other justification than doing it?*

Don't you find it curious that "justification" comes up only now in relation with your philosophical question about theory? In the midst of engagement with images, we never felt we had to justify what we are doing. Your question leads away from the actual work into philosophy of life:

Why work? Why live? Why make soul? Suddenly we have left the kitchen and are sitting in the salon discussing over port and cigars. While we were cooking, we didn't ask whether this dinner is justified. It would have spoiled the beans.

Our differences cannot be argued out because they do not reside in the difference between tactical method on my side and overarching strategy on yours. Our argument is between two kinds of consciousness, two time periods, perhaps two gods. We are engaged in a psychological conflict rather than a philosophical argument. Moreover, between us is a piece of history.

You're older than I am, with the formation of your mind having taken place at the height of modernism, between the 1930s and the 1950s. A time of substantial statements in which the author's intentions, his or her philosophy, was instrumental for grasping the work. You are quite right to demand an overarching theory. This is a psychological requirement of your position; universals, general theories belong to its rhetorical style. Jung's self, individuation, symbolic interpretation, etc. meet this need.

There is something else around now—even though it has been here in a variety of guises for centuries from Socrates's dialectic, Hume's skepticism, Nietzsche's perspectives, James's pragmatics. Now it's called "postmodern," and it shows itself as an confluence of dozens of meandering streams: electronics, phenomenology, altered states, linguistics, pop art, catastrophe theory, incurable disease, philosophy as conversation, holocaust theology, biogenetics, plastics, corporate finance, urban architecture, perestroika, deconstruction, meditative mysticism, show business, government, terrorism, high-energy physics, and TV.

An essential aspect of these streams—and already my language subverts what I am writing about since singling out an "aspect" and speaking of using the word "essential" are alien rhetoric to postmodern style—is the absence of positivism. It will not posit anything, take a position, or favor positive attitudes. It refuses to take anything whatsoever literally including its own consciousness. Although it seems profoundly hermetic ("mercurial," you called me), slipping away from fixity and, by always displacing and thieving, allowing doors to open to death and soul—upward to unspoken transcendents, outward to exchange with the popular, and inward to body and reflexiveness—consciousness will not allow its winged heels to be held and planted into the immortal fixity of definition.

Jung is on the banks of these streams with one foot in the water and one foot out, as were his literary contemporaries Eliot and Joyce, Mann and Hesse. All of them were very much aware of the unconscious and the role of subjectivity in their works. But, in the clutch, they fell back onto the prepared positions, for they had positive programs of one sort or another; they were moralists, if not about society then about aesthetics, literature, and psychology. Jung's everlasting reference to himself as an empiricist meant not a scientific claim but a defense against his not being taken seriously, as if his statements were not in touch with the positive notion of facts to which his letters love to appeal.

Today, we seek for no such support, neither to empiricism nor to facts. We tend to see facts just as the word says, "made," even "made-up," to fit whatever works, like made-up news, made-up photos, and made-up wildlife scenes on TV. The hard line between fiction and fact does not exist as it once did. Besides, for every fact there is a counterfact. The adversarial style derives from the devotion to facts, so that you and I, in this chapter, are also caught in that earlier mode of consciousness. Today, show is more relevant than fact, and that is why I have again turned away from your theoretical questions to showing the method at work.

Skepticism has gone far further than Hume's, and no one provides more background to our minds (except, of course, the French minds that can never shake Descartes) than Nietzsche because all he really wanted was to wake us all up. Skepticism is in our bones now, where with you it was merely a refinement of the mind in an age of belief, where everything was quite what it was, and delusions only what our minds do mistakenly to things. Today, however, skepticism, as the hermeneutic of suspicion, follows E.B. White's dictum that "everything... is something it isn't."[62] Our consciousness does not reflect the moral skepticism in a confident age of enlightenment but media skepticism in a darkened age of the confidence man.

Don't now think that I am claiming a new mind for a new people, and that what I have sketched just now and laid out through the book is better than what you are insisting upon.

Please don't think that I am using the one-upmanship of the historical argument by saying to you that times have changed and that you are old-fashioned. Your romantic idealism and my skepticism, or whatever you

62 E.B. White, "The Door," *The New Yorker* (March 25, 1939): 17.

charge me with, like nihilism, are archetypal positions, ever-recurrent, ever-challenging each other, and both give satisfaction to the soul. So I am not claiming that we are in a new age, which is so skeptical and so nihilistic that it is dotty with light-headed and aggressively fundamental positions, but that skepticism has so riddled us that it has become an impulse, less a quality of the tempered mind than an instinct of self-preservation. If I don't meet the world with *both* love for its beauty and sensitivity to it suffering *and* with doubt, suspicion, and seeing through, I will be conned out of existence. While Jung thought that the self creates and individuates, I think that the self (whatever that may be) today skepticizes in order to stay alive.

No overarching idea or feeling can guarantee my activities; they must be valid in themselves with each step they take, each move they make, providing background as they proceed. The soul indeed takes but one day at a time; its entire strategy is tactical.

The many chapters to which you have so patiently submitted each gave an intention, but not as an overarching theory. An operational inquiry does not separate theory from practice, isolating theory as a set of principles and goals that are then applied in practice. Instead, theory lives in the operation itself and informs its doing. For instance, by sticking to the image, we give it primary place without having to declare a general principle about the priority of images. When we use gadgets to move the images, we demonstrate the depth, substantiality, and analogizing power of images without having to argue a theoretical position about imagination. When we compare the image with the *temenos* of sacred space, we feel the religious implications of the work without having to speak in the language of high-minded spiritual goals, and we have shown how that practice with images is akin to ritual.

What you ask for is present all through the chapters if you read them for their undertones. What keeps you from that reading is your own literalism: having been told that this is an operational inquiry, you are looking for the theory as something apart from the operations—the old mistake of separating theory and practice, aesthetics and ethics. The moral moment in this inquiry is present throughout; it is not something reached only at the end through practical operations. The goal of activating imagination and attending to images is present in each chapter. My approach keeps the goal in the way of doing. It follows the moral precept that says that the ends must show in the means. Your error lies in the fact that you are literalizing goals as distinctive from methods, separating practice and theory, and locating operations only in overarching principles. In other words, what I am struggling with in you are the stubborn remnants of positivistic consciousness, the demand for positional statements and positive goals. All I can do in response is analyze ("see through") your "position" rather than answer it in kind. In fact, my seeing through is my answer.

PROTESTOR: *Then the realm of values means nothing to you. You are just another mercenary, another terrorist, or another black humorist. You use the term "soul," but you refuse to fill it with substance, even though in some of your writing you call for a soul of stuff and substance. Like a hired gun, you will let your method be used by anyone. Suppose you were asked to work for the Mafia, for the extremist left (or right), or for an industrial cartel. They want a man who sees through, who can analyze consciousness. Will you take the job?*

The answer depends here not only on my ethical and political positions but on my "gods." What will they allow me to do? What does the soul want? And what the *animus*? But have these anything to do with an inquiry into image? With psychology or psychotherapy? I am a rather law-abiding, petit bourgeois, liberal Democrat, so I would consider their job offers in terms of these other considerations. But the definitions of my political positions and ethical values do not belong here. We must here distinguish another aspect of postmodern consciousness. It is not concerned with opinions. Multiple personality has many levels of awareness. Some complexes are clever, others stupid. Some are in the nineteenth century, some in the eighteenth, some even further back as if in a Mosaic tribal code. I don't fit it all together, so where I advance my discretion, as in this inquiry, into subtleties, it's not the same as my view of the justice system, the pleas for insanity, or the case of Patricia Hearst and the like. Now, the elder generation, going back to Freud and to Jung especially, again did not make this distinction. Jung opined on everything–race, culture, politics, religion, nation, marriage, education, family. But his refined awareness was elsewhere and some of what he had to say about marriage, for instance, or Jews, or Blacks (the contained and the container) in my opinion is hogwash.

The world, it seems to me, is full of ethics, morals, values, political doctrine—they have been accumulating for centuries, and they are our inheritance from some very fine thinkers and some very fine commentators. Do we need more? Or, do we need to sift what we have and see through their implications, their suppositions, and how they affect us (the Bible, Kant's ethics, etc.), until we can get to the images that are at work in them on us?

PROTESTOR: *Aha, we are getting adumbrations of your social philosophy after all. The task, you are saying, is not the formulation of philosophies but the seeing through them.*

Oh yes. I have held to that consistently.

PROTESTOR: *Then why? What's the point of this seeing through?*

To become aware of what holds us.

PROTESTOR: *So as to be freer?*

No "so as." To see through *is* awareness, is therapy, gives soul a satisfaction. Its eye is ever hungry. If this is called liberation or awareness or whatever in various meditative disciplines or psychological schools, then all seem to me to refer to the same activity of psychologizing. And this, like beauty, like education, like love, like knowledge, is its own end.